The Prophet's
PRAYER

sallallaahu 'alaihi wasallam

described

from the beginning to the end
as though you see it

by:
Shaikh Muhammad Naasir-ud-Deen Al-Albaani

Translated by:
Usama ibn Suhaib Hasan

Seventh reprint, Jumada Al-Thania 1428 AH/July 2007

Published by:
Jam'iat Ihyaa Minhaaj Al-Sunnah
P.O. Box 24
Ipswich, Suffolk,
IP3 8ED
UK

Tel/Fax : 01473 251578
Email: mail@jimas.org
http://www.jimas.org
http://www.islaam.com

Typesetting and Editing by Jam'iat Ihyaa' Minhaaj Al-Sunnah

ISBN 0 9533019 1 5

Printed & Bound by :
De-Luxe Printers Ltd.
London NW10 7NR
Tel: 020 8965 1771
email: deluxeprinters1@aol.com

CONTENTS

A Brief Biography of Ash-Shaikh Al-Muhaddith Abu 'Abdir-Rahmaan Muhammad Naasir-ud-Deen Al-Albaani

(Taken from the Biography of him by Dr. 'Aasim 'Abdullaah al-Qaryooti)

He was born in the city of Ashkodera, then the capital of Albania in the year 1332 H (1914 C.E.) into a poor family. His father al-Haaj Nooh Najjaatee al-Albaani had completed Sharee'ah studies in Istanbul and returned a scholar to Albania. After Albania was taken over by atheism the family made Hijrah to Damascus. In Damascus Shaikh al-Albaani completed his initial education and was then taught the Qur'an, Tajweed, sciences of 'Arabic language, fiqh of the Hanafee madhab and further branches of the Deen by various Shaikhs and friends of his father.

He also learnt from his father the art of clock and watch repair - and became highly skilled in that and famous for it and derived his earnings through it. He began to specialize in the field of hadeeth and its related sciences by the age of 20 - being influenced by articles in 'al-Manaar' magazine.

He began to work in this field by transcribing al-Haafiz al'Iraaqee's monumental 'al-Mughnee 'an-hamlil-Asfaar fil-Asfaar fee takhreej maafil-Ihyaa minal-Akhbaar' and adding notes to it.

He delved further into the field of Hadeeth and its various sciences despite discouragement from his father. Furthermore, the books he needed were not to be found in his father's library which was composed mainly of various works of Hanafee Fiqh - and since he could not afford many of the books he required he would borrow them from the famous library of Damascus - 'al-Maktabatuz-Zaahiriyyah' or sometimes from book sellers.

He became engrossed with the science of Hadeeth to the extent that he would sometimes close up his shop and remain in the library for up to twelve hours - breaking off his work only for prayer - he would not even leave to eat, but would take two light snacks with him.

Eventually the library authorities granted him a special room to himself for his study and his own key for access to the library before normal opening time. Often he would remain at work from early morning until after 'Ishaa. During this time he produced many useful works - many of which are still waiting to be printed.

The Shaikhs studies of Hadeeth of Allah's Messenger. (sallallaahu 'alaihi wasallam) had a great effect on him and resulted in his turning away from blind following of his former madhab and instead to accept and act upon the Book and the Sunnah - with the understanding of the pious predecessors (As-Salafus Saalih) This naturally meant he was sometimes at variance with some of the local Shaikhs who blindly followed the Hanafee Madhhab, and likewise with the local Soofi imams and innovators who began to oppose him and incite the common people against him by calling him a, "Wahhaabi deviant". He was however, encouraged by some of the noble Shaikhs of Damascus who urged him to continue, amongst them Shaikh Bahjatul Baijaar, Shaikh 'Abdul-Fattaah - the imam, and Tawfeeq al-Barzah-rahimahumullaah.

The Shaikh therefore faced much opposition in his efforts to promote Tawheed and the Sunnah but he bore this with patient perseverance.

After some time he started giving two weekly classes attended by students of knowledge and university teachers - in which he taught various books of 'Aqeedah, Fiqh, Usool and Hadeeth sciences.

He also began organised monthly journeys for Da'wah to the various cities of Syria and then Jordan.

After a number of his works appeared in print the Shaikh was chosen to teach Hadeeth in the new University in al-Madeenah, Saudi Arabia, for three years from 1381 to 1383H - where he was also a member of the University board.

After this he returned to his former studies and work in 'Maktabatuz-Zaahiriyyah' leaving his shop in the hands of one of his brothers.

He visited various countries for Da'wah and lectures - amongst them Qatar, Egypt, Kuwait, the Emirates, Spain and England.

He was forced to emigrate a number of times moving from Syria to Jordan, then Syria again, then Beirut, then the Emirates, then again to 'Ammaan, Jordan where he now resides.

His works - mainly in the field of Hadeeth and its sciences number over 100.

His students are many and include many Shaikhs of the present day amongst them: Shaikh Hamdee 'Abdul-Majeed as-Salafee, Shaikh Muhammad 'Eed 'Abbaasee, Dr. 'Umar Sulaimaan al-Ashqar, Shaikh Muhammad Ibraheem Shaqrah, Shaikh Muqbil ibn Haadee al-Waadi'ee, Shaikh 'Alee Khushshaan, Shaikh Muhammad Jameel Zainoo, Shaikh 'Abdur-Rahman 'Abdus-Samad, Shaikh 'Alee Hasan 'Abdul-Hameed al-Halabee, Shaikh Saleem al-Hilaalee and Shaikh 'Abdur-Rahmaan 'Abdul-Khaaliq.

INTRODUCTION

Praise be to Allaah, who made Prayer compulsory on his slaves and ordered them to establish it and perform it well; who linked success and felicity to humility in Prayer; who made it the criterion to distinguish between *Eeman* and *Kufr* ; and who made it a restrainer from shameful and unjust deeds.

Prayers and peace be upon our Prophet Muhammad, who was addressed in the Words of the Exalted:

وَأَنزَلْنَآ إِلَيْكَ ٱلذِّكْرَ لِتُبَيِّنَ لِلنَّاسِ مَا نُزِّلَ إِلَيْهِمْ وَلَعَلَّهُمْ يَتَفَكَّرُونَ

"And We have sent down to you the Message, that you may explain clearly to the people what is sent for them"[1], and who fully carried out this task. The Prayer was one of the most important things which he explained to the people, verbally and practically, even praying on the pulpit once - standing, bowing and prostrating, and then saying to them, *I have done this so that you may follow me and learn my prayer.*[2] He obligated us to copy him in his prayer, saying, *Pray as you have seen me praying.*[3] He also gave the good tidings to whoever prayed like him that such a person has a covenant with Allaah that He will enter him into the Garden, saying, *There are five prayers which Allaah, Mighty and Sublime, has made compulsory: he who performs ablution well for them, prays them at their proper times, and is complete in their bowings, prostrations and humility, he has a guarantee from Allaah that He will forgive him; but he who does not do so, has no guarantee from Allaah: if He wishes, He will forgive him or if He wishes, He will punish him.*[4]

Prayers and peace be also on his family and his pious and just Companions, who passed on to us his worship, prayer, sayings and actions (sallallaahu 'alaihi wa sallam), and who made these, and these alone, a Madhhab and a path for them to follow ; and also on those who follow in their footsteps and tread their path until the Day of Judgment.

* * *

When I finished reading the book of prayer in *At-Targheeb wat-Tarheeb* by al-Haafiz al-Mundhiri (rahimahullaah) and teaching it to our brothers, four years ago, it became clear to us all the important position of the Prayer in Islam; and the reward, grace and respect awaiting those who establish and perform it well;

---

[1] Soorah an-Nahl, 16:44

[2] Bukhaari & Muslim - it will later follow in full.

[3] Bukhaari & Ahmad.

[4] Maalik, Abu Daawood, Nasaa'i, & Ibn Hibbaan. A saheeh hadeeth, declared saheeh by several Imaams. I have given its takhreej in *Saheeh Abi Daawood* (451, 1276).

and that all this varies, depending on its closeness to the Prophet's prayer (sallallaahu 'alaihi wa sallam). This is what he indicated in his saying, *Verily the slave prays a prayer of which nothing is written down for him except a tenth, ninth, eighth, seventh, sixth, fifth, quarter, third or half of it.*[5] Therefore, I reminded the brothers that it is not possible for us to perform prayer as it should be performed, or even approach that, unless we know the detailed description of the Prophet's prayer (sallallaahu 'alaihi wa sallam), including its essentials, manners, forms, supplications (*du'aas*) and remembrances (*adhkaar*), and then we make an effort to put that knowledge into practice carefully, for then we could hope that our prayers would restrain us from shameful and unjust deeds, and that the reward and blessings mentioned in the narrations would be written down for us.

However, detailed familiarity with all these aspects of prayer is unlikely to be achieved by most people nowadays, even many scholars, because of their limiting themselves to a particular Madhhab. But, as anyone concerned with assisting in compiling and studying the purified Sunnah knows, in every Madhhab there are sunnahs which are not found in other Madhhabs; moreover, in every Madhhab there are sayings and actions which cannot be authentically traced back to the Prophet (sallallaahu 'alaihi wa sallam) - most of these are found in the sayings of the later scholars[6], many of whom we see firmly

---

5 Saheeh - collected by Ibn al-Mubaarak in *az-Zuhd* (10/21/1-2), Abu Daawood & Nasaa'i with a good sanad; I have given its takhreej in *Saheeh Abi Daawood* (761).

6 Abul-Hasanaat Al-Lucknowi says in *An-Naafi' al-Kabeer liman yutaali' al-Jaami' as-Sagheer* (p. 122-3), after ranking the books of Hanafi fiqh and saying which of them are dependable and which are not: "All that we have said about the relative grades of these compilations is related to their content of fiqh issues; however, as for their content with regards to ahaadeeth of the Prophet (sallallaahu 'alaihi wa sallam), then it does not apply, for many books on which the cream of the fuqahaa' rely are full of fabricated ahaadeeth, let alone rulings of the scholars. It is clear to us from a broad analysis that although their authors were otherwise competent, they were careless in their quotation of narrations."

One of these false, fabricated ahaadeeth which are found in some of the best books is: "He who offers the compulsory prayers on the last Friday of Ramadaan, that will make up for every prayer he missed during his life up to the age of seventy years" ! Lucknowi (rahimahullaah) says in *Al-Aathaar al-Marfoo'ah fil-Akhbaar al-Mawdoo'ah* (p. 315), after giving this hadeeth, "'Ali al-Qaari says in his *al-Mawdoo'aat as-Sughraa* and *al-Kubraa*: this is totally false, for it contradicts the ijmaa' (consensus of opinion) that one act of worship cannot make up for those missed over years. Hence, there is no point in quoting the author of *an-Nihaayah* nor the rest of the commentators on *al-Hidaayah*, for they are not scholars of Hadeeth, nor did they reference this hadeeth to any of the collectors of Hadeeth."

Shawkaani also mentioned this hadeeth in *Al-Fawaa'id al-Majmoo'ah fil-Ahaadeeth al-Mawdoo'ah* with a similar wording and then said (p. 54), "This is fabricated beyond doubt - I do not even find it in any of the compilations of fabricated ahaadeeth! However, it has become popular among some students of fiqh in the city of San'aa' in this age of ours, and many of them have started acting according to it. I do not know who has fabricated it for them - May Allaah disgrace the liars."

Lucknowi further says, "To establish that this hadeeth, which is found in books of rituals and formulas, is fabricated, I have composed a brief essay, with intellectual and narrated evidence, called *Repelling the Brethren from the Inventions of the Last Friday of Ramadaan*, in which I

attributing these to the Prophet (sallallaahu 'alaihi wa sallam)![7] This is why the scholars of Hadeeth - may Allaah reward them well - have produced books of Takhreej on the famous books of the later scholars, explaining the rank of each hadeeth given in them: whether e.g. authentic, weak or fabricated. Examples of these books of Takhreej are: *Al-'Inaayah fi Ma'rifah Ahaadeeth al-Hidaayah* and *At-Turuq wal-Wasaa'il fi Takhreej Ahaadeeth Khulaasah ad-Dalaa'il* by Shaikh 'Abdul Qaadir ibn Muhammad al-Qurashi al-Hanafi; *Nasb ar-Raayah li Ahaadeeth al-Hidaayah* by Haafiz Zayla'i, and its abridged version *ad-Dirayah* by Haafiz Ibn Hajr al-Asqalaani, who also wrote *Talkhees al-Habeer fi Takhreej Ahaadeeth ar-Raafi'i al-Kabir*; there are many others, naming which will only lengthen this discussion.[8]

Reasons behind the Compilation of this Book, & some of its Features

Since I had not come across a comprehensive book covering this topic, I felt obliged to produce a book which collected together as many features of the Prophet's prayer (sallallaahu 'alaihi wa sallam) from the *takbeer* to the *tasleem* as possible, for the benefit of my Muslim brothers who wished to follow the guidance of their Prophet (sallallaahu 'alaihi wa sallam) in their worship, such that it would be easy for any who truly loved the Prophet (sallallaahu 'alaihi wa sallam) to use this book to fulfil his command, *"Pray as you have seen me praying."*

---

have filed points which will enlighten minds and to which ears will hearken, so consult it, for it is valuable in this topic and of high quality."

The occurrence of similar false ahaadeeth in the books of fiqh destroys the reliability of other ahaadeeth which they do not quote from dependable books of Hadeeth. The words of 'Ali al-Qaari contain an indication towards this: a Muslim must take Hadeeth from the people who are experts in that field, as the old Arabic sayings go, "The people of Makkah know its mountain-paths best" and "The owner of the house knows best what is in it."

[7] Imaam Nawawi(rahimahullaah)'s words in *Al-Majmoo' Sharh al-Muhadhdhab* (1/60) can be summed up as follows: "The researching scholars of the People of Hadeeth and others say that if the hadeeth is weak, it will not be said regarding it, 'The Messenger of Allaah (sallallaahu 'alaihi wa sallam) said/did/commanded/forbade ...' or any other phrase designating certainty, but instead it will be said, 'It is reported/quoted/narrated from him ...' or other phrases suggesting uncertainty. They say that phrases of certainty are for saheeh and hasan ahaadeeth, and phrases of uncertainty are for anything else. This is because phrases designating certainty mean that what follows is authentic, so they can only be used in the case of what is authentic, otherwise one would effectively be lying about him (sallallaahu 'alaihi wa sallam).

This convention is one ignored by most of the fuqahaa' of our age, in fact, by most scholars of any discipline, except for the skilled muhadditheen. This is disgusting carelessness, for they often say about a saheeh hadeeth, 'It is reported from him that ...', and about a da'eef one, 'he said' and 'so-and-so reported ...', and this is far from correct."

[8] Publisher's note: Also in this category are the works of our teacher, author of e.g. *Irwaa' al-Ghaleel fi takhreej Manaar as-Sabeel* in 8 volumes, & *Ghaayah al-Maraam fi takhreej ahaadeeth al-Halaal wal-Haraam*, a takhreej of the ahaadeeth found in Dr. Yoosuf al-Qaradaawi's *The Lawful and the Prohibited in Islam*, (which contains many da'eef ahaadeeth).

Thus I en.barked on a difficult task, and researched the relevant ahaadeeth from the various sources of Hadeeth, the book in your hands being the end result of it all. I stipulated on myself that I would only give ahaadeeth which had an authentic sanad according to the principles and regulations of the science of Hadeeth. I disregarded any hadeeth which depended on unknown or weak narrators, whether it dealt with the outward form, adhkaar, excellence, etc. of the Prayer. This is because I hold that the authentic ahadeeth[9] are sufficient, leaving no need for anything weak, for the latter does not amount to anything except zann (conjecture, suspicion), and incorrect conjecture at that; as the Exalted says:

$$ وَإِنَّ ٱلظَّنَّ لَا يُغْنِى مِنَ ٱلْحَقِّ شَيْئًا $$

"... And conjecture is of no use against the truth"[10]; and the Prophet (sallallaahu 'alaihi wa sallam) said, Beware of suspicion, for truly, suspicion is the most false of speech.[11] Therefore, we cannot worship Allaah by acting according to inauthentic ahaadeeth; in fact, the Messenger of Allaah (sallallaahu 'alaihi wa sallam) forbade us from this saying, Keep away from saying things about me, except what you know[12]; since he has forbidden us from relating weak narrations, it goes without saying that it is forbidden to act according to them.

I have compiled the book as two texts: the main text and the subsidiary text.

The main text includes the text of ahaadeeth or phrases taken from them, as well as appropriate words to string them together to give the book a fluency from start to finish. I have been careful to preserve the text of each hadeeth as it is found in the books of Sunnah; where a hadeeth has different wordings, I have chosen the version which best fits the fluency etc., but I have brought together other wordings thus: "(in one version: ...)" or "(in one narration: ...)". Only rarely have I given the Companion who narrated the hadeeth, or explained in the main text which of the Imaams of Hadeeth have collected each hadeeth, in order to provide easier reading and reference.

As for the subsidiary text, it is a commentary on the main text. In it I have traced the ahaadeeth to their sources, exploring their various versions and routes of narration. Along with this, I have commented on their isnaads and supporting narrations, with authenticating and disparaging remarks on narrators, whether

---

[9]The term, "authentic hadeeth" includes saheeh and hasan in the eyes of the muhadditheen, whether the hadeeth is saheeh li dhaatihi or saheeh li ghairihi, or hasan li dhaatihi or hasan li ghairihi.

[10] an-Najm, 53:28

[11] Bukhaari & Muslim.

[12] Saheeh - collected by Tirmidhi, Ahmad & Ibn Abi Shaibah.

Later, I discovered that this hadeeth is actually da'eef: I had relied on Manaawi in declaring saheeh the isnaad of Ibn Abi Shaibah, but then I happened to come across it myself, and found that it was clearly weak, being the same isnaad as Tirmidhi and others - see my book Silsilah al-Ahaadeeth ad-Da'eefah (1783). However, its place is taken by the Prophet's saying (sallallaahu 'alaihi wa sallam), "He who relates from me a saying which he knows is a lie is indeed one of the liars", collected by Muslim and others.

iv

authentic or weak, judged according to the rules of the science of Hadeeth. Often, one route of narration has additional words which are not found in other routes, so I have inserted these into the original hadeeth in the main text whenever it is possible to do so without destroying the fluency, enclosing the addition in square brackets: [...], usually without stating which of the sources were alone in containing that addition. This has been done only if the hadeeth is originally on the authority of the same Companion, otherwise I have given it separately, e.g. in the opening supplications etc. This insertion of additional wordings is a tremendous advantage which you will not find in many books - Praise be to Allaah, by Whose Favour good actions are completed.

Next, I have mentioned in the subsidiary text the madhhabs of the scholars regarding the hadeeth traced, as well as the evidence and counter-evidence for each view, along with the strengths and weaknesses of each argument. We have then selected out of that the correct view which we have given in the main text. Also in the subsidiary text, we have given some issues for which there is no text in the Sunnah, but which require *ijtihaad*, and do not come under the title of this book.

Since the publication of this book with both main and subsidiary texts is not feasible right now due to various reasons, we have decided to publish only the main text of the book (along with brief footnotes) by Allaah's Will, and named it *"Sifah Salaah an-Nabi (sallallaahu 'alaihi wa sallam), min at-takbeer ilaa at-tasleem ka'annaka taraahaa* (The Prophet's Prayer Described, from beginning to end, as though you were watching it)"

I ask Allaah to make this work sincerely for His Face, and to help my brothers in faith to benefit from it, for He is the Hearer, the Answerer.

Methodology of this Book

Since the purpose of this book is to convey the guidance of the Prophet (sallallaahu 'alaihi wa sallam) regarding Prayer, it was elementary that I would not limit myself to a particular Madhhab, for the reasons mentioned previously. Therefore, I would give whatever is authentically proved from him (sallallaahu 'alaihi wa sallam), as has always been the way of the scholars of Hadeeth[13], whether of old or of the recent past[14], as the excellent saying goes:

> *The People of Hadeeth are the People of the Messenger, although*
> *They accompany him not, they are with his every movement.*[15]

Thus this book would, Allaah Willing, gather whatever is relevant to each topic from the various contents of the books of Hadeeth and the books on the differences between the Madhhabs, such that the correct verdicts found in this book would not be found totally in any one Madhhab. Hence the one acting on it, Allaah Willing, would be among those whom Allaah had guided **"by His Grace to the Truth concerning that in which they differed, for Allaah guides whom He will to a path that is straight."**[16]

When I adopted these principles for myself, i.e. to adhere to the authentic Sunnah, and to implement them in this book as well as others, I knew for sure

---

[13] 'Abdul Hayy Al-Lucknowi says in *Imaam al-Kalaam fimaa yata'allaq bil-Qiraa'ah Khalf al-Imaam* (p. 156), as follows:
"Whoever dives into the oceans of fiqh and the fundamentals of jurisprudence with an open mind, and does not allow himself to be prejudiced, will know with certainty that in most of the principal and subsidiary issues in which the scholars have differed, the madhhab of the scholars of Hadeeth is firmer than other madhhabs. Every time I go into the branches of difference of opinion, I find the view of the muhadditheen nearest to justice - their reward is with Allaah, and He will thank them. How could it be otherwise, when they are the true inheritors of the Prophet (sallallaahu 'alaihi wa sallam), and the sincere agents of his Law; may Allaah include us in their company and make us die loving them."

[14] Subki says in *al-Fataawaa* (1/148):
"The most important affair of the Muslims is the Prayer, which every Muslim must care about and ensure its performance and the establishment of its essentials. Related to Prayer are issues on which there is consensus and there is no escaping the truth, and other issues in which the scholars have differed. The correct approach is either to keep clear of dispute if possible, or to look for what is authentically-proven from the Prophet (sallallaahu 'alaihi wa sallam) and adhere to that. When one does this, his Prayer will be correct and righteous, and included in the words of the Exalted, **"So whoever expects to meet his Lord, let him work correct, righteous deeds."** (Al-Kahf, 18:110)

I say: The latter approach is superior, nay, obligatory; this is because the former appeoach, as well as being impossible many issues, does not fulfil his command (sallallaahu 'alaihi wa sallam), **"Pray as you have seen me praying"**, but instead leads to one's prayer being decidedly different to that of the Prophet (sallallaahu 'alaihi wa sallam).

[15] From the poetry of Hasan ibn Muhammad an-Nasawi, as narrated by Haafiz Diyaa' ad-Deen al-Maqdisi in his article on the excellence of the Hadeeth and its People.
[16] Baqarah, 2:213

that this would not satisfy every group of people or sect; in fact, it would result in some, if not most of them, insulting or criticising me. This does not matter to me, for I also know that to please everyone is an unattainable notion, and that **"He who pleases the people by angering Allaah, Allaah will entrust him to the people"**, as the Messenger of Allaah (sallallaahu 'alaihi wa sallam) said.[17] The reward is with Allaah for the author of the following lines:

Nor could I ever escape from abuse,
   Even were I in a cave in a rugged mountain;
For who can escape from the people unharmed,
   Even if he hides behind the eagle's wings?

It is enough for me that I believe that this is the most upright way, which Allaah has commanded the believers to take; which our Prophet Muhammad (sallallaahu 'alaihi wa sallam), Chief of the Messengers, has explained. This is the path which was trodden by the Pious Predecessors: the Companions, their Successors and those after them, including the four Imaams to whose Madhhabs the majority of Muslims today attribute themselves. All of them were agreed on the obligation to stick to the Sunnah and to refer to it; to ignore every view contradictory to it, no matter how great the holder or propounder of that view, for the status of the Messenger of Allaah (sallallaahu 'alaihi wa sallam) is far greater, and his example is far truer. Because of this, I have acted on their guidance, followed in their footsteps and carried out their commands to stick to the authentic hadeeth, even if this opposes their view. These commands of theirs have influenced me greatly in my perusal of this path, and my rejection of blind *taqleed* (following of opinion). I ask Allaah Exalted to reward them greatly.

SAYINGS OF THE IMAAMS REGARDING FOLLOWING THE SUNNAH AND IGNORING THEIR VIEWS CONTRADICTORY TO IT

It would be beneficial if we gave some of these here, for perhaps this will admonish or remind those who follow the opinion of the Imaams - nay, of those far below the Imaams in rank - blindly[18], sticking to their madhhabs or views as if these had descended from the heavens! But Allaah, Mighty and Sublime, says:

اتَّبِعُوا مَا أُنزِلَ إِلَيْكُم مِّن رَّبِّكُمْ وَلَا تَتَّبِعُوا مِن دُونِهِ أَوْلِيَاءَ قَلِيلًا مَّا تَذَكَّرُونَ

---

[17] Tirmidhi, Qudaa'i, Ibn Bushraan & others.

[18] This is the sort of *taqleed* (blind following) which Imaam Tahaawi was referring to when he said, "Only someone with party-spirit or a fool blindly follows opinion" - quoted by Ibn 'Aabideen in *Rasm al-Mufti* (vol. 1, p. 32 from the Compilation of his Essays).

"Follow (O men!) the revelation given to you from your Lord, and follow not, as friends and protectors, other than Him. Little is it you remember of admonition."[19]

1) Abu Haneefah (rahimahullaah)

The first of them is Abu Haneefah Nu'maan ibn Thaabit, whose companions have narrated from him various sayings and diverse warnings, all of them leading to one thing: the obligation to accept the Hadeeth, and to give up following the opinions of the imaams which contradict it:

1. "When a hadeeth is found to be saheeh, then that is my madhhab."[20]

2. "It is not permitted[21] for anyone to accept our views if they do not know from where we got them "[22]

---

[19] al-A'raaf, 7:3

[20] Ibn 'Aabideen in al-Haashiyah (1/63), and in his essay Rasm al-Mufti (1/4 from the Compilation of the Essays of Ibn 'Aabideen), Shaikh Saalih al-Fulaani in Eeqaaz al-Himam (p. 62) & others. Ibn 'Aabideen quoted from Sharh al-Hidaayah by Ibn al-Shahnah al-Kabeer, the teacher of Ibn al-Humaam, as follows:

"When a hadeeth contrary to the Madhhab is found to be saheeh, one should act on the hadeeth, and make that his madhhab. Acting on the hadeeth will not invalidate the follower's being a Hanafi, for it is authentically reported that Abu Haneefah said, 'When a hadeeth is found to be saheeh, then that is my madhhab', and this has been related by Imaam Ibn 'Abdul Barr from Abu Haneefah and from other imaams."

This is part of the completeness of the knowledge and piety of the Imaams, for they indicated by saying this that they were not versed in the whole of the Sunnah, and Imaam Shaafi'i has elucidated this thoroughly (see later). It would happen that they would contradict a sunnah because they were unaware of it, so they commanded us to stick to the Sunnah and regard it as part of their Madhhab. May Allaah shower His mercy on them all.

[21] Ar.: halaal

[22] Ibn 'Abdul Barr in Al-Intiqaa' fi Fadaa'il ath-Thalaathah al-A'immah al-Fuqahaa' (p. 145), Ibn al-Qayyim in I'laam al-Mooqi'een (2/309), Ibn 'Aabideen in his Footnotes on Al-Bahr ar-Raa'iq (6/293) and in Rasm al-Mufti (pp. 29,32) & Sha'raani in Al-Meezaan (1/55) with the second narration. The last narration was collected by 'Abbaas ad-Dawri in At-Taareekh by Ibn Ma'een (6/77/1) with a saheeh sanad on the authority of Zafar, the student of Imaam Abu Haneefah. Similar narrations exist on the authority of Abu Haneefah's companions Zafar, Abu Yoosuf and 'Aafiyah ibn Yazeed; cf. Eeqaaz (p. 52). Ibn al-Qayyim firmly certified its authenticity on the authority of Abu Yoosuf in I'laam al-Mooqi'een (2/344). The addition to the second narration is referenced by the editor of Eeqaaz (p. 65) to Ibn 'Abdul Barr, Ibn al-Qayyim and others.

If this is what they say of someone who does not know their evidence, what would be their response to one who knows that the evidence contradicts their saying, but still gives verdicts opposed to the evidence?! Therefore, reflect on this saying, for it alone is enough to smash blind following of opinion; that is why one of the muqallid shaikhs, when I criticised his giving a verdict using Abu Haneefah's words without knowing the evidence, refused to believe that it was a saying of Abu Haneefah!

In one narration, "It is prohibited[23] for someone who does not know my evidence to give verdicts[24] on the basis of my words."

Another narration adds, "... for we are mortals: we say one thing one day, and take it back the next day."

In another narration, "Woe to you, O Ya'qub[25]! Do not write down everything you hear from me, for it happens that I hold one opinion today and reject it tomorrow, or hold one opinion tomorrow and reject it the day after tomorrow."[26]

3. "When I say something contradicting the Book of Allaah the Exalted or what is narrated from the Messenger (sallallaahu 'alaihi wa sallam), then ignore my saying."[27]

---

[23] Ar.: *haraam*

[24] Ar.: *fatwaa*

[25] i.e. Imaam Abu Haneefah's illustrious student, Abu Yoosuf (rahimahullaah).

[26] This was because the Imaam would often base his view on *Qiyaas* (Analogy), after which a more potent analogy would occur to him, or a hadeeth of the Prophet (sallallaahu 'alaihi wa sallam) would reach him, so he would accept that and ignore his previous view. Sha'raani's words in *Al-Meezaan* (1/62) are summarised as:

"Our belief, as well as that of every researcher into Imaam Abu Haneefah (radi Allaahu 'anhu), is that, had he lived until the recording of the Sharee'ah, and the journeys of the Preservers of Hadeeth to the various cities and frontiers in order to collect and acquire it, he would have accepted it and ignored all the analogies he had employed. The amount of *qiyaas* in his Madhhab would have been just as little as that in other Madhhabs, but since the evidences of the Sharee'ah had been scattered with the Successors and their successors, and had not been collected in his lifetime, it was necessary that there be a lot of *qiyaas* in his Madhhab compared to that of other imaams. The later scholars then made their journeys to find and collect ahaadeeth from the various cities and towns and wrote them down; hence, some ahaadeeth of the Sharee'ah explained others. This is the reason behind the large amount of *qiyaas* in his Madhhab, whereas there was little of it in other Madhhabs."

Abul-Hasanaat Al-Lucknowi quoted his words in full in *An-Naafi' al-Kabeer* (p. 135), endorsing and expanding on it in his footnotes, so whoever wishes to consult it should do so there.

Since this is the justification for why Abu Haneefah has sometimes unintentionally contradicted the authentic ahaadeeth - and it is a perfectly acceptable reason, for Allaah does not burden a soul with more than it can bear - it is not permissible to insult him for it, as some ignorant people have done. In fact, it is obligatory to respect him, for he is one of the imaams of the Muslims through whom this Deen has been preserved and handed down to us, in all its branches; also, for he is rewarded under any circumstance: whether he is correct or wrong. Nor is it permissible for his devotees to continue sticking to those of his statements which contradict the authentic ahaadeeth, for those statements are effectively not part of his Madhhab, as the above sayings show. Hence, these are two extremes, and the truth lies in between. "Our Lord! Forgive us, and our brethren who came before us into the Faith; and leave not, in our hearts, any rancour against those who have believed. Our Lord! You are indeed Full of Kindness, Most Merciful." (Al-Hashr 59:10)

[27] Al-Fulaani in *Eeqaaz al-Himam* (p. 50), tracing it to Imaam Muhammad and then saying, "This does not apply to the mujtahid, for he is not bound to their views anyway, but it applies to the muqallid."

2) Maalik ibn Anas (rahimahullaah)

As for Imaam Maalik ibn Anas, he said:

1. "Truly I am only a mortal: I make mistakes (sometimes) and I am correct (sometimes). Therefore, look into my opinions: all that agrees with the Book and the Sunnah, accept it; and all that does not agree with the Book and the Sunnah, ignore it."[28]

2. "Everyone after the Prophet (sallallaahu 'alaihi wa sallam) will have his sayings accepted and rejected - not so the Prophet (sallallaahu 'alaihi wa sallam)."[29]

3. Ibn Wahb said: "I heard Maalik being asked about cleaning between the toes during ablution. He said, 'The people do not have to do that.' I did not approach him until the crowd had lessened, when I said to him, 'We know of a sunnah about that.' He said, 'What is that ?' I said, 'Laith ibn Sa'd, Ibn Lahee'ah and 'Amr ibn al-Haarith narrated to us from Yazeed ibn 'Amr al-Ma'aafiri from Abu 'Abdur-Rahman al-Hubuli from Mustawrid ibn Shaddaad al-Qurashi who said, 'I saw the Messenger of Allaah (sallallaahu 'alaihi wa sallam) rubbing between his toes with his little finger.' He said, 'This hadeeth is sound; I had not heard of it at

---

Sha'raani expanded on that in *Al-Meezaan* (1/26):

"If it is said: 'What should I do with the ahaadeeth which my Imaam did not use, and which were found to be authentic after his death?' The answer which is fitting for you is: 'That you act on them, for had your Imaam come across them and found them to be authentic, he would have instructed you to act on them, because all the Imaams were captives in the hand of the Sharee'ah.' He who does so will have gathered all the good with both his hands, but he who says, 'I will not act according to a hadeeth unless my Imaam did so', he will miss a great amount of benefit, as is the case with many followers of the Imaams of the Madhhabs. It would be better for them to act on every hadeeth found to be authentic after the Imaam's time, hence implementing the will of the Imaams; for it is our firm belief about the Imaams that had they lived longer and come to know of those ahaadeeth which were found authentic after their time, they would have definitely accepted and acted according to them, ignoring any analogies they may have previously made, and any views they may have previously held."

[28] Ibn 'Abdul Barr in *Jaami' Bayaan al-'Ilm* (2/32), Ibn Hazm, quoting from the former in *Usool al-Ahkaam* (6/149), & similarly Al-Fulaani (p. 72)

[29] This is well known among the later scholars to be a saying of Maalik. Ibn 'Abdul Haadi declared it saheeh in *Irshaad as-Saalik* (227/1); Ibn 'Abdul Barr in *Jaami' Bayaan al-'Ilm* (2/91) & Ibn Hazm in *Usool al-Ahkaam* (6/145, 179) had narrated it as a saying of Al-Hakam ibn 'Utaibah and Mujaahid; Taqi ad-Deen as-Subki gave it, delighted with its beauty, in *al-Fataawaa* (1/148) as a saying of Ibn 'Abbaas, and then said: "These words were originally those of Ibn 'Abbaas and Mujaahid, from whom Maalik (radi Allaahu 'anhu) took them, and he became famous for them." It seems that Imaam Ahmad then took this saying from them, as Abu Daawood has said in *Masaa'il of Imaam Ahmad* (p. 276): "I heard Ahmad say, 'Everyone is accepted and rejected in his opinions, with the exception of the Prophet (sallallaahu 'alaihi wa sallam)'."

all until now.' Afterwards, I heard him being asked about the same thing, on which he ordered cleaning between the toes."[30]

3) Shaafi'i (rahimahullaah)

As for Imaam Shaafi'i, the quotations from him are most numerous and beautiful[31], and his followers were the best in sticking to them:

1. "The sunnahs of the Messenger of Allaah (sallallaahu 'alaihi wa sallam) reach, as well as escape from, every one of us. So whenever I voice my opinion, or formulate a principle, where something contrary to my view exists on the authority of the Messenger of Allaah (sallallaahu 'alaihi wa sallam), then the correct view is what the Messenger of Allaah (sallallaahu 'alaihi wa sallam) has said, and it is my view."[32]

2. "The Muslims are unanimously agreed that if a sunnah of the Messenger of Allaah (sallallaahu 'alaihi wa sallam) is made clear to someone, it is not permitted[33] for him to leave it for the saying of anyone else."[34]

3. "If you find in my writings something different to the Sunnah of the Messenger of Allaah (sallallaahu 'alaihi wa sallam), then speak on the basis of the Sunnah of the Messenger of Allaah (sallallaahu 'alaihi wa sallam), and leave what I have said."

In one narration: "... then follow it (the Sunnah), and do not look sideways at anyone else's saying."[35]

4. "When a hadeeth is found to be saheeh, then that is my madhhab."[36]

---

[30] From the Introduction to *Al-Jarh wat-Ta'deel* of Ibn Abi Haatim, pp. 31-2.

[31] Ibn Hazm says in *Usool al-Ahkaam* (6/118):

"Indeed, all the fuqahaa' whose opinions are followed were opposed to taqleed, and they forbade their companions from following their opinion blindly. The sternest among them in this regard was Shaafi'i (rahimahullaah), for he repeatedly emphasised, more than anyone else, following the authentic narrations and accepting whatever the proof dictated; he also made himself innocent of being followed totally, and announced this to those around him. May this benefit him in front of Allaah, and may his reward be of the highest, for he was the cause of great good."

[32] Related by Haakim with a continuous sanad up to Shaafi'i, as in *Taareekh Dimashq* of Ibn 'Asaakir (15/1/3), *I'laam al-Mooqi'een* (2/363, 364) & *Eeqaaz* (p. 100).

[33] Ar.: *halaal*

[34] Ibn al-Qayyim (2/361) & Fulaani (p. 68)

[35] Harawi in *Dhamm al-Kalaam* (3/47/1), Khateeb in *Al-Ihtijaaj bi ash-Shaafi'i* (8/2), Ibn 'Asaakir (15/9/10), Nawawi in *Al-Majmoo'* (1/63), Ibn al-Qayyim (2/361) & Fulaani (p. 100); the second narration is from *Hilyah al-Awliyaa'* of Abu Nu'aim.

[36] Nawawi in Al-Majmoo' (1/63), Sha'raani (1/57), giving its sources as Haakim and Baihaqi, & Fulaani (p. 107). Sha'raani said, "Ibn Hazm said, 'That is, ... found to be saheeh by him or by any other Imaam'." His saying given next confirms this understanding.

5. "You[37] are more knowledgeable about Hadeeth than I, so when a hadeeth is saheeh, inform me of it, whether it is from Kufah, Basrah or Syria, so that I may take the view of the hadeeth, as long as it is saheeh."[38]

Nawawi says: "Our companions acted according to this in the matter of tathweeb (calling to prayer in addition to the adhaan), the conditions on coming out of ihraam due to illness, and other issues well-known in the books of the Madhhab. Among those of our companions who are reported to have passed judgment on the basis of the hadeeth (i.e. rather than the saying of Shaafi'i) are Abu Ya'qoob al-Buweeti and Abu l-Qaasim ad-Daariki. Of our companions from the muhadditheen, Imaam Abu Bakr Al-Baihaqi and others employed this approach. Many of our earliest companions, if they faced an issue for which there was a hadeeth, and the madhhab of Shaafi'i was contrary to it, would act according to the hadeeth and give verdicts based on it, saying, 'The madhhab of Shaafi'i is whatever agrees with the hadeeth.' Shaikh Abu 'Amr (Ibn as-Salaah) says, 'Whoever among the Shaafi'is found a hadeeth contradicting his Madhhab, he would consider whether he fulfilled the conditions of ijtihaad generally, or in that particular topic or issue, in which case he would be free to act on the hadeeth; if not, but nevertheless he found it hard to contradict the hadeeth after further analysis, he would not be able to find a convincing justification for opposing the hadeeth. Hence, it would be left for him to act according to the hadeeth if an independent imaam other than Shaafi'i had acted on it, and this would be justification for his leaving the Madhhab of his Imaam in that issue.' What he (Abu 'Amr) has said is correct and established. Allaah knows best."

There is another possibility which Ibn as-Salaah forgot to mention: what would one do if he did not find anyone else who acted according to the hadeeth? This has been answered by Taqi ad-Deen as-Subki in his article, *The Meaning of Shaafi'i's saying, "When a hadeeth is found to be saheeh, then that is my madhhab"* (p. 102, vol. 3): "For me, the best thing is to follow the hadeeth. A person should imagine himself in front of the Prophet (sallallaahu 'alaihi wa sallam), just having heard it from him: would there be leeway for him to delay acting on it? No, by Allaah ... and everyone bears a responsibility according to his understanding."

The rest of this discussion is given and analysed in *I'laam al-Muwaqqi'een* (2/302, 370) and in the book of al-Fulaane, (full title:) *Eeqaaz Himam ulu l-Absaar, lil-Iqtidaa' bi Sayyid al-Muhaajireen wal-Ansaar, wa Tahdheeruhum 'an al-Ibtidaa' ash-Shaa'i' fi l-Quraa wal-Amsaar, min Taqleed al-Madhaahib ma'a l-Hamiyyah wal-'Asabiyyah bain al-Fuqahaa' al-A'saar* (*Awakening the Minds of those who have Perception, towards following the Leader of the Emigrants and Helpers, and Warning them against the Innovation Widespread among Contemporary Jurists in the Towns and Cities, of following Madhhabs with Zeal and Party-Spirit*). The latter is a unique book in its field, which every desirer of truth should study with understanding and reflection.

[37] addressing Imaam Ahmad ibn Hanbal (rahimahullaah).

[38] Related by Ibn Abi Haatim in *Aadaab ash-Shaafi'i* (pp. 94-5), Abu Nu'aim in *Hulyah al-Awliyaa'* (9/106), al-Khateeb in *Al-Ihtijaaj bish-Shaafi'i* (8/1), and from him Ibn 'Asaakir (15/9/1), Ibn 'Abdul Barr in *al-Intiqaa'* (p. 75), Ibn al-Jawzi in *Manaaqib al-Imaam Ahmad* (p. 499) & Harawi (2/47/2) with three routes from 'Abdullaah ibn Ahmad ibn Hanbal from his father that Shaafi'i said to him: ...etc; thus, it is authentic on the authority of Shaafi'i. This is why Ibn al-Qayyim attributed it definitely to him in *I'laam* (2/325), as did Fulaani in *Eeqaaz* (p. 152) and then said: "Baihaqi said, 'This is why he - i.e. Shaafi'i - used hadeeth so much, because he gathered knowledge from the people of Hijaaz, Syria, Yemen and 'Iraq, and so accepted all that he found to be authentic, without leaning towards or looking at what he had considered out of the Madhhab of the people of his land when the truth was clear to him elsewhere. Some of those before him would limit themselves to what they found in the Madhhab of the people of their land, without attempting to ascertain the authenticity of what opposed it. May Allaah forgive all of us'."

6. "In every issue where the people of narration find a report from the Messenger of Allaah (sallallaahu 'alaihi wa sallam) to be saheeh which is contrary to what I have said, then I take my saying back, whether during my life or after my death."[39]

7. "If you see me saying something, and contrary to it is authentically-reported from the Prophet (sallallaahu 'alaihi wa sallam), then know that my intelligence has departed."[40]

8. "For everything I say, if there is something authentic from the Prophet (sallallaahu 'alaihi wa sallam) contrary to my saying, then the hadeeth of the Prophet (sallallaahu 'alaihi wa sallam) comes first, so do not follow my opinion."[41]

9. "Every statement on the authority of the Prophet (sallallaahu 'alaihi wa sallam) is also my view, even if you do not hear it from me."[42]

4) Ahmad ibn Hanbal (rahimahullaah)

Imaam Ahmad was the foremost among the Imaams in collecting the Sunnah and sticking to it, so much so that he even "disliked that a book consisting of deductions and opinions be written."[43] Because of this he said:

1. "Do not follow my opinion; neither follow the opinion of Maalik, nor Shaafi'i, nor Awzaa'i, nor Thawri, but take from where they took."[44]

In one narration: "Do not copy your Deen from anyone of these, but whatever comes from the Prophet (sallallaahu 'alaihi wa sallam) and his Companions, take it; next are their Successors, where a man has a choice."

Once he said: "Following[45] means that a man follows what comes from the Prophet (sallallaahu 'alaihi wa sallam) and his Companions; after the Successors, he has a choice."[46]

---

[39] Abu Nu'aim (9/107), Harawi (47/1), Ibn al-Qayyim in *I'laam al-Muwaqqi'een* (2/363) & Fulaani (p. 104).

[40] Ibn Abi Haatim in *al-Aadaab* (p. 93), Abul Qaasim Samarqandi in *al-Amaali*, as in the selection from it by Abu Hafs al-Mu'addab (234/1), Abu Nu'aim (9/106) & Ibn 'Asaakir (15/10/1) with a saheeh sanad.

[41] Ibn Abi Haatim, Abu Nu'aim & Ibn 'Asaakir (15/9/2).

[42] Ibn Abi Haatim (pp. 93-4).

[43] Ibn al-Jawzi in *al-Manaaqib* (p. 192)

[44] Fulaani (p. 113) & Ibn al-Qayyim in *I'laam* (2/302).

[45] Ar.: *ittibaa'*

[46] Abu Daawood in *Masaa'il of Imaam Ahmad* (pp. 276-7)

2. "The opinion of Awzaa'i, the opinion of Maalik, the opinion of Abu Haneefah: all of it is opinion, and it is all equal in my eyes. However, the proof is in the narrations (from the Prophet (sallallaahu 'alaihi wa sallam) and his Companions)."[47]

3. "Whoever rejects a statement of the Messenger of Allaah (sallallaahu 'alaihi wa sallam) is on the brink of destruction."[48]

* * *

These are the clear, lucid sayings of the Imaams (Allaah Exalted be pleased with them) about sticking to the Hadeeth and forbidding the following of their opinion without clearly-visible evidence, such that mere opinion and interpretation is not acceptable.

Hence, whoever adhered to whatever of the Sunnah that was proved authentic, even if it opposed some of the Imaams' sayings, he would not be conflicting with their madhhab, nor straying from their path; rather, such a person would be following all of them and would be grasping the most trustworthy hand-hold, which never breaks. However, this would not be the case with the one who abandoned any of the authentic Sunnah simply because it contradicted their views; nay, such a person would be being disobedient to them and opposing their above mentioned sayings, while Allaah says:

$$ فَلَا وَرَبِّكَ لَا يُؤْمِنُونَ $$
$$ حَتَّىٰ يُحَكِّمُوكَ فِيمَا شَجَرَ بَيْنَهُمْ ثُمَّ لَا يَجِدُوا $$
$$ فِي أَنفُسِهِمْ حَرَجًا مِّمَّا قَضَيْتَ وَيُسَلِّمُوا تَسْلِيمًا $$

"But no, by Your Lord, they can have no (real) faith, until they make you judge in all disputes between them, and find in their souls no resistance against your decisions, but accept them with the fullest conviction."[49]. He also says:

$$ فَلْيَحْذَرِ الَّذِينَ يُخَالِفُونَ عَنْ أَمْرِهِ $$
$$ أَن تُصِيبَهُمْ فِتْنَةٌ أَوْ يُصِيبَهُمْ عَذَابٌ أَلِيمٌ $$

"Then let those beware who withstand the Messenger's order, lest some trial befall them or a grievous penalty be inflicted on them."[50]

Haafiz Ibn Rajab al-Hanbali (rahimahullaah) says:

---

[47] Ibn 'Abdul Barr in *Jaami' Bayaan al-'Ilm* (2/149).
[48] Ibn al-Jawzi (p. 182).
[49] an-Nisaa', 4:65
[50] an-Noor, 24:63

"Therefore it is obligatory on anyone who hears of a command of the Messenger of Allaah (sallallaahu 'alaihi wa sallam) or knows it, to explain it to the Ummah, advise them sincerely, and order them to follow his command, even if it contradicts the opinion of someone great. This is because the authority of the Messenger of Allaah (sallallaahu 'alaihi wa sallam) has the most right to be respected and followed, over and above the opinion of anyone great who has unknowingly contradicted the Messenger's command in any matter. This is why the Companions and those after would refute anyone who contradicted the authentic Sunnah, sometimes being very stern in their refutation[51], not out of hatred for that person, for they loved and respected him, but because the Messenger of Allaah was more beloved to them, and his command was superior to the command of any other created being. Hence, when the order of the Messenger and that of someone else conflicted, the order of the Messenger would be more fitting to be enforced and followed. None of this would stop them respecting the person they had opposed because they knew that he would be forgiven[52]; in fact, the latter would not mind his instruction being opposed when the command of the Messenger of Allaah (sallallaahu 'alaihi wa sallam) was clearly shown to be opposite."[53]

---

[51] Even against their fathers and learned men, as Tahaawi in *Sharh Ma'aani al-Aathaar* (1/372) & Abu Ya'laa in his *Musnad* (3/1317) have related, with an isnaad of trustworthy men, from Saalim ibn 'Abdullaah ibn 'Umar, who said:

"I was sitting with Ibn 'Umar (radi Allaahu 'anhu) in the mosque once, when a man from the people of Syria came to him and asked him about continuing the 'Umrah onto the Hajj (known as *Hajj Tamattu'*). Ibn 'Umar replied, 'It is a good and beautiful thing.' The man said, 'But your father (i.e. 'Umar ibn al-Khattaab) used to forbid it!' So he said, 'Woe to you! If my father used to forbid something which the Messenger of Allaah (sallallaahu 'alaihi wa sallam) practised and commanded, would you accept my father's view, or the order of the Messenger of Allaah (sallallaahu 'alaihi wa sallam) ?' He replied, 'The order of the Messenger of Allaah (sallallaahu 'alaihi wa sallam).' He said, 'So go away from me.' Ahmad (no. 5700) related similarly, as did Tirmidhi (2/82) and declared it saheeh.

Also, Ibn 'Asaakir (7/51/1) related from Ibn Abi Dhi'b, who said:

"Sa'd ibn Ibraaheem (i.e. the son of 'Abdur Rahmaan ibn 'Awf) passed judgment on a man on the basis of the opinion of Rabee'ah ibn Abu 'Abdur Rahmaan, so I informed him of the saying of the Messenger of Allaah (sallallaahu 'alaihi wa sallam) which was contradictory to the judgment. Sa'd said to Rabee'ah, 'We have Ibn Abi Dhi'b, whom I regard to be reliable, narrating from the Prophet (sallallaahu 'alaihi wa sallam) contrary to what I ruled.' Rabee'ah said to him, 'You have made your effort, and your judgment has been passed.' Sa'd said, 'Most amazing! I enforce the decree of Sa'd, and not the decree of the Messenger of Allaah (sallallaahu 'alaihi wa sallam)! No, I shall withdraw the decree of Sa'd, son of the mother of Sa'd, and enforce the decree of the Messenger of Allaah (sallallaahu 'alaihi wa sallam).' So Sa'd called for the written decree, tore it up and gave a new verdict."

[52] In fact, he would be rewarded, because of the Prophet's saying (sallallaahu 'alaihi wa sallam): **"When a judge passes judgment, if he makes his effort (ijtihaad) and rules correctly, he will have two rewards; if he makes his effort (ijtihaad) and rules wrongly, he will have one reward."** (Related by Bukhaari, Muslim & others.)

[53] Quoted in the notes on *Eeqaaz al-Himam* (p. 93)

Indeed, how could they mind that, when they had ordered their followers to do so, as we have seen, and had enjoined on them to abandon any of their views which contradicted the Sunnah. In fact, Imaam Shaafi'i (rahimahullaah) told his companions to attribute the authentic Sunnah to him also, even if he had not adopted it or had adopted something contradictory to it. Hence, when the analyst Ibn Daqeeq al-'Eid (rahimahullaah) collected together, in a bulky volume, the issues in which one or more of the four Imaams' madhhabs had contradicted the authentic hadeeth, he wrote at the beginning of it, "It is prohibited to attribute these answers to the Mujtahid Imaams, and obligatory on the jurists who follow their opinions to know of these so that they do not quote them regarding these and thus lie against them."[54]

The Imaams' Followers Leaving their Views if these Contradicted the Sunnah

Due to all that we have mentioned, the disciples of the Imaams, **a number of people from those of old, and a few from those of later time**[55], would not accept all of their Imaam's views; they actually ignored many when they found them to be clearly against the Sunnah. Even the two Imaams, Muhammad ibn al-Hasan and Abu Yoosuf (rahimahullaah) differed from their shaikh Abu Haneefah "in about a third of the Madhhab"[56], as the books of masaa'il prove. Similarly is said about Imaam al-Muzani[57] and other followers of Shaafi'i and other Imaams; were we to start giving examples, the discussion would become exceedingly, long, and we would digress from what we set out to do in this Introduction, so we shall limit ourselves to two instances:

1) Imaam Muhammad says in his *Muwatta'*[58](p. 158), "As for Abu Haneefah, he did not regard there being a prayer to ask for rain, but we hold that the imaam prays two rak'ahs and then supplicates and holds out his wrapping garment ..."

---

[54] Fulaani (p. 99)

[55] cf. al-Waaqi'ah 56:13-14

[56] Ibn 'Aabideen in *Haashiyah* (1/62), & Lucknowi gave its source in *an-Naafi' al-Kabeer* (p. 93) as Ghazaali .

[57] He himself says at the beginning of his *Concise Shaafi'i Fiqh* (printed in the margin of Imaam Shaafi'i's *Al-Umm*):

"This book is a selection from the knowledge of Muhammad ibn Idrees al-Shaafi'i (rahimahullaah) and from the meanings of his sayings, to aid the understanding of whoever wants it, knowing of his forbidding the following of his, or anyone else's, opinion, so that such a person may carefully look for his Deen in it."

[58] In which he has explained his opposing his Imaam in about twenty masaa'il (nos. 42, 44, 103, 120, 158, 169, 172, 173, 228, 230, 240, 244, 274, 275, 284, 314, 331, 338, 355, 356 - from *Ta'leeq al-Mumajjid 'alaa Muwatta' Muhammad (Important Notes on Muhammad's Muwatta')*)

2) We have 'Isaam ibn Yoosuf al-Balkhi, one of the companions of Imaam Muhammad[59] and a servant of Imaam Abu Yoosuf[60], who "would give verdicts contrary to Imaam Abu Haneefah because he did not know the latter's evidence, and other evidence would present itself to him, so he would give verdicts using that."[61] Hence, "he would raise his hands on bowing (in prayer) and on rising from it"[62], as is the *mutawaatir* sunnah of the Prophet (sallallaahu 'alaihi wa sallam); the fact that his three Imaams (i.e. Abu Haneefah, Abu Yoosuf and Muhammad) said otherwise did not prevent him from practising this sunnah. This is the approach which every Muslim is obliged to have, as we have already seen from the testimony of the Four Imaams, and others.

To sum up: I sincerely hope that no follower of an Imaam will race to condemn the principles of this book and abandon benefiting from the sunnahs of the Prophet (sallallaahu 'alaihi wa sallam) which it contains, with the argument that they are contrary to his Madhhab. I hope that such a person will instead consider what we have given of the exhortations of the Imaams towards the obligation to act on the Sunnah and ignore their sayings contradictory to it. I hope also that he will realise that to condemn the attitude of this book is to condemn whichever Imaam he is following, for we have taken these principles from those Imaams, as we have explained. Therefore, whoever refuses to be guided by them on this path is in great danger, for such refusal necessitates turning away from the Sunnah, the Sunnah to which we have been ordered to refer in cases of difference of opinion and on which we have been commanded to depend.

I ask Allaah to make us among those about whom He says,

---

[59] Ibn 'Aabideen mentioned him among them in *Haashiyah* (1/74) & in *Rasm al-Mufti* (1/17). Qurashi mentioned him in *Al-Jawaahir al-Madiyyah fi Tabaqaat al-Hanafiyyah* (p. 347) and said, "He was a reliable transmitter of Hadeeth. He and his brother Ibraaheem were the two shaikhs of Balakh of their time."

[60] *Al-Fawaa'id al-Bahiyyah fi Taraajum al-Hanafiyyah* (p. 116)

[61] *Al-Bahr ar-Raa'iq* (6/93) & *Rasm al-Mufti* (1/28).

[62] *Al-Fawaa'id* ... (p. 116); the author then added a useful note:

"From this can be deduced the falsity of Makhool's narration from Abu Haneefah: 'that he who raises his hands during Prayer, his Prayer is ruined', by which Ameer, the scribe of Itqaani, was deceived, as has been mentioned under his biography. 'Isaam ibn Yoosuf, a companion of Abu Yoosuf, used to raise his hands, so if the above-mentioned narration had any foundation, Abu Yoosuf and 'Isaam would have known about it ... It can also be deduced that if a Hanafi ignored the madhhab of his Imaam in an issue due to the strength of the evidence against it, this would not take him outside the ranks of the Imaam's followers, but this would in fact be proper taqleed in the guise of leaving taqleed; do you not see that 'Isaam ibn Yoosuf left Abu Haneefah's madhhab of not raising the hands, but he is stil counted as a Hanafi?... To Allaah I complain of the ignorance of our time, when they insult anyone who does not follow his Imaam in an issue because of the strength of evidence against it, and expel him from the fold of that Imaam's followers! This is not surprising when those who do this are from the ordinary masses, but it is amazing when it comes from those who imitate men of learning but plod along that path like cattle!"

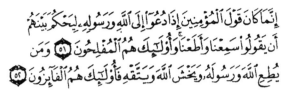

"The answer of the believers, when summoned to Allaah and His Messenger, in order that he may judge betweeen them, is no other than this: they say, "We hear and we obey" - it is such as these that will attain Success. It is those who obey Allaah and His Messenger, and fear Allaah, and keep their duty to Him, who will triumph."[63]

---

[63] an-Noor 24:51-52

MISCONCEPTIONS CLEARED

The preceding Introduction was written ten years ago, during which time it has become apparent to us that our words have had a positive effect on Muslim youth in guiding them towards the obligation in matters of their Deen and worship to return to the pure sources of Islaam: the Book and the Sunnah. Among them, there was an increase in the ranks of of those who practised the Sunnah and devoted themselves to it, - Praise be to Allaah - such that they became conspicuous for it. However, I still found among some of them a steadfastness in failing to practise the Sunnah: not due to any doubt about its obligation after reading the Qur'aanic verses and narrations from the Imaams about going back to the Sunnah, but because of some objections and misconceptions which they had heard from some muqallid shaikhs. Therefore, I decided to mention these incorrect notions and refute them, so that perhaps ths would encourage more people to practise the Sunnah and thus be among the Saved Sect, Allaah Willing.

Misconception One: Some of them say, *"There is no doubt that it is obligatory to return to the guidance of our Prophet (sallallaahu 'alaihi wa sallam) in the matters of our Deen, especially in the recommended acts of worship such as Prayer, where there is no room for opinion or ijtihaad, due to their immutable nature. However, we hardly hear any of the muqallid shaikhs propounding this; in fact, we find them upholding difference of opinion, which they regard as flexibility for the Ummah. Their proof for this is the hadeeth which they repeatedly quote in such circumstances, when refuting the helpers of the Sunnah, 'The difference of opinion (ikhtilaaf) among my Ummah is a mercy (rahmah)' It seems to us that this hadeeth contradicts the principles to which you invite and based on which you have compiled this book and others. So, what do you say about this hadeeth ?"*

Answer: The answer is from two angles:

A) Firstly: This hadeeth is not authentic; in fact, it is false and without foundation. 'Allaamah Subki said, "I have not come across an authentic or weak or fabricated chain of narration for it", i.e. no chain of narrators exists for this "hadeeth"!

It has also been related with the wordings: "... the difference of opinion among my Companions is a mercy for you" and "My Companions are like the stars, so whichever of them you follow, you will be guided." Both of these are not authentic: the former is very feeble; the latter is fabricated. (*See Appendix 1*)

B) Secondly: This hadeeth contradicts the Glorious Qur'aan, for the aayaat forbidding division in the Deen and enjoining unity are too well-known to need reminding. However, there is no harm in giving some of them by way of example: Allaah says,

وَلَا تَنَازَعُوا فَتَفْشَلُوا وَتَذْهَبَ رِيحُكُمْ

"... and do not fall into disputes, lest you lose heart and your power depart"[1];

وَلَا تَكُونُوا مِنَ الْمُشْرِكِينَ ۝ مِنَ الَّذِينَ فَرَّقُوا دِينَهُمْ وَكَانُوا شِيَعًا كُلُّ حِزْبٍ بِمَا لَدَيْهِمْ فَرِحُونَ

"And do not be among those join deities with Allaah, those who split up their Deen and become sects - each party rejoicing with what it has !"[2];

وَلَا يَزَالُونَ مُخْتَلِفِينَ ۝ إِلَّا مَن رَّحِمَ رَبُّكَ

"But they will not cease to differ, except those on whom your Lord bestows His Mercy"[3].

Therefore, if those on whom your Lord has mercy do not differ, and the people of falsehood differ, how can it make sense that differing is a mercy?!

Hence, it is established that this hadeeth is not authentic, neither in the chain of narration, nor in meaning; therefore, it is clear and obvious that it cannot be used to justify resistance towards acting on the Book and the Sunnah, which is what our Imaams have commanded us anyway.

Misconception Two: Others say, *"If differing in the Deen is forbidden, what do you say about the differences among the Companions and among the Imaams after them? Is there any distinction between their differing and that of later generations ?"*

Answer: Yes, there is a big difference between these two examples of differing, which manifests itself in two ways: firstly, in cause; secondly, in effect.

A) As for the differing among the Companions, that was unavoidable, natural difference of understanding: they did not differ by choice. Other factors of their time contributed to this, necessitating difference of opinion, but these vanished after their era.[4] This type of differing is impossible to totally remove and such

---

[1] al-Anfaal, 8:46

[2] ar-Room, 30:31-2

[3] Houd, 11:118-9

[4] cf. *Al-Ihkaam fi Usool al-Ahkaam* by Ibn Hazm, *Hujjatullaah al-Baalighah* by al-Dehlawi, & the latter's essay dealing specifically with this issue, *'Iqd al-Jeed fi Ahkaam al-Ijtihaad wat-Taqleed.*

people cannot be blamed in the light of the above mentioned aayaat because of the absence of the appropriate conditions, i.e. differing on purpose and insisting on it.

However, as for the differing found among the muqallideen today, there is no overriding excuse for it. To one of them, the proof from the Book and the Sunnah is shown, which happens to support a Madhhab other than his usual one, so he puts the proof aside for no other reason except that it is against his Madhhab. It is as though his Madhhab is the original, or it is the Deen which Muhammad (sallallaahu 'alaihi wa sallam) brought, while other Madhhabs are separate Deens which have been abrogated! Others take the opposite extreme, regarding the Madhhabs - for all their differences - as parallel codes of Law, as some of their later adherents explain[5]: there is no harm in a Muslim taking what he likes from them and leaving what he likes, because they are all valid codes of Law !

Both these categories of people justify their remaining divided by this false hadeeth, "*The differing among my Ummah is a mercy*" - so many of them we hear using this as evidence! Some of them give the reason behind this hadeeth and its purpose by saying that it ensures flexibility for the Ummah! Apart from the fact that this "reason" is contrary to the clear Qur'aanic verses and to the meanings of the Imaam's words mentioned, there is also text fom some Imaams to refute it.

Ibn al-Qaasim said,

> "I heard Maalik and Laith saying about the differing of the Companions of the Messenger of Allaah (sallallaahu 'alaihi wa sallam), 'It is not as people say: "There is flexibility in it"; no, it is not like that, but it is a matter of some being mistaken and some being correct'."[6]

Ashhab said,

> "Maalik was asked about the person who accepted a hadeeth narrated by reliable people in the authority of the Companions of the Messenger of Allaah (sallallaahu 'alaihi wa sallam): 'Do you see any flexibility there?' He said, 'No, by Allaah, so that he may be on the truth. Truth can only be one. Two contradictory views, can both be correct?! Truth and right are only one."[7]

Imaam Muzani, a companion of Imaam Shaafi'i said,

> "The Companions of the Messenger of Allaah (sallallaahu 'alaihi wa sallam) indeed differed, and some of them corrected others. Some

---

[5] See *Faid al-Qadeer* by al-Manaawi (1/209) or *Silsilah al-Ahaadeeth ad-Da'eefah* (1/76, 77)
[6] Ibn 'Abdul Barr in *Jaami' Bayaan al-'Ilm* (2/81-2)
[7] ibid. (2/82, 88-9)

scrutinised others' views and found fault with them. If all their views had been correct, they would not have done so.

'Umar ibn al-Khattab became angry at the dispute between Ubayy ibn Ka'b and Ibn Mas'ood about prayer in a single garment. Ubayy said, 'Prayer in one garment is good and fine; Ibn Mas'ood said, 'That is only if one does not have many clothes.' So 'Umar came out in anger, saying, 'Two men from among the companions of the Messenger of Allaah (sallallaahu 'alaihi wa sallam), who are looked up to and learnt from, disputing? Ubayy has spoken the truth and not cared about Ibn Mas'ood. But if I hear anyone disputing about it after this I will do such-and-such to him'."[8]

Imaam Muzani also said,

"There is the one who allows differing and thinks that if two scholars make ijtihaad on a problem and one says, 'Halaal', while the other says, 'Haraam', then both have arrived at the truth with their ijtihad! It can be said to such a person, 'Is this view of yours based on the sources or on qiyaas (analogy) ?' If he says, 'On the sources', it can be said, 'How can it be based on the sources, when the Qur'aan negates differing ?' And if he says, 'On analogy', it can be said, 'How can the sources negate differing, and it be allowed for you to reason by analogy that differing is allowed?! This is unacceptable to anyone intelligent, let alone to a man of learning."[9]

If it is said further: "What you have quoted from Imaam Maalik that truth is only one, not plural, is contradicted by what is found in Al-Madkhal al-Fiqhi by Shaikh Zarqaa' (1/89), "The Caliphs Abu Ja'far al-Mansoor and later ar-Rasheed proposed to select the Madhhab of Imaam Maalik and his book Al-Muwatta' as the official code of Law for the 'Abbaasi empire, but Maalik forbade them from this, saying, "Indeed, the Companions of the Messenger of Allaah (sallallaahu 'alaihi wa sallam) differed in the non-fundamental issues and were scattered in various towns, but each of them was correct."

I say: This incident of Imaam Maalik (rahimahullaah) is well-known, but his saying at the end, "but each of them was correct" is one for which I find no basis in any of the narrations or sources I have come across[10], by Allaah, except for one narration collected by Abu Nu'aim in Hilyah al-Awliyaa' (6/332), but with a chain of narrators which includes al-Miqdaam ibn Daawood who is classified among the weak narrators by Dhahabi in ad-Du'afaa'; not only this, but the wording of it is, "... but each of them was correct in his own eyes." Hence the phrase "in his own eyes" shows that the narration in Madkhal is fabricated; indeed, how could it be otherwise, when it contradicts what has been reported

---

[8] ibid. (2/83-4)

[9] ibid (2/89)

[10] cf. Al-Intiqaa' by Ibn 'Abdul Barr (41), Kashf al-Mughatta fi Fadl al-Muwatta' (pp. 6-7) by Ibn 'Asaakir, & Tadhkirah al-Huffaaz by Dhahabi (1/195).

on reliable authority from Imaam Maalik that truth is only one and not plural, as we have mentioned, and this is agreed on by all the Imaams of the Companions and the Successors as well as the four Mujtahid Imaams and others. Ibn 'Abdul Barr says, "If the conflicting views could both be right, the Salaf would not have corrected each other's ijtihaad, judgments, and verdicts. Simple reasoning forbids that something and its opposite can both be correct; as the fine saying goes,

To prove two opposites simultaneously is the most hideous absurity."[11]

If it is said further, "Given that this narration from Imaam Maalik is false, why did he forbid al-Mansoor from bringing the people together on his book *Al-Muwatta'* rather than acceding to the Caliph's wish ?"

I say: The best that I have found in answer to this is what Haafiz Ibn Katheer has mentioned in his *Sharh Ikhtisaar 'Uloom al-Hadeeth* (p.31), that Imaam Maalik said, "Indeed the people have come together on, and know of, things which we are not acquainted with." This was part of the excellence of his wisdom and impartiality, as Ibn Katheer (rahimahullaah) says.

Hence, it is proved that all differing is bad, not a mercy! However, one type of differing is reprehensible, such as that of staunch followers of the Madhhabs, while another type is not blameworthy, such as the differing of the Companions and the Imaams who succeeded them - May Allaah raise us in their company, and give us the capability to tread their path.

Therefore, it is clear that the differing of the Companions was not like that of the muqallideen. Briefly: the Companions only differed when it was inevitable, but they used to hate disputes, and would avoid them whenever possible; as for the muqallideen, even though it is possible in a great many cases to avoid differing, they do not agree nor strive towards unity; in fact, they uphold differing. Hence there is an enormous gulf between these two types of people in their difference of opinion.

This was from the point of view of cause.

B) The difference in effect is more obvious.

The Companions (radi Allaahu 'anhum), despite their well-known differing in non-fundamental issues, were extremely careful to preserve outward unity, staying well-away from anything which would divide them and split their ranks. For example, there were among them those who approved of saying the *basmalah* loudly (in prayer) and those who did not; there were those who held that raising the hands (in prayer) was recommended and those who did not; there were those who held that touching a woman nullified ablution, and those who did not; - but despite all that, they would all pray together behind

---

[11] *Jaami' Bayaan al-'Ilm* (2/88)

one imaam, and none of them would disdain from praying behind an imaam due to difference of opinion.

As for the muqallideen, their differing is totally opposite, for it has caused Muslims to be divided inthe mightiest pillar of faith after the two testifications of faith: none other than the Salaah (Prayer). They refuse to pray together behind one imaam, arguing that the imaam's prayer is invalid, or at least detestable, for someone of a different Madhhab. This we have heard and seen, as others beside us have seen[12]; how can it not be, when nowadays some famous books of the Madhhabs rule such cases of invalidity or detestability. The result of this has been that you find four Mihraabs (alcoves) in some large congregational mosques, in which four imaams successively lead the Prayer, and you find people waiting for their imaam while another imaam is already standing in Prayer!!!

In fact, to some muqallideen, the difference between the Madhhabs has reached a worse state than that, such as a ban in marriage between Hanafees and Shaafi'is; one well known Hanafi scholar, later nicknamed *Mufti ath-Thaqalayn (The Mufti for Humans and Jinn)*, issued a fatwaa allowing a Hanafi man to marry a Shaafi'i woman, because "her position is like that of the People of the Book"[13] ! This implies - and implied meanings are acceptable to them - that the reverse case is not allowed, i.e. a Hanafi woman marrying a Shaafi'i man, just as a Muslim woman cannot marry a Jew or Christian?!!

These two examples, out of many, are enough to illustrate to anyone intelligent the evil effects of the differing of the later generations and their insistence upon it, unlike the differing of the earlier generations (the Salaf), which did not have any adverse effect on the Ummah. Because of this, the latter are exempt from the verses prohibiting division in the Deen, unlike the later generations. May Allaah guide us all to the Straight Path.

Further, how we wish that the harm caused by such differing be limited to among themselves and not extend to the other peoples being given da'wah, for then it would not be that bad, but it is so sad when they allow it to reach the non-believers in many areas around the world, and their differing obstructs the entry of people in large numbers into the Deen of Allaah! The book *Zalaam min al-Gharb* by Muhammad al-Ghazaali (p. 200) records the following incident,

> "It so happened during a conference held at the University of Princeton in America that one of the speakers raised a question, one which is a favourite of the Orientalists and the attackers of Islaam: 'Which teachings do the Muslims advance to the world in order to specify the Islaam towards which they are inviting ? Is it Islamic teachings as understood by the Sunnis? Or is it as understood by the Imaami or

---

12 see Chapter Eight of the book, *Maa Laa Yajooz min al-Khilaaf* (pp. 65-72), where you will find numerous examples of what we have indicated, some of them involving scholars of Al-Azhar.
13 *Al-Bahr ar-Raa'iq.*

Zaidi Shee'ahs? Moreover, all of these are divided further amongst themselves, and further, some of them believe in limited progression in thought, while others believe obstinately in fixed ideas.'

The result was that the inviters to Islaam left those being invited in confusion, for they were themselves utterly confused."[14]

In the Preface to *Hadiyyah as-Sultaan ilaa Muslimee Bilaad Jaabaan* by 'Allaamah Sultaan al-Ma'soomi (rahimahullaah), the author says,

A query was posed to me by the Muslims from Japan, from the cities of Tokyo and Osaka in the far east, "What is the actual Deen of Islaam? What is a Madhhab? Is it necessary for one ennobled by the Deen of Islaam to adhere to one of the four Madhhabs? That is, should he be Maaliki, Hanafi, Shaafi'i or Hanbali, or is it not necessary?"

This was because a major differing, a filthy dispute, had occured here, when a number of groups of Japanese intellectuals wanted to enter into the Deen of Islaam, and be ennobled by the nobility of Eeman. When they proposed this to some Muslims present in Tokyo, some people from India said, "It is best that they choose the Madhhab of Abu Haneefah, for he is the Lamp of the Ummah"; some people from Indonesia (Java) said, "No, they should be Shaafi'i!" So when the Japanese heard these statements, they were extremely perplexed and were thrown off their original purpose. Hence the issue of the Madhhabs became a barrier in the path of their accepting Islaam!!

---

[14] I now say: Muhammad al-Ghazaali's recent writings such as his newly-released book entitled *As-Sunnah an-Nabawiyyah bayna Ahl al-Hadeeth wa Ahl al-Fiqh* (The Prophetic Sunnah between the People of Hadeeth and the People of Fiqh) have confirmed that he himself is one of those inviters to Islaam who are "themselves utterly confused"! His writings have for long betrayed his confusion, his distortion of the Sunnah, and his using his intellect to authenticate or falsify ahaadeeth, not by turning to the principles and science of Hadeeth, nor to the experts of that field; instead, whatever appeals to him, he authenticates, even if it is weak, and declares unreliable whatever is not to his liking, even if it is agreed to be authentic!

His above approach is shown most obviously in his discussion of the ahaadeeth in his previous book *Fiqh as-Seerah* , where he explains his methodology of accepting unreliable ahaadeeth and discarding authentic ones on the basis of the text of the hadeeth alone, from which the reader can see that the objective criticism of Hadeeth has no value in his eyes if it contradicts a "reasoned analysis", which varies enormously from person to person, for what is truth to one is falsehood to another! Thus the whole of Islaam becomes subject to personal whims, having no principles nor reference points except personal opinion; this is poles apart from the position of the early leading 'ulamaa of Islaam, "that the Isnaad is part of the religion; were it not for the Isnaad, people would have said whatever they wished."

His latest above-mentioned book has exposed to the people his Mu'tazilite methodology, his blatant disregard for the Imaams of Hadeeth and their efforts over the ages in serving the Sunnah, and distinguishing the genuine traditions from the unreliable ones, and his lack of appreciation of the efforts of the Imaams of Fiqh in their laying down principles and developing issues on that basis, for he takes from these and leaves from them whatever he wishes, with no consistency towards any set of principles or fundamentals!

Misconception Three: *Others have the idea that what we invite to, of following the Sunnah and not accepting the views of the Imaams contrary to it, means to completely abandon following their views and benefiting from their opinions and ijtihaad.*

Answer: This idea is as far as can be from the truth - it is false and obviously flawed, as is clearly evident from our previous discussion, all of which suggests otherwise. All that we are calling to is to stop treating the Madhhab as a Deen, placing it in the position of the Qur'aan and the Sunnah, such that it is referred to in the case of dispute or when extracting a new judgment for unexpected cirumstances, as the so-called jurists of this age do when setting new rules for personal matters, marriage, divorce, etc, instead of referring to the Qur'aan and the Sunnah to distinguish the right from the wrong, the truth from falsehood - all of this on the basis of their "Differing is a mercy" and their idea of pursuing every concession, ease and convenience! How fine was the saying of Sulaiman at-Taymi (rahimahullaah):

> Were you to accept the concessions of every scholar,
> In you would gather every evil.

Related by Ibn 'Abdul Barr in *Jaami' Bayaan al-'Ilm* (2/91-91), who said after it, "There is ijmaa' (consensus of opinion) on this: I know of no contrary view."

All this pursuing of concessions for the sake of it is what we reject, and it agrees with ijmaa', as you see.

As for referring to the Imaams' views, benefiting from them, and being helped by them in understanding the truth where they have differed and there is no text in the Qur'aan and the Sunnah, or when there is need for clarification, we do not reject it. In fact, we enjoin it and stress upon it, for there is much benefit expected in this for whoever treads the path of being guided by the Qur'aan and the Sunnah. 'Allaamah Ibn 'Abdul Barr (rahimahullaah) says (2/182),

> "Hence, my brother, you must preserve the fundamentals and pay attention to them. You should know that he who takes care over preserving the sunnahs and the commandments stated in the Qur'aan, considers the views of the jurists to assist him in his ijtihaad, open up different angles of approach and explain sunnahs which carry different possible meanings, does not blindly follow the opinion of anyone of them the way the Sunnah should be followed without analysis, nor ignores what the scholars themselves achieved in preserving and reflecting on the sunnahs, but follows them in discussion, understanding and analysis, is grateful to them for their efforts through which they have benefited him and alerted him about various points, praises them for their correct conclusions, as in the majority of cases, but does not clear them of errors just as they did not clear themselves:

such is the pursuer of knowledge who is adhering to the way of the pious predecessors; such is the really fortunate and truly guided; such is the follower of the Sunnah of his Prophet (sallallaahu 'alaihi wa sallam), and the guidance of the Companions (radi Allaahu 'anhum).

But he who refrains from analysis, forsakes the method we have mentioned, disputes the sunnahs with his opinion and desires to accommadate them only where his own view allows: such a one is straying and leading others astray. Further, he who is ignorant of all we have mentioned, and plunges carelessly into giving verdicts without knowledge: such a one is even more blind, and on a path more astray."

Misconception Four: There exists another common misconception among muqallideen which bars them from practising the Sunnah which it is apparent to them that their Madhhab is different to it in that issue: they think that practising that sunnah entails faulting the founder of the Madhhab. To them, finding fault means insulting the Imaam; if it is no. allowed to insult any individual Muslim, how can they insult one of their Imaams ?

Answer: This reasoning is totally fallacious, and borne of not understanding the Sunnah; otherwise, how can an intelligent Muslim argue in such a way?!

The Messenger of Allaah (sallallaahu 'alaihi wa sallam) himself said, *When the one making a judgment strives his outmost and arrives at the correct result, he has two rewards; but if he judges, striving his utmost and passes the wrong judgment, he has one reward.*[15] This hadeeth refutes the above argument and explains lucidly and without any obscurity that if someone says, "So-and-so was wrong", its meaning under the Sharee'ah is "So-and-so has one reward." So if he is rewarded in the eyes of the one finding fault, how can you accuse the latter of insulting him?! There is doubt that this type of accusation is baseless and anyone who makes it must retract it: otherwise it is he who is insulting Muslims, not just ordinary individuals among them, but their great Imaams among the Companions, Successors the subsequent Mujtahid Imaams and others. This is because we know for sure that these illustrious personalities used to fault and refute each other[16]; is it reasonable to say, "They used to insult each other"? No! In fact, it is authentically-reported that the Messenger of Allaah (sallallaahu 'alaihi wa sallam) himself faulted Abu Bakr (radi Allaahu 'anhu) in his interpretation of a man's dream, saying to him, *"You were right in some of it and wrong in some of it"*[17]- so did he (sallallaahu 'alaihi wa sallam) insult Abu Bakr by these words?!

One of the astonishing effects this misconception has on its holders is that it prevents them from following the Sunnah when it is different to their

---

[15] Bukhaari & Muslim.

[16] See the previous words of Imaam Muzani and Haafiz Ibn Rajab al-Hanbali.

[17] Bukhaari & Muslim; see Appendix Two for the full hadeeth.

Madhhab, since to them practising it means insulting the Imaam, whereas following him, even when contrary to the Sunnah, means respecting and loving him! Hence they insist on following his opinion to escape from this supposed disrespect.

These people have forgotten - I am not saying: ... pretended to forget - that because of this notion, they have landed in something far worse than that from which they were fleeing. It should be said to them, "If to follow someone means that you are respecting him, and to oppose him means that you are insulting him, then how do you allow yourselves to oppose the example of the Prophet (sallallaahu 'alaihi wa sallam) and not follow it, preferring to follow the Imaam of the Madhhab in a path different to the Sunnah, when the Imaam is not infallible and insulting him is not Kufr?! If you interpret opposing the Imaam as insulting him, then opposing the Messenger of Allaah (sallallaahu 'alaihi wa sallam) is more obviously insulting him; in fact, it is open Kufr, from which we seek refuge with Allaah!" If this is said to them, they cannot answer to it, by Allaah, except one retort which we hear time and time again from some of them: "We have left this sunnah trusting in the Imaam of the Madhhab, and he was more learned about the Sunnah than us."

Our answer to this is from many angles, which have already been discussed at length in this Introduction. This is why I shall briefly limit myself to one approach, a decisive reply by the permission of Allaah. I say:

> "The Imaam of your Madhhab is not the only one who was more learned about the Sunnah than you: in fact, there are dozens, nay hundreds, of Imaams who too were more knowledgeable about the Sunnah than you. Therefore, if an authentic sunnah happens to differ from your Madhhab, and it was taken by one of these other Imaams, it is definitely essential that you accept this sunnah in this circumstance. This is because your above-mentioned argument is of no use here, for the one opposing you will reply, 'We have accepted this Sunnah trusting in our Imaam, who accepted it' - in this instance, to follow the latter Imaam is preferable to following the Imaam who has differed from the Sunnah."

This is clear and not confusing to anyone, Allaah Willing.

Because of all of the above, I am able to say:

Since this book of ours has collected the authentic sunnahs reported from the Messenger of Allaah (sallallaahu 'alaihi wa sallam) about the description of his Prayer, there is no excuse for anyone to not act on it, for there is nothing in it which the scholars have unanimously rejected, as they would never do. In fact, in every instance several of them have adopted the authentic sunnah; any one of them who did not do so is excused and rewarded once, because the text was not conveyed to him at all, or it was conveyed but in such a way that to him it did not constitute proof, or due to other reasons which are well-known among the scholars. However, those after him in front of whom the text is firmly established have no excuse for following his opinion; rather, it is obligatory to follow the infallible text.

This message has been the purpose of this Introduction. Allaah, Mighty and Sublime, says,

"O you who believe! Give your response to Allaah and His Messenger when he calls you to that which will give you life, and know that Allaah comes in between a man and his heart, and it is He to whom you shall all be gathered."[18]

Allaah says the Truth; He shows the Way; and He is the Best to Protect and the Best to Help. May Allaah send prayers and peace on Muhammad, and on his family and his Companions. Praise be to Allaah, Lord of the Worlds.

Muhammad Naasir ad-Deen al-Albaani

Damascus 28/10/1389 AH

---

[18] al-Anfaal, 8:24

THE PROPHET'S PRAYER DESCRIBED

(PEACE AND MERCY OF ALLAAH BE UPON HIM)

from beginning to end, as though you were watching it.

"Pray as you have seen me praying." (transmitted by al-Bukhaari)

1

FACING THE KA'BAH

When the Messenger of Allaah (sallallaahu 'alaihi wa sallam) stood for prayer, he would face the Ka'bah in both obligatory and voluntary prayers[1], and he (sallallaahu 'alaihi wa sallam) ordered that, saying to the "one who prayed badly"[2] : *When you stand for prayer, perform ablution prefectly, then face the qiblah and say takbeer.*[3]

"During a journey, he (sallallaahu 'alaihi wa sallam) would pray voluntary prayers and witr on his mount, wherever it faced carrying him [east or west]."[4]

The saying of Allaah, the Exalted,

$$\text{فَأَيْنَمَا تُوَلُّوا فَثَمَّ وَجْهُ اللَّهِ}$$

"Wherever you turn, there is the Face of Allaah" (Baqarah, 2:115) applies to this.[5]

"[Sometimes] when he intended to pray non-obligatory prayers on his she-camel, he would make it face the qiblah, say takbeer, and pray towards wherever his mount turned its face."[6]

"He would make rukoo' and sajdah on his mount by lowering his head, making the sajdah lower than the rukoo'."[7]

"When he intended to pray obligatory prayers, he would dismount and face the qiblah."[8]

In prayer during severe fear, he (sallallaahu 'alaihi wa sallam) set the example for his ummah to pray "on foot, standing on their feet, or mounted; facing the qiblah or not facing it"[9], and he also said, *When they (the armies) meet, then it (i.e. the prayer) is takbeer and indication with the head.*[10]

---

[1] This is a *mutawaatir* fact, so detail is not necessaary, although some of the evidence for it will follow.

[2] see Appendix 3.

[3] Collected by Bukhaari, Muslim & Siraaj.

[4] Collected by Bukhaari, Muslim & Siraaj. Its takhreej is given in *Irwaa' al-Ghaleel* (289 & 588)

[5] Muslim; Tirmidhi declared it saheeh.

[6] Abu Daawood, Ibn Hibbaan in *Thiqaat* (1/12), Diyaa' in *Mukhtaarah* with a hasan sanad,; Ibn as-Sukn declared it saheeh, as did Ibn Al-Mulaqqin in *Khulasah Badr al-Muneer* (22/1) and, before them, 'Abdul Haqq al-Ishbeeli in his *Ahkaam* (no. 1394 with my checking). Ahmad used it as proof, as Ibn Haani reported from him in his *Masaa'il* (1/67).

[7] Ahmad & Tirmidhi , who declared it saheeh.

[8] Bukhaari & Ahmad.

[9] Bukhaari & Muslim.

[10] Baihaqi with a sanad meeting the requirements of Bukhaari and Muslim.

He (sallallaahu 'alaihi wa sallam) also used to say: *What is between the east and the west is qiblah.* [1]

Jaabir (radiallaahu 'anhu) said:

"Once, when we were with the Messenger of Allaah (sallallaahu 'alaihi wa sallam) on an expedition, the sky was cloudy, so we tried to find the Qibla but we differed, so each one of us prayed in a different direction, and each of us drew marks in front of him in order to mark our positions. In the morning, we looked at it and found that we had not prayed towards the Qiblah. So we mentioned this to the Prophet (sallallaahu 'alaihi wa sallam) [but he did not order us to repeat (the prayer)] and he said: *Your prayer was sufficient.*"[2]

"He (sallallaahu 'alaihi wa sallam) used to pray towards Bait al-Muqaddas [with the Ka'bah in front of him] before the following verse was revealed:

$$ قَدْ نَرَىٰ تَقَلُّبَ وَجْهِكَ فِى ٱلسَّمَآءِ $$

$$ فَلَنُوَلِّيَنَّكَ قِبْلَةً تَرْضَىٰهَا فَوَلِّ وَجْهَكَ شَطْرَ ٱلْمَسْجِدِ ٱلْحَرَامِ $$

"We see the turning of your faces to the heavens; now shall we turn you to a Qiblah that shall please you: turn then your faces in the direction of the Sacred Mosque" (Baqarah 2:144). When it was revealed he faced the Ka'bah. There were people at Qubaa' praying Fajr when someone came to them and said, 'Verily the Messenger of Allaah (sallallaahu 'alaihi wa sallam) has had some of the Qur'aan revealed to him last night and he has been ordered to face the Ka'bah, [verily] so face it'. Their faces were towards Shaam, so they turned round [and their Imaam turned round to face the qiblah along with them]."[3]

STANDING IN PRAYER

He (sallallaahu 'alaihi wa sallam) used to stand in prayer for both obligatory and voluntary prayers, carrying out the command of the Exalted:

$$ وَقُومُوا۟ لِلَّهِ قَـٰنِتِينَ $$

"And stand before Allaah devoutly." (Baqarah, 2:238).

---

1 Tirmidhi and Haakim, who declared it saheeh, and I have given it in *Irwaa' al-Ghaleel* (292), the publication of which Allaah has made easy.

2 Daaraqutni, Haakim, Baihaqi, Tirmidhi, Ibn Maajah & Tabaraani; it is given in *Iruaa'* (296)

3 Bukhaari, Muslim, Ahmad, Siraaj, Tabaraani (3/108/2) & Ibn Sa'd (1/234). It is also in *Irwaa'* (290)

As for during a journey, he would pray voluntary prayers on his riding beast.

He set the example for his ummah to pray during severe fear on foot or while mounted, as has been mentioned, and that is the purpose of the saying of Allaah:

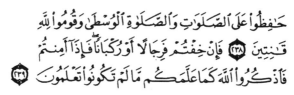

"Guard strictly your (habit of) prayers, especially the Middle Prayer[1], and stand before Allaah devoutly. If you fear (an enemy) then pray on foot, or while riding. But when you are in security, celebrate Allaah's praises in the manner He has taught you, which you did not know before." (Baqarah, 2:238-9)

He (sallallaahu 'alaihi wa sallam) prayed sitting during the illness of which he died."[2] He also prayed sitting on another occasion before that, when he was injured, and the people behind him prayed standing; so he indicated to them to sit, so they sat (and prayed). When he finished, he said, *You were going to do as the Persians and the Romans do: stand for their kings who sit. So do not do so, for the Imaam is there to be followed: when he makes rukoo', make rukoo', when he rises, rise; and when he prays sitting, pray sitting [all of you].* [3]

The Prayer of a Sick Person in a Sitting Position

'Imran ibn Husain (radiallaahu 'anhu) said, "I was suffering from haemorrhoids (piles), so I asked the Messenger of Allaah (sallallaahu 'alaihi wa sallam) and he said, *Pray standing; if you are not able, then sitting down; if you are not able to do so, then pray lying down.*[4]

'Imraan ibn Husain also said, "I asked him (sallallaahu 'alaihi wa sallam) about the prayer of a man while sitting, so he said: *He who prays standing, that is better; he who prays sitting, his reward is half that of the former. He who prays lying down (and in another narration: reclining), has half the reward of the one*

---

[1] i.e.,the 'Asr prayer according to the correct saying of the majority of scholars, among them Abu Haneefah and his two students. There are ahaadeeth about this which Ibn Katheer has given in his Tafseer of the Qur'aan.

[2] Tirmidhi, who declared it saheeh, and Ahmad.

[3] Muslim and Bukhaari, and it is given in my book *Irwaa' al-Ghaleel* under Hadeeth 394.

[4] Bukhaari, Abu Daawood and Ahmad.

who sits.[1] This applies to the sick person, for Anas (radiallaahu 'anhu) said, "The Messenger of Allaah (sallallaahu 'alaihi wa sallam) came out to the people while they were praying sitting due to illness, so he said: *Verily, the prayer of one who sits is (worth) half of the prayer of the one who stands.* [2]

Once "he (sallallaahu 'alaihi wa sallam) visited a sick person and saw him praying (leaning) on a pillow, so he took it and cast it aside. So the man took a stick to pray (leaning) on it, but he took it and cast it aside and said: *Pray on the ground if you can, but otherwise make movements with your head, making your sujood lower than your rukoo'.*"[3]

Prayer on a Ship

He (sallallaahu 'alaihi wa sallam) was asked about prayer on a ship, so he said, *Pray on it standing, unless you are afraid of drowning.*[4]

When he grew old he took a support at his place of prayer to lean on.[5]

Sitting and Standing in the Night Prayer (Tahajjud)

He (sallallaahu 'alaihi wa sallam), used to pray long through the night standing, and long through the night sitting, and if he recited standing, he would bow standing, and if he recited sitting, he would bow sitting."[6]

Sometimes, "He would pray sitting, so he would recite sitting until about thirty or forty verses of his recitation wre left; he would then stand up to recite these standing and then bow and prostrate, and he would do likewise in the second raka'ah."[7]

---

[1] ibid. Khattaabi said, "The meaning of 'Imran's hadeeth is intended for a sick person who is able to undergo hardship and stand with difficulty. Hence the reward of praying sitting has been made half of the reward of praying standing: encouraging him to pray standing while allowing him to sit." Ibn Hajr said in *Fath al-Baari* (2/468): "This deduction is valid".

[2] Ahmad & Ibn Maajah with a saheeh sanad.

[3] Tabaraani, Bazzaar, Ibn as-Samaak in his hadeeth book (67/2) & Baihaqi . It has a saheeh isnaad as I have explained in *Silsilah al-Ahaadeeth as-Saheehah* (323).

[4] Bazzaar (68), Daaraqutni, 'Abdul Ghani al-Maqdisi in his Sunan (82/2) and Haakim declared it saheeh and Dhahabi agreed.

[5] Abu Daawood and Haakim, who declared it saheeh, as did Dhahabi. I have given it in *as-Saheehah* (319) and *Irwaa'* (383)

[6] Muslim and Abu Daawood.

[7] Bukhaari and Muslim.

In fact, "he prayed as-subhah[1] sitting down towards the end of his life when he had grown old, and that was a year before his death."[2]

Also "he would sit cross-legged."[3]

Prayer Wearing Shoes and the Command to do so

"He used to stand (in prayer) bare-footed sometimes and wearing shoes sometimes."[4]

He allowed this for his ummah, saying: *When one of you prays, he should wear his shoes or take them off and put them between his feet, and not harm others with them.*[5]

He encouraged prayer wearing them sometimes, saying: *Be different from the Jews, for they do not pray in their shoes nor in their khuffs* (leather socks).[6]

Occasionally he would remove them from his feet while in prayer and then continue his prayer, as Abu Sa'eed al-Khudri has said:

"The Messenger of Allaah (sallallaahu 'alaihi wa sallam) prayed with us one day. Whilst he was engaged in the prayer he took off his shoes and placed them on his left. When the people saw this, they took off their shoes. When he finished his prayer he said, *Why did you take your shoes off?* They said, 'We saw you taking your shoes off, so we took our shoes off.' He said, *Verily Jibreel came to me and informed me that there was dirt - or he said: something harmful - (in another narration: filth)on my shoes, so I took them off. Therefore, when one of you goes to the mosque, he should look at his shoes: if he sees in them dirt - or he said: something harmful - (in another narration: filth) he should wipe them and pray in them.*[7]

"When he removed them, he would place them on his left"[8] and he would also say: *When one of you prays, he should not place his shoes on his right nor*

---

[1] i.e. voluntary prayer (night or forenoon), named so due to its content of *tasbeeh* (glorification).
[2] Muslim and Ahmad.
[3] Nasaa'i, Ibn Khuzaimah in his Saheeh (1/107/2), 'Abdul Ghani al-Maqdisi in his Sunan (80/1) & Haakim, who declared it saheeh and Dhahabi agreed.
[4] Abu Daawood & Ibn Maajah. It is a mutawatir hadeeth as Tahaawi has mentioned.
[5] Abu Daawood & Bazzaar (53, az-Zawa'id); Haakim declared it saheeh and Dhahabi agreed.
[6] ibid.
[7] Abu Daawood, Ibn Khuzaimah & Haakim, who declared it saheeh and Dhahabi and Nawawi agreed. The first one is given in *Irwaa'* (284)
[8] ibid.

on his left, where they will be on someone else's right, except if there is no one on his left, but he should place them between his feet.[1]

Prayer on the Pulpit (Minbar)

"Once he (sallallaahu 'alaihi wa sallam) prayed on the pulpit (in another narration: '... which had three steps')[2]. Hence [he stood on it and said takbeer and the people behind him said takbeer while he was on the pulpit,] [then he made rukoo' on the pulpit,] then he rose and descended backwards to make sajdah at the foot of the pulpit. Then he returned, [and did on it as he had done in the first rak'ah], until he completed his prayer. He then turned to the people and said: *O people! I have done this so that you may follow me and learn my prayer*.[3]

The *Sutrah*[4], and the Obligation to have one

"He (sallallaahu 'alaihi wa sallam) used to stand near to the sutrah, so that there was (a distance of) three cubits between him and the wall"[5] and "between the place of his prostration and the wall, (there was) enough space for a sheep to pass."[6]

He used to say: "Do not pray except towards a sutrah, and do not let anyone pass in front of you, but if someone continues (to try to pass) then fight him, for he has a companion (i.e. a shaytaan) with him."[7]

He would also say: "When one of you prays towards a sutrah, he should get close to it so that Shaytaan cannot break his prayer."[8]

---

[1] Abu Daawood, Nasaa'i & Ibn Khuzaimah (1/110/2) with a saheeh isnaad.

[2] This is the sunnah about the pulpit: that it should have three steps, not more, To have more is an innovation, from the period of Bani Umayyah, which often causes an interruption in the row, and to get out of that by having it in the western corner of the mosque or in the mihrab is another innovation, as is the raising of it in the wall like a balcony to which one ascends by means of steps in the wall! Whereas the best guidance is the guidance of Muhammad (sallallaahu 'alaihi wa sallam). See *Fath al-Baari* (2/331).

[3] Bukhaari , Muslim (who collected the other narration) & Ibn Sa'd (1/253). It is given in *Irwaa'* (545)

[4] lit., "screen, cover"; in the context of prayer, it refers to an object just beyond the place of prostration, within which nothing should pass, as is detailed in this section.

[5] Bukhaari & Ahmad.

[6] Bukhaari & Muslim.

[7] Ibn Khuzaimah in his Saheeh (1/93/1) with a sound isnaad.

[8] Abu Daawood, Bazzaar (p. 54 - Zawaaid) & Haakim, who declared it saheeh and Dhahabi and Nawawi agreed.

Sometimes "he would seek to pray at the pillar which was in his mosque."[1]

"When he prayed [in an open space where there was nothing to use as sutrah] he would plant a spear in the ground in front of him and pray towards it with the people behind him"[2]; Sometimes "he would to set his mount sideways and pray towards it"[3] but this is not the same as prayer in the resting-place of camels[4], which "he forbade"[5], and sometimes "he would take his saddle; set it lengthways and pray towards its end."[6]

He would say: *When one of you places in front of him something such as the stick on the end of a saddle, he should pray and not mind anyone who passes beyond it.*[7]

Once "he prayed towards a tree"[8] and sometimes "he would pray towards the bed on which 'Aa'ishah (radi Allaahu anhaa) was lying [under her sheet]."[9]

He (sallallaahu 'alaihi wa sallam), would not let anything pass between him and his sutrah, hence once "he was praying, when a sheep came running in front of him, so he raced it until he pressed his belly against the wall [and it passed behind him]."[10]

Also, once "while praying an obligatory prayer, he clenched his fist (during it), so when he had finished, the people said: 'O Messenger of Allaah, did something happen during the prayer?' He said: *No, except that the devil wanted to pass in front of me, so I strangled him until I could feel the coldness of his tongue on my hand By Allaah! Had my brother Sulaimaan not beaten*

---

[1] Bukhaari. The sutrah is a must for the Imaam or a person praying alone, even in a large mosque. Ibn Haani said in his *Masaa'il from Imaam Ahmad* (1/66): "Abu 'Abdullaah (i.e. Imaam Ahmad ibn Hanbal) saw me one day when I was praying without a sutrah in front of me, and I was in a (large) congregational mosque, so he said to me: 'Take something as a sutrah', so I took a man as a sutrah." This contains an indication that Imaam Ahmad did not differentiate between big or small mosques in taking a sutrah - and that is surely correct, but this is something neglected by most people, including imaams of mosques, in every land that I have visited, including Arabia which I was able to tour in Rajab of this year (1410), so the 'ulamaa should tell the people and advise them of this, explaining its ruling and that it is also required in the Two Sacred Mosques.

[2] Bukhaari, Muslim & Ibn Maajah

[3] Bukhaari & Ahmad.

[4] i.e., their kneeling place.

[5] Bukhaari & Ahmad.

[6] Muslim, Ibn Khuzaimah (92/2) & Ahmad.

[7] Muslim & Abu Daawood.

[8] Nasaa'i & Ahmad with a saheeh isnaad.

[9] Bukhaari , Muslim & Abu Ya'laa (3/1107).

[10] Ibn Khuzaimah in his Saheeh (1/95/1), Tabaraani (3/140/3) & Haakim who declared it saheeh and Dhahabi agreed.

me to it[1], I would have tied him (the devil) to one of the pillars of the mosque so that the children of Madinah could walk round him. [So whoever can prevent something intervening between him and the qiblah, he must do so]."[2]

He also used to say:

When one of you prays towards something which is a sutrah between him and the people and someone intends to cross in front of him, then he should push him in the throat [and repel, as much as he can], (in one narration: he should stop him, twice) but if he refuses (to not pass) then he should fight him, for verily he is a devil.[3]

He also used to say: *If the person who passed in front of someone praying knew (the sin) on him, it would be better for him to wait forty than to pass in front.* (Abu an-Nadr said, "I do not remember exactly whether he said forty days, months or years.").[4]

What Breaks the Prayer

He used to say: *A man's prayer is cut off when there is nothing such as the end of a saddle in front of him, by: a [menstruating][5] woman, a donkey or a black dog.* Abu Dharr said, 'I said: "O Messenger of Allaah, why the black dog rather than the red one?" He said, *The black dog is a shaytaan.[6]*

---

[1] Referring to the following prayer of the Prophet Sulaimaan ('alaihis salaam) which was answered by Allaah, as described in the Qur'aan: "**My Lord! Forgive me, and *grant me sovereignty not allowed to anyone after me,* for You are indeed the Granter of Bounties. So we subjected to his power: the Wind, gently flowing to his order, wherever he wished; and *the devils,* every kind of builder and diver, and also others bound together in fetters.**" (Saad 38: 35-38)

[2] Ahmad, Daaraqutni & Tabari with a saheeh isnaad, and similar in meaning to this hadeeth is found in Bukhaari and Muslim and others on the authority of several Companions. It is one of the many ahaadeeth which the Qadiani group disbelieve, for they do not believe in the world of the jinn which is mentioned in the Qur'aan and the Sunnah. Their method of discarding the texts is well-known: if it is from the Qur'aan, they change its meaning e.g. the saying of the Exalted "**Say, it has been revealed to me that a group of jinns listened**" (72:1); they say "i.e. a group of humans"! making the word "jinn" synonymous with "human"! Hence they play with the language and the religion; if it is from the Sunnah, then if it is possible for them to change it with a false interpretation they do so, otherwise they find it easy to declare it to be false, even if all the Imaams of Hadeeth and the whole ummah behind them are agreed on its authenticity, nay its being mutawaatir. May Allaah guide them.

[3] Bukhaari & Muslim, and the additional narration is from Ibn Khuzaimah (1/94/1).

[4] ibid.

[5] i.e. mature, and what is meant by 'cut off' is 'rendered futile'. As regards the hadeeth: "Nothing cuts off the prayer", then it is a weak hadeeth as I have shown in *Tamaam al-Minnah* (p. 306).

[6] Muslim, Abu Daawood and Ibn Khuzaimah (1/95/2).

Prohibition of Prayer Facing the Grave

He used to forbid prayer facing the grave, saying: *Do not pray towards the graves, and do not sit on them.*[1]

INTENTION[2]

He (sallallaahu 'alaihi wa sallam) used to say: *All actions are by intention, and every man shall have what he intended.*[3]

TAKBEER

Then he (sallallaahu 'alaihi wa sallam) would commence the prayer by saying:

اللّهُ أَكْبَر

Allaah is the Greatest[4];

he ordered "the man who prayed badly" to do likewise as has been mentioned, and he said to him: *Verily, the prayer of a person is not complete until he has made an ablution which has included the necessary parts of the body and has then said: 'Allaahu Akbar'.*[5]

He would also used to say: *The key to the prayer is purification, it is entered by takbeer and exited by tasleem.*[6]

---

[1] ibid.

[2] Nawawi says in *Rawdah at-Taalibeen* (1/224 published by Maktab al-Islami):
"The intention is the purpose, so the person about to pray brings to mind that prayer and what is relevant of its characteristics, such as which prayer it is, whether it is obligatory etc. & he brings these things together in his intention with the first takbeer."

[3] Bukhaari, Muslim and others. It is given in *Irwaa'* (no. 22)

[4] Muslim & Ibn Maajah. The hadeeth contains an indication that he did not use to commence it with the words of some people: "I intend to pray ...etc." which is in fact agreed to be an innovation. But they differ as to whether it is a good or bad innovation, to which we say: "Indeed all innovations in worship are misguided, from the generality of his statement ('alaihis salaatu was salaam), '...and all innovations are misleading, and every misleading thing is in the Fire'." But this is not the place for a detailed discussion of this.

[5] Tabaraani with a saheeh isnaad.

[6] Abu Daawood, Tirmidhi and Haakim who declared it saheeh and Dhahabi agreed. It is given in *Irwaa'* (no. 301).
Literally, "the takbeer makes it haraam", i.e. the actions which Allaah has made haraam during it, "and the tasleem makes it halaal" i.e. what is allowed outside prayer. Just as the hadeeth proves that the door to prayer is shut, no worshipper being able to open it except with purification, it similarly proves that the prayer cannot be entered except with takbeer, and that it cannot be exited except with tasleem. This is the view of the majority of scholars.

Also, "he used to raise his voice for the takbeer such that those behind him could hear."[1] But, "when he fell ill Abu Bakr used to raise his voice to convey the takbeer of the Messenger (sallallaahu 'alaihi wa sallam) to the people."[2]

He would also say: *When the Imaam says: Allaahu Akbar, then say: Allaahu Akbar.*[3]

Raising the Hands

He would raise his hands sometimes with the takbeer,[4] sometimes after the takbeer,[5] and sometimes before it.[6]

"He would raise them with fingers apart [not spaced out, nor together]",[7] and "he would put them level with his shoulders"[8], although occasionally, "he would raise them until they were level with [the tops of] his ears."[9]

To Place the Right Arm on the Left Arm, and the Command for it

"He (sallallaahu 'alaihi wa sallam) used to place his right arm on his left arm"[10], and he used to say: *We, the company of prophets, have been commanded to hasten the breaking of the fast, to delay the meal before the fast, and to place our right arms on our left arms during prayer.*[11]

Also "he passed by a man who was praying and had placed his left arm on his right, so he pulled them apart and placed the right on the left."[12]

---

[1] Ahmad & Haakim, who declared it saheeh and Dhahabi agreed.

[2] Muslim & Nasaa'i.

[3] Ahmad & Baihaqi with a saheeh isnaad.

[4] Bukhaari & Nasaa'i.

[5] ibid.

[6] Bukhaari & Abu Daawood.

[7] Abu Daawood, Ibn Khuzaimah (1/62/2, 64/1), Tammaam & Haakim who declared it saheeh and Dhahabi agreed.

[8] Bukhaari & Nasaa'i.

[9] Bukhaari & Abu Daawood.

[10] Muslim & Abu Daawood. It is also given in *Irwaa'* (352).

[11] Ibn Hibbaan & Diyaa', with a saheeh isnaad.

[12] Ahmad & Abu Daawood, with a saheeh isnaad.

To Place the Hands on the Chest

"He used to place the right arm on the back of his left palm, wrist and forearm"[1], "and he commanded his companions to do likewise"[2], and (sometimes) "he would grasp his left arm with his right."[3]

"He used to place them on his chest."[4]

Also "he used to forbid putting one's hand on the waist during prayer [and he put his hand on his waist *(to demonstrate)*]"[5]. And this is the "silb" which he used to forbid.[6]

To Look at the Place of Prostration, and Humility

"He (sallallaahu 'alaihi wa sallam) used to incline his head during prayer and fix his sight towards the ground"[7] - "while he was in the Ka'bah, his sight did

---

[1] Abu Daawood, Nasaa'i & Ibn Khuzaimah (1/54/2) with a saheeh isnaad, and Ibn Hibbaan declared it saheeh (485).

[2] Maalik, Bukhaari & Abu 'Awaanah.

[3] Nasaa'i and Daaraqutni with a saheeh isnaad. In this hadeeth there is evidence that grasping is from the sunnah, and in the previous hadeeth that so is placing, so both are sunnah. As for the combination of holding and placing, which some of the later Hanafis hold to be good, then that is an innovation; its form as they state is to place the right hand on the left, holding the wrist with the little finger and the thumb, and laying flat the remaining three fingers, as described in Ibn 'Aabideen's Footnotes on *Durr al-Mukhtaar* (1/454); so do not be confused by what they say.

[4] Abu Daawood, Ibn Khuzaimah in his saheeh (1/54/2), Ahmad & Abu Shaikh in *Taareekh Isbahaan* (p. 125); Tirmidhi declared one of its isnaads hasan, and its meaning is found in *Al-Muwatta'* and *Saheeh Al-Bukhaari* if considered carefully. I have fully quoted the isnaads of this hadeeth in my book *Ahkaam al-Janaa'iz* (p. 118)

NOTE: To place them on the chest is what is proved in the Sunnah, and all that is contrary to it is either da'eef or totally baseless. In fact, Imaam Ishaaq ibn Raahawaih acted on this sunnah, as Marwazi said in *Masaa'il* (p. 222): "Ishaaq used to pray witr with us ...he would raise his hands in qunoot, and make the qunoot before bowing, and place his hands on his breast or just under his breast." Similar is the saying of Qaadi 'Iyaad al-Maaliki in *Mustahabbaat as-Salaah* in his book *al-I'laam* (p.15, 3rd edition, Rabat): "the right arm is to be placed on the back of the left, on the upper part of the chest." Close to this is what 'Abdullaah ibn Ahmad ibn Hanbal related in his *Masaa'il* (p. 62): "I saw that when praying, my father placed his hands, one on the other, above the navel." See Appendix 4.

[5] Bukhaari & Muslim. It is given in *Irwaa'* (374) as well as the following one.

[6] Abu Daawood, Nasaa'i and others.

[7] Baihaqi and Haakim, who declared it saheeh and it is as he said. It also has a strengthening hadeeth reported by ten of his Companions: transmitted by Ibn 'Asaakir (17/202/2). See *Irwaa'* (354).

=

not leave the place of his prostration until he came out from it"[1]; and he said, *It is not fitting that there should be anything in the House which disturbs the person praying.*[2]

"He used to forbid looking up at the sky"[3], and he emphasised this prohibition so much that he said: *People must refrain from looking up at the sky in prayer, or their sight will not return to them* (and in one narration: *...or their sight will be plucked away*).[4]

In another hadeeth: *So when you pray, do not look here and there, for Allaah sets His Face for the face of his slave in his prayer as long as he does not look away"*[5], and he also said about looking here and there, *"it is a snatching away which the devil steals from the slave during prayer.*[6]

He (sallallaahu 'alaihi wa sallam) also said: *Allaah does not cease to turn to a slave in his prayer as long as he is not looking around; when he turns his face away, Allaah turns away from him*[7]; he "forbade three things: pecking like a hen, squatting *(iq'aa')*, like a dog and looking around like a fox"[8]; he also used to say, *Pray a farewell prayer as if you see Him, but if you do not see Him, surely He sees you*[9]; and, *Any person who, when an obligatory prayer is due, excels in its ablution, humility and bowings, will have it as a remission for his previous minor sins as long as he does not commit a major sin, and this (opportunity) is for all times.*[10]

Once he (sallallaahu 'alaihi wa sallam), prayed in a *khameesah*[11] and (during the prayer) he looked at its marks. So when he finished, he said: *Take this khameesah of mine to Abu Jahm and bring me his anbijaaniyyah*[12], for it has

---

*NB: These two ahaadeeth show that the sunnah is to fix one's sight on the place of prostration on the ground, so the action of some worshippers of closing their eyes during Prayer is misdirected piety, for the best guidance is the guidance of Muhammad (sallallaahu 'alaihi wa sallam).

[1] ibid.

[2] Abu Daawood & Ahmad with a saheeh isnaad (*Irwaa'*, 1771); what is meant here by 'the House' is the Ka'bah, as the context of this hadeeth shows.

[3] Bukhaari & Abu Daawood.

[4] Bukhaari, Muslim & Siraaj.

[5] Tirmidhi & Haakim, who declared it saheeh, cf. *Saheeh at-Targheeb* (no. 353)

[6] Bukhaari and Abu Daawood.

[7] Transmitted by Abu Daawood and others. Ibn Khuzaimah and Ibn Hibbaan declared it saheeh. See *Saheeh at-Targheeb* (no.555)

[8] Ahmad and Abu Ya'laa. See *Saheeh at-Targheeb* (no. 556).

[9] Mukhlis in *Ahaadeeth Muntaqaah*, Tabaraani, Rooyaani, Diyaa' in *al-Mukhtaarah*, Ibn Maajah, Ahmad and Ibn 'Asaakir. Haitami declared it saheeh in *Asnaa al-Mataalib*.

[10] Muslim.

[11] A woollen garment having marks.

[12] A coarse garment without marks.

13

diverted my attention from the prayer (in one narration: ... for I have looked at its marks during the prayer and it almost put me to trial).[1]

Also "'Aaishah had a cloth with pictures spread towards a *sahwah*[2], towards which the Prophet (sallallaahu 'alaihi wa sallam) prayed and then said: *Take it away from me [for its pictures did not cease to thwart me in my prayer].*[3]

He would also say: *Prayer is not valid when the food has been served, nor when it is time to relieve oneself of the two filths.*[4]

OPENING SUPPLICATIONS (DU'AA'S)

Next, he (sallallaahu 'alaihi wa sallam) would commence his recitation with many kinds of supplications in which he would praise Allaah the Exalted, and glorify and extol Him. He in fact ordered "the man who prayed badly" to do so, saying to him: *No person's prayer is complete unless he says takbeer, praises Allaah the Mighty and Sublime and extols Him, recites of the Qur'aan what is easy for him ...*[5]

He would say any one of the following supplications: -

اَللَّهُمَّ بَاعِدْ بَيْنِي وَبَيْنَ خَطَايَايَ كَمَا بَاعَدْتَ بَيْنَ الْمَشْرِقِ وَالْمَغْرِبِ،اَللَّهُمَّ نَقِّنِي مِنْ خَطَايَايَ -1
كَمَا يُنَقَّى الثَّوْبُ الأَبْيَضُ مِنَ الدَّنَسِ، اللَّهُمَّ اغْسِلْنِي مِنْ خَطَايَايَ بِالْمَاءِ وَالثَّلْجِ وَالْبَرَدِ .

O Allaah! Separate me (far) from my sins as you have separated (far) the East and West. O Allaah! Cleanse me of my sins as white cloth is cleansed from dirt. O Allaah! Wash me of my sins with water, ice and snow.
He used to say this in obligatory prayers[6].

2-

---

[1] Bukhaari , Muslim & Maalik. It is given in *Irwaa'* (376).

[2] "A small room embedded in the ground slightly, like a small chamber or cupboard" (*Nihaayah*).

[3] Bukhaari , Muslim & Abu 'Awaanah. The Messenger (sallallaahu 'alaihi wa sallam) did not order the wiping out or tearing of the pictures but only removed them because - and Allaah knows best - they were not pictures of things having souls. The evidence for this is that he (sallallaahu 'alaihi wa sallam) tore other pictures as proved by many narrations in Bukhaari and Muslim, and whoever wishes to explore this further should consult *Fath al-Baari* (10/321) and *Ghaayah al-Maraam fi Takhreej Ahaadeeth al-Halaal wal-Haraam* (nos. 131-145).

[4] Bukhaari and Muslim.

[5] Bukhaari , Muslim & Ibn Abi Shaibah (12/110/2). It is given in *Irwaa'* (no. 8)

[6] Abu Daawood & Haakim, who declared it saheeh and Dhahabi agreed.

وَجَّهْتُ وَجْهِيَ لِلَّذِي فَطَرَ السَّمَاوَاتِ وَالْأَرْضَ حَنِيفاً، [مُسْلِماً]، وَمَا أَنَا مِنَ الْمُشْرِكِينَ، إِنَّ صَلاَتِي وَنُسُكِي وَمَحْيَايَ وَمَمَاتِي لِلَّهِ رَبِّ الْعَالَمِينَ، لاَ شَرِيكَ لَهُ، وَبِذَلِكَ أُمِرْتُ وَأَنَا أَوَّلُ الْمُسْلِمِينَ، اَللَّهُمَّ أَنْتَ الْمَلِكُ، لاَ إِلَهَ إِلاَّ أَنْتَ، سُبْحَانَكَ وَبِحَمْدِكَ، أَنْتَ رَبِّي وَأَنَا عَبْدُكَ، ظَلَمْتُ نَفْسِي، وَاعْتَرَفْتُ بِذَنْبِي، فَاغْفِرْ ذَنْبِي جَمِيعاً إِنَّهُ لاَ يَغْفِرُ الذُّنُوبَ إِلاَّ أَنْتَ، وَاهْدِنِي لِأَحْسَنِ الْأَخْلاَقِ لاَ يَهْدِي لِأَحْسَنِهَا إِلاَّ أَنْتَ، وَاصْرِفْ عَنِّي سَيِّئَهَا لَا يَصْرِفُ عَنِّي سَيِّئَهَا إِلاَّ أَنْتَ، لَبَّيْكَ وَسَعْدَيْكَ، وَالْخَيْرُ كُلُّهُ فِي يَدَيْكَ، وَالشَّرُّ لَيْسَ إِلَيْكَ، وَالْمَهْدِيُّ مَنْ هَدَيْتَ، أَنَا بِكَ وَإِلَيْكَ، لاَ مَنْجَا وَلاَ مَلْجَأَ مِنْكَ إِلَّا إِلَيْكَ، تَبَارَكْتَ وَتَعَالَيْتَ، أَسْتَغْفِرُكَ وَأَتُوبُ إِلَيْكَ.

I have set my face towards the Originator of the heavens and the earth sincerely [in Islam] and I am not among the Mushrikeen. Indeed my prayer, my sacrifice, my living and my dying are for Allaah, the Lord of the Worlds: no partner has He. With this I have been commanded, and I am the first of the Muslims (those who submit to Him)[1]. O Allaah! You are the King, none has the right to br worshipped but You, [You are the Most Perfect & all Praise is for You] You are my Lord and I am Your slave[2]. I have wronged myself, and have acknowledged my sins, so forgive all my sins, for no-one forgives sins except You. Guide me to the best of characters, to which no-one can guide except You, and save me from the worst of characters, from which no-one can save except You. I am here and happy to serve you[3]. All good is in your Hands, and evil is not from You.[4] [The

---

[1] It is thus in most of the narrations; in some, it is *wa ana min al-muslimeen* ("I am one of the Muslims"). It is likely that this is because of the mistake of one of the narrators, and other evidence points to that, so the worshipper should say: *wa ana awwal-ul-muslimeen* ("I am the first of the Muslims"). There is nothing wrong with that, contrary to what some people say under the impression that this means "I am the first person who has this quality, while the rest of the people do not." But it is not so; this phrase actually represents competing to fulfil orders - similar to this is **"Say: if the Merciful God has a son, then I am the first of the worshippers"** (Zukhruf 43:81) and the saying of Moosa ('alaihis salam), **"and I am the first of the believers."** (A'raaf 7:143)

[2] Azhari said: i.e. 'I do not worship anything other than You.'

[3] *labbaik*: I am firmly & continually present in Your obedience; *sa'daik*: extremely happy under Your order and devoutly following the deen which You have chosen.

[4] i.e. Evil cannot be traced back to Allaah because there is nothing bad in His actions, for they are all good, ranging from justice to grace to wisdom, all of which are good with no bad in them. But evil is evil because it cannot be traced back to Allaah. Ibn al-Qayyim (rahimahullaah) said: "He is the Creator of good and evil, but the evil exists in some of His creatures, not in His act of creating nor in His actions. Hence the Exalted is cleared of any *zulm*, which is fundamentally to put something in other than its proper place. He does not put anything except in its suitable place, so that is all good. But evil is to put something in other than its proper place: when it is put in its proper place it is not evil, so be sure that evil is not from Him. ...But if it is said: Why did He create something which is evil? I would say: He did the creating, and His action is good not evil, for creation and action is with Allaah, and it is impossible for evil to be with, or attributed to, Allaah. Anything evil in the created cannot be traced back to Allaah, but His actions and His creation can be attributed to Him, so they are good." The rest of this important discussion as well as its conclusion is to be found in his book *Shifaa' al-'Aleel fi Masaa'il al-Qadaa' wal-Qadr wat-Ta'leel* (pp. 178-206).

guided one is he who is guided by you.] I exist by your will and belong to You. [There is no escape or shelter from You except to You.] You are blessed and exalted. I seek Your forgiveness and repent to You.

He used to say this in obligatory and voluntary prayers[1].

3- Similar to the above, without

أَنْتَ رَبِّي وَأَنَا عَبْدُكَ

You are my Lord and I am Your slave... to the end, with the following addition:

اَللّهُمَّ أَنْتَ الْمَلِكُ، لاَ إِلهَ إِلاَّ أَنْتَ، سُبْحَانَكَ وَبِحَمْدِكَ،

O Allaah! You are the King, there is no (true) deity except You, glorified be You and praised.[2]

4- Similar to no. 2 until

وَأَنَا أَوَّلُ الْمُسْلِمِين

...and I am the first of the Muslims, adding:

اَللّهُمَّ أَهْدِني لِأَحْسَنِ الْأَخْلاقِ وَأَحْسَنِ الْأَعْمَالِ لاَ يَهْدِي لِأَحْسَنِهَا إِلاَّ أَنْتَ، وَقِني سَيِّءَ الْأَخْلاقِ وَالْأَعْمَالِ لاَ يَقِي سَيِّئَهَا إِلاَّ أَنْتَ

O Allaah, guide me to the best of characters and the best of actions, no one to which can guide except You, and save me from the evil characters and actions, from which no one except You can save (others) except You[3].

5-

سُبْحَانَكَ اَللّهُمَّ وَبِحَمْدِكَ وَتَبَارَكَ اسْمُكَ وَتَعَالَى جَدُّكَ وَلاَ إِلهَ غَيْرُكَ

You are Glorified[4]*, O Allaah, and Praised*[5]*; Your Name is Blessed*[6]*; Your Majesty*[7] *is Exalted, and none has the right to worshipped but You.*[8] H e

---

[1] Muslim, Abu 'Awaanah, Abu Daawood, Nasaa'i Ibn Hibbaan, Ahmad, Shaafi'i & Tabaraani; those who specify it to optional prayers are mistaken.

[2] Nasaa'i with a saheeh isnaad.

[3] Nasaa'i & Daaraqutni with a saheeh isnaad.

[4] i.e I glorify You, meaning I consider You totally free from any deficiency.

[5] i.e. we are submerged in Your praise.

[6] i.e. the blessings of Your Name are great, for great good springs from the remembrance of Your Name.

[7] i.e. Your Glory and Might.

(sallallaahu 'alaihi wa sallam) also said, *Indeed, the words most loved by Allaah are when His slave says: You are glorified, O Allaah ...*1

6- Similar to the above, adding in prayer at night:

لَا إِلَهَ إِلَّا اللهُ

There is no true god except Allaah, three times, and

اللهُ أَكْبَرُ كَبِيراً

Allaah is the Greatest, Very Great, three times.

7-
اللهُ أَكْبَرُ كَبِيراً، وَالْحَمْدُ لِلهِ كَثِيراً، وَسُبْحَانَ اللهِ بُكْرَةً وَأَصِيلاً

Allaah is the Greatest, very great. Praise be to Allaah, again and again. Glorified is Allaah morning and evening - one of the Companions commenced with this, to which the Messenger (sallallaahu 'alaihi wa sallam) said: *Wonderful for it (the supplication) is that the doors of the heavens were opened for it.*2

8-
اَلْحَمْدُ لِلهِ حَمْداً كَثِيراً طَيِّباً مُبَارَكاً فِيهِ

Praise be to Allaah, many, pure, blessed praises. Another man commenced with this, to which he (sallallaahu 'alaihi wa sallam) said: *I saw twelve angels competing as to which of them would take it up.*3

9-
اَللَّهُمَّ لَكَ الْحَمْدُ، أَنْتَ نُورُ السَّمَاوَاتِ وَالْأَرْضِ وَمَنْ فِيهِمْ، وَلَكَ الْحَمْدُ، أَنْتَ قَيِّمُ السَّمَاوَاتِ وَالْأَرْضِ وَمَنْ فِيهِنَّ، [وَلَكَ الْحَمْدُ، أَنْتَ مَلِكُ السَّمَاوَاتِ وَالْأَرْضِ وَمَنْ فِيهِمْ]، وَلَكَ الْحَمْدُ، أَنْتَ الْحَقُّ، وَوَعْدُكَ حَقٌّ، وَقَوْلُكَ حَقٌّ، وَلِقَاؤُكَ حَقٌّ، وَالْجَنَّةُ حَقٌّ، وَالنَّارُ حَقٌّ، وَالسَّاعَةُ حَقٌّ، وَالنَّبِيُّونَ حَقٌّ، وَمُحَمَّدٌ حَقٌّ، اَللَّهُمَّ لَكَ أَسْلَمْتُ

---

8 Abu Daawood & Haakim, who declared it saheeh and Dhahabi agreed. 'Uqaili said (p. 103): "this has been narrated via several routes with good isnaads." It is given in *Irwaa'* (no. 341) Transmitted by Ibn Mandah in *At-Tawheed* (123/2) with a saheeh isnaad & Nasaa'i in *al-Yawm wal-Laylah* as *mawqoof* and *marfoo'*, as in *Jaami' al-Masaaneed* of Ibn Katheer (vol. 3 part 2 p. 235/2)

1 Abu Daawood & Tahaawi with a hasan isnaad.

2 Muslim & Abu 'Awaanah; declared saheeh by Tirmidhi. Abu Nu'aim also narrated it in *Akhbaar Isbahaan* (1/210) from Jubair ibn Mut'am who heard the Prophet (sallallaahu 'alaihi wa sallam) saying it in voluntary prayer.

3 Muslim & Abu 'Awaanah.

عَلَيْكَ تَوَكَّلْتُ، وَبِكَ آمَنْتُ، وَإِلَيْكَ أَنَبْتُ، وَبِكَ خَاصَمْتُ، وَإِلَيْكَ حَاكَمْتُ، [أَنْتَ رَبُّنَا وَإِلَيْكَ الْمَصِيرُ، فَاغْفِرْ لِي مَا قَدَّمْتُ، وَمَا أَخَّرْتُ، وَمَا أَسْرَرْتُ وَمَا أَعْلَنْتُ]، [وَمَا أَنْتَ أَعْلَمُ بِهِ مِنِّي]، أَنْتَ الْمُقَدِّمُ وَأَنْتَ الْمُؤَخِّرُ، [أَنْتَ إِلهِي]، لَا إِلهَ إِلَّا أَنْتَ

O Allaah, to You belongs all Praise. You are the Light[1] of the heavens and the earth and all those in them; to You belongs all Praise. You are the Maintainer[2] of the heavens and the earth and all those in them; [to You belongs all Praise. You are the King of the heavens and the earth and all those in them] to You belongs all Praise. You are the Haqq[3]; Your promise is haqq; Your saying is haqq; meeting You is haqq; Paradise is haqq; the Fire is haqq; the Hour is haqq; the Prophets are haqq; Muhammad is haqq. O Allaah! to You I have submitted; in You I have placed my trust; in You I have believed; to You I have turned; for Your sake I have fought; to You I have referred for judgement; [You are our Lord and to You is the end of all journeys: so forgive me my earlier and later sins, what I have concealed and what I have showed] [and whatever else You know about more than I.] You are the Bringer-Forward and You are the Delayer; [You are my deity;] and none has the right to worshipped but You.[4] [and there is no might nor power except with You].

He (sallallaahu 'alaihi wa sallam) used to say this in prayer at night, as he did the following supplications:[5]

10-

هُمَّ رَبَّ جِبْرَائِيلَ وَمِيكَائِيلَ وَإِسْرَافِيلَ، فَاطِرَ السَّمَاوَاتِ وَالْأَرْضِ، عَالِمَ الْغَيْبِ وَالشَّهَادَةِ، أَنْتَ تَحْكُمُ بَيْنَ عِبَادِكَ فِيمَا كَانُوا فِيهِ يَخْتَلِفُونَ، إِهْدِنِي لِمَا اخْتُلِفَ فِيهِ مِنَ الْحَقِّ بِإِذْنِكَ، إِنَّكَ تَهْدِي مَنْ تَشَاءُ إِلَى صِرَاطٍ مُسْتَقِيم

O Allaah, Lord of Jibraa'eel, Meekaa'eel and Israafeel, Creator of the heavens and the earth, Knower of all that is hidden and open! It is You that will judge between Your servants in those matters about which they used to differ. Guide me by Your Grace to the Truth concerning that about which they differed, for indeed You guide whomsoever You wish to a path that is straight.[6]

---

[1] i.e. You are the Giver of Light to them, and those in them are guided by You.
[2] i.e. the Protector and the constant Watcher over them.
[3] *haqq*: truth, reality.
[4] Bukhaari , Muslim, Abu 'Awaanah, Abu Daawood, Ibn Nasr & Daarimi.
[5] Although that clearly does not rule out using them in the obligatory prayers also, except for the imaam, so that he does not prolong the prayer for the followers.
[6] Muslim & Abu 'Awaanah.

11- He would say *takbeer*, *tahmeed*, *tasbeeh*, *tahleel* and *istighfaar* ten times each, and then say,

$$\text{اَللّٰهُمَّ اغْفِرْ لِي وَاهْدِنِي وَارْزُقْنِي [وَعَافِنِي]}$$

O Allaah! forgive me and guide me and give me sustenance and [overlook my sins] ten times, and then say:

$$\text{اَللّٰهُمَّ إِنِّي أَعُوذُ بِكَ مِنَ الضِّيقِ يَوْمَ الْحِسَابِ}$$

O Allaah! I seek refuge with You from the distress of the Day of Account ten times.[1]

12-

$$\text{اللهُ أَكْبَرُ [ثَلاَثاً] ذُو الْمَلَكُوتِ وَالْجَبَرُوتِ وَالْكِبْرِيَاءِ وَالْعَظَمَةِ}$$

"Allaah is the Greatest [three times], Possessor of Kingdom, Power, Magnificence and Might."[2]

RECITATION

Next, he (sallallaahu 'alaihi wa sallam) would seek refuge with Allaah the Exalted, saying:

$$\text{أَعُوذُ بِاللهِ مِنَ الشَّيْطَانِ الرَّجِيمِ مِنْ هَمْزِهِ وَنَفْخِهِ وَنَفْثِهِ}$$

I seek refuge with Allaah from the Evil One, the Rejected, from his madness[3], his arrogance, and his poetry[4]: Sometimes he would add to this, saying:

$$\text{أَعُوذُ بِاللهِ السَّمِيعِ الْعَلِيمِ مِنَ الشَّيْطَانِ ...}$$

I seek refuge with Allaah, the all-Hearing, the all-Knowing, from the Evil One ...[5]

---

[1] Ahmad, Ibn Abi Shaibah (12/119/2), Abu Daawood & Tabaraani in *Mu'jam al-Awsat* (62/2) with one isnaad saheeh, and another hasan.

[2] Tayaalisi & Abu Daawood with a saheeh isnaad.

[3] The three 'Arabic words *hamz*, *nafkh*, and *nafth*, were interpreted such by the narrator; all three interpretations are also traced back to the Prophet (sallallaahu 'alaihi wa sallam) with a saheeh mursal isnaad. By "poetry" here is meant the vain kind, for the Prophet (on whom be peace and blessings) said: "Truly, some poetry is wisdom" (Bukhaari).

[4] Abu Daawood, Ibn Maajah, Daaraqutni & Haakim who, along with Ibn Hibbaan and Dhahabi, declared it saheeh. It is given along with the next one in *Irwaa' al-Ghaleel* (342).

[5] Abu Daawood & Tirmidhi with a hasan isnaad. Ahmad endorsed it (*Masaa'il of Ibn Haani* 1/50).

19

Then he would recite,

$$\text{بِسْمِ اللَّهِ الرَّحْمَنِ الرَّحِيمِ}$$

In the Name of Allaah, the Most Merciful, the Bestower of Mercy, but not loudly[1].

Recitation of one Verse at a Time

Next, he would recite Soorah al-Faatihah and divide his recitation, reciting one verse at a time. He would say:

$$\text{بِسْمِ اللَّهِ الرَّحْمَنِ الرَّحِيمِ}$$

[Here he would pause, and then say:]

$$\text{الْحَمْدُ لِلَّهِ رَبِّ الْعَالَمِينَ}$$

[Then he would pause, and then say:]

$$\text{الرَّحْمَنِ الرَّحِيمِ}$$

[Then he would pause, and then say:]

$$\text{مَالِكِ يَوْمِ الدِّينِ}$$

... and so on, until the end of the soorah. The rest of his recitation was also like this: stopping at the end of the verse and not joining it with the one after.[2]

Sometimes, he would recite,

$$\text{مَلِكِ يَوْمِ الدِّينِ}$$

(*King of the Day of Judgment*) instead of

$$\text{مَالِكِ يَوْمِ الدِّينِ}$$

(*Master of the Day of Judgment*).[3]

---

[1] Bukhaari , Muslim, Abu 'Awaanah, Tahaawi & Ahmad.

[2] Abu Daawood & Sahmi (64 -65); Haakim declared it saheeh and Dhahabi agreed. It is given in *Irwaa'* (343). Abu 'Amr ad-Daani transmitted it *al-Muktafaa* (5/2) and said: "This hadeeth has many routes, and it is what is depended upon in this regard, and several of the past imaams and reciters preferred to stop at every verse, even if some were connected (in meaning) to the one after." I say: This is a sunnah which has been neglected by the majority of the reciters of this age, let alone others.

[3] Tammaam ar-Raazi in *al-Fawaa'id*, Ibn Abi Dawood in *al-Masaahif* (7/2), Abu Nu'aim in *Akhbaar Isbahaan* (1/104) & Haakim who declared it saheeh and Dhahabi agreed. Both of these recitations are *mutawaatir*.

The Necessity of al-Faatihah, and its Excellence

He would vehemently emphasise the importance of this soorah, saying: "There is no prayer for the one who did not recite [in it] the opening chapter [at least]"[1], and in another saying: *That prayer is not sufficient in which a man does not recite the Opening of the Book*[2]. He also said: *He who performs a prayer in which he does not recite the Opening of the Book, then it (i.e. the prayer) is deficient, it is deficient, it is deficient, incomplete.*[3]. He also said:

Allaah the Blessed and Exalted has said: "I have divided the prayer[4] between Myself and My servant, into two halves: half of it is for Me and half is for My servant, and My servant shall have what he has asked for." Then the Messenger of Allaah (sallallaahu 'alaihi wa sallam) said: *Recite! The servant says "Praise be to Allaah, the Lord of the Worlds"; Allaah the Exalted says "My servant has praised Me". The servant says, "The Most Merciful, the Bestower of Mercy"; Allaah says, "My servant has extolled Me". The servant says "Master of the Day of Judgment"; Allaah the Exalted says, "My servant has glorified Me". The servant says, "It is You (alone) we worship and it is You (alone) we ask for help"; [He says:], "This is between Me and My servant, and My servant shall have what he has asked for".* The servant says, *"Guide us to the Straight Path, the Path of those whom You have favoured, not of those who receive Your anger, nor of those who go astray".* [He says:], *"All these are for My servant, and My servant shall have what he has asked for."*[5]

He also used to say: *Allaah did not reveal in the Torah or the Gospel anything like the Mother of the Qur'aan. It is the Seven Oft-Repeated[6] [and the Grand Recitation which have been bestowed upon me].*[7]

He (sallallaahu 'alaihi wa sallam) commanded "the one who prayed badly" to recite it in his prayer[8], but said to one who could not remember it, *Say:*

---

[1] Bukhaari, Muslim, Abu 'Awaanah & Baihaqi. It is given in *Irwaa'* (302).

[2] Daaraqutni, who declared it saheeh, and Ibn Hibbaan in his Saheeh. It is also in *Irwaa'* (302).

[3] Muslim & Abu 'Awaanah.

[4] i.e. soorah al-Fatihah. It is an example of the wording including the whole prayer but intending only a part, as a way of emphasis on that part.

[5] Muslim, Abu 'Awaanah & Maalik, and Sahmi has a supporting hadeeth of Jaabir in *Taareekh Jurjaan* (144)

[6] Baaji said: "He is referring to the saying of the Exalted **"And We have bestowed upon you seven of the Oft-Repeated and the Grand Recitation."** (Hijr 15:87). It is named the "seven" because it has seven verses, and "oft-repeated" because it is repeated again and again in prayer. It has been called "the grand recitation" to specify this name for it, even though every part of the Qur'aan is a grand recitation; similarly, the Ka'bah is "the House of Allaah" even though all houses belong to Allaah; this is by way of specifying it and emphasising its importance."

[7] Nasaa'i & Haakim, who declared it saheeh and Dhahabi agreed.

[8] Bukhaari in his article on "Recitation behind the Imaam" with a saheeh isnaad.

سُبْحَانَ اللهِ، وَالْحَمْدُ للهِ، وَلاَ إِلَهَ إِلاَّ اللهُ، وَاللهُ أَكْبَرُ، وَلاَ حَوْلَ وَلاَ قُوَّةَ إِلاَّ بِاللهِ

(I declare Allaah free from all defects; all Praise be to Allaah; none has the right to be worshipped but Allaah; Allaah is the Greatest; there is no might or power except by Allaah)[1].

He also said to "the one who prayed badly": *If you know some of the Qur'aan, then recite it, otherwise praise Allaah, declare His Greatness and declare that none has the right to be worshipped but Allaah;* [2]

The Abrogation of Recitation behind the Imaam in the Loud Prayers

He had given permission for those being led by the Imaam to recite Soorah al-Faatihah in the loud prayers, when once:

> "he was praying Fajr and the recitation became difficult for him. When he finished, he said: *Perhaps you recite behind your imaam.* We said: "Yes, quickly[3], O Messenger of Allaah." He said: *Do not do so, except for [each of you reciting] the opening chapter of the Book, for the prayer is not valid of the one who does not recite it.*[4]

Later, he forbade them from reciting in the loud prayers at all, when:

> "He finished a prayer in which he was reciting loudly (*in one narration:* it was the dawn prayer) and said: *Were any of you reciting with me just now?!* A man said: "Yes, I was, O Messenger of Allaah". He said: *I say, why am I contended with?* [Abu Hurairah said:] So the people stopped reciting with the Messenger of Allaah (sallallaahu 'alaihi wa sallam) when he was reciting loudly after hearing that from him [but they recited to themselves quietly when the imaam was not reciting loudly]."[5]

He also made silence during the imaam's recitation part of the completeness of following the imaam, saying: *The imaam is there to be followed, so when he says takbeer, say takbeer, and when he recites, be silent*[6], just as he made listening to the imaam's recitation enough to not have to recite behind him, saying: *He who*

---

[1] Abu Daawood, Ibn Khuzaimah (1/80/2), Haakim, Tabaraani & Ibn Hibbaan who, along with Haakim, declared it saheeh and Dhahabi agreed. It is in *Irwaa'* (303).

[2] Abu Daawood & Tirmidhi, who declared it hasan; its isnaad is saheeh. (Saheeh Abi Dawood no. 807)

[3] *hadhdhan*: reciting quickly, implying racing or hurrying.

[4] Bukhaari in his pamphlet, Abu Daawood & Ahmad. Tirmidhi & Daaraqutni declared it hasan.

[5] Maalik, Humaidi, Bukhaari in his pamphlet, Abu Daawood & Mahaamali (6/139/1). Tirmidhi declared it *hasan*; Abu Haatim ar-Raazi, Ibn Hibbaan & Ibn Qayyim declared it *saheeh*.

[6] Ibn Abi Shaibah (1/97/1), Abu Daawood, Muslim, Abu 'Awaanah & Ruwayaani in his musnad (24/119/1). It is given in *Irwaa'* (332, 394).

has an imaam, then the recitation of the imaam is recitation for him[1] - this applying in the loud prayers.

The Obligation to Recite in the Quiet Prayers

As for the quiet prayers, he urged them to recite during them; Jaabir said, "We used to recite behind the imaam in Zuhr and 'Asr: soorah al-Faatihah and another soorah in the first two rak'ahs, and soorah al-Fatihah in the last two."[2]

However, he dissuaded them from confusing him with their recitation, when:

> "he prayed Zuhr with his Companions and said (afterwards): *Which of you recited "Glorify the name of your Lord the Most High"* (soorah al-A'laa, 87) ? Someone said: It was I [but I was only intending nothing but good by doing so]. So he said: *I knew that someone was contending with me by it.*[3] In another hadeeth: "They used to recite behind the Prophet (sallallaahu 'alaihi wa sallam) [loudly], so he said: *You have mixed up my (recitation of the) Qur'aan.*[4]

He also said: *Truly, the person praying is privately consulting his Lord, so he should be careful about what he consults him with, and you should not recite the Qur'aan loudly over each other.*[5]

He also used to say: *Whoever recited a harf (letter) from the Book of Allaah, it will count for him as one good deed, and a good deed is worth ten times over. I do not mean that "alif laam meem" is a harf, but "alif" is a harf, "laam" is a harf, and "meem" is a harf.*[6]

---

[1] Ibn Abi Shaibah (1/97/1), Daaraqutni, Ibn Maajah, Tahaawi & Ahmad from numerous routes, *musnad* and *mursal*. Shaikh-ul-Islam Ibn Taymiyyah declared it strong, as in *al-Furoo'* of Ibn 'Abdul Haadi (48/2). Boosayri declared some of its isnaads saheeh. I have discussed it in detail and investigated its routes of narration in the manuscript version and then in *Irwaa' al-Ghaleel* (no. 500)

[2] Ibn Maajah with a saheeh isnaad. It is given in *Irwaa'* (506)

[3] Muslim, Abu 'Awaanah & Siraaj.

[4] Bukhaari in his article, Ahmad & Siraaj with a hasan isnaad.

[5] Maalik & Bukhaari in *Af'aal al-'Ibaad* with a saheeh isnaad.

* NB The view of the validity of recitation behind the imaam in quiet but not loud prayers was taken by Imaam Shaafi'i initially, and by Muhammad the student of Abu Haneefah in a narration from him which was preferred by Shaikh 'Ali al-Qaari and other shaikhs of the madhhab; it was also the position of, among others, the Imaams Zuhri, Maalik, Ibn al-Mubaarak, Ahmad ibn Hanbal, several of the muhadditheen, and it is the preference of Shaikh-ul-Islam Ibn Taymiyyah.

[6] Tirmidhi & Ibn Maajah with a saheeh isnaad. Transmitted also by Aajuri in *Aadaab Haml al-Qur'aan*. As for the hadeeth, "He who recites behind the imaam, his mouth is filled with fire", it is fabricated *(mawdoo')* and this is explained in *Silsilat al-ahaadeeth al-da'eefah* (no. 569) - see Appendix 5.

The *aameen*, and the Imaam's saying it Loudly

When he (sallallaahu 'alaihi wa sallam) finished reciting al-Faatihah, he would say:

أَمِين

("aameen") loudly, prolonging his voice.[1]

He also used to order the congregation to say aameen: *When the imaam says,*

غَيْرِ الْمَغْضُوبِ عَلَيْهِمْ وَلاَ الضَّالِّينَ

"Not of those who receive (Your) anger, nor of those who go astray", *then say "aameen" [for the angels say "aameen" and the imaam says aameen"]* (in another narration: *when the imaam says "aameen" say "aameen"*), *so he whose aameen coincides with the aameen of the angels* (in another narration: *when one of you says "aameen" in prayer and the angels in the sky say "aameen", and they coincide), his past sins are forgiven.*[2]
In another hadeeth: *... then say aameen; Allaah will answer you.*[3]

He also used to say: *The Jews do not envy you over anything as much as they envy you over the salutation and aameen [behind the imaam].*[4]

---

[1] Bukhaari in *Juz' al-Qiraa'ah* & Abu Daawood with a saheeh isnaad.

[2] Bukhaari , Muslim, Nasaa'i, & Daarimi; the additional wordings are reported by the latter two, and prove that this hadeeth cannot justify that the imaam does not say aameen, as reported from Maalik; hence, Ibn Hajar says in *Fath al-Baari*, "It clearly shows that the imaam says aameen." Ibn 'Abdul Barr says in *Tamheed* (7/13), "It is the view of the majority of the Muslims, including Maalik as the people of Madeenah report from him, for it is authentic from Allaah's Messenger (sallallaahu 'alaihi wa sallam) through the ahaadeeth of Abu Hurairah (i.e. this one) and that of Waa'il ibn Hujr (i.e. the previous one)."

[3] Muslim & Abu 'Awaanah.

[4] Bukhaari in *al-Adab al-Mufrad*, Ibn Maajah, Ibn Khuzaimah, Ahmad & Siraaj with two saheeh isnaads.

*NB The aameen of the congregation behind the imaam should be done loudly and simultaneously with the imaam, not before him as the majority of worshippers do, nor after him. This is what I finally find most convincing, as I have explained in some of my works, among them *Silsilat al-ahaadeeth ad-da'eefah* (no. 952, vol. 2) which has been printed and published by the grace of Allaah, and *Saheeh at-Targheeb wat-Tarheeb* (1/205). See Appendix 6.

The Recitation after al-Faatihah

Next, he (sallallaahu 'alaihi wa sallam) would recite another soorah after al-Faatihah, making it long sometimes, and on other occasions making it short because of travel, cough, illness or the crying of infants.

Anas ibn Maalik (may Allaah be pleased with him) said: "He (sallallaahu 'alaihi wa sallam) made it [i.e. the recitation] short one day in the dawn prayer." (In another hadeeth: he prayed the morning prayer and recited the two shortest soorahs in the Qur'aan.) So it was said: "O Messenger of Allaah, why did you make it short?" He said: *I heard the crying of a child, and I supposed that his mother was praying with us, so I wanted to free his mother for him.*[1]

He also used to say: *I enter into prayer intending to lengthen it, but I hear the crying of a child so I shorten my prayer because I know how deeply his mother feels about his crying.*[2]

He used to start from the beginnning of a soorah, completing it most of the time.[3]

He used to say: *Give every soorah its share of rukoo' and sujood.*[4]
In another narration: *Every soorah should have a rak'ah.*[5]

Sometimes he would divide the soorah into two rak'ahs[6] and sometimes he would repeat the whole soorah in the second rak'ah[7].

Sometimes he would combine two or more soorahs in one rak'ah.[8]

One of the Ansaar used to lead them in the mosque of Qubaa', and every time he recited a soorah[9] for them, he would begin with "Say: He is Allaah, the One and

---

[1] Ahmad with a saheeh isnaad; the other hadeeth was transmitted by Ibn Abi Dawood in *al-Masaahif* (4/14/2). This and other similar hadeeths contain permission for infants to enter the mosque. As for the hadeeth on many lips: "Keep your small children away from your mosques...", it is *da'eef* and cannot be used for proof at all; among those who have declared it da'eef are Ibn al-Jawzi, Mundhiri, Haitami, Ibn Hajar al-Asqalaani and Boosayri. 'Abdul Haqq al-Ishbeeli said, "It is baseless".

[2] Bukhaari & Muslim.

[3] There are many ahaadeeth mentioned further on which prove this.

[4] Ibn Abi Shaibah (1/100/1), Ahmad & 'Abdul Ghani al-Maqdisi in his *Sunan* (9/2) with a *saheeh* isnaad.

[5] Ibn Nasr & Tahaawi with a *saheeh* isnaad; I take the meaning of the hadeeth as: Make every rak'ah have a complete soorah. The order is one of preference, not compulsion, from the evidence which follows.

[6] Ahmad & Abu Ya'laa from two routes. Also see "Recitation in Fajr prayer".

[7] As he did in Fajr, as will follow.

[8] Details and sources will follow shortly.

[9] i.e. a soorah after al-Fatihah.

Only..." (*soorah al-Ikhlaas, 112*) until its end, and then recite another soorah with it, and he would do this in every rak'ah. Because of this, his people spoke to him, saying: "You begin with this soorah, and then you do not regard it as enough until you recite another one: you should either recite it (only) or leave it and recite another one. He said: "I will not leave it: if you do not mind me leading you with it, I shall carry on, but if you do not like it, I shall leave you." They knew that he was one of their best, and they did not like to be led by anyone else, so when the Prophet (sallallaahu 'alaihi wa sallam) came to them, they told him the story. He said: *O so-and-so, what stops you from doing what your people ask you to? What makes you recite this soorah in every rak'ah?* He said: "I love this soorah." He said: *Your love for it will enter you into the Garden.*[1]

Combining Similar Soorahs and others in One Rak'ah

He used to combine the pairs[2] of the *mufassal*[3] soorahs, so he used to recite one of the following pairs of soorahs in one rak'ah[4]:

ar-Rahmaan (55:78)[5] & an-Najm (53:62);
al-Qamar (54:55) & al-Haaqqah (69:52);
at-Toor (52:49) & Dhaariyaat (51:60);
al-Waaqi'ah (56:96) & al-Qalam (68:52);
al-Ma'aarij (70:44) & an-Naazi'aat (79:46);
al-Mutaffifeen (83:36) & 'Abasa (80:42);
al-Muddaththir (74:56) & al-Muzzammil (73:20);
ad-Dahr (76:31) & al-Qiyaamah (75:40);
an-Naba (78:40) & al-Mursalaat (77:50);
ad-Dukhaan (44:59) & at-Takweer (81:29).

Sometimes he would combine soorahs from the seven *tiwaal* (long soorahs), such as al-Baqarah, an-Nisaa' and aal-Imraan in one rak'ah during night prayer (below). He used to say: *The most excellent prayer is one with long standing.*[6]

When he recited,

---

[1] Bukhaari as *ta'leeq* & Tirmidhi as *mawsool*, and he declared it *saheeh*.

[2] *nazaa'ir*: soorahs which are similar in meaning, e.g. they both contain advice, commandments, or stories.

[3] These are agreed to end at the end of the Qur'aan; the soundest view is that they begin with soorah Qaaf (no. 50).

[4] Bukhaari & Muslim.

[5] The first number is that of the soorah, while the second is the number of aayaat in the soorah. By inspecting the first of the two numbers in each case, it is easy to see that in many of these combinations, he (sallallaahu 'alaihi wa sallam) did not stick to the Qur'aanic order of the soorahs, so this is evidence for the permissibility of doing this, even though it is better to follow the sequence of the Qur'aan. A similar case is to be found later under "Night prayer".

[6] Muslim & Tahaawi.

$$\text{أَلَيْسَ ذَٰلِكَ بِقَادِرٍ عَلَىٰ أَن يُحْيِيَ ٱلْمَوْتَىٰ}$$

"Does He not have the power to give life to the dead?" (Qiyaamah 75:40), he would say,

$$\text{سُبْحَانَكَ فَبَلَى}$$

(Glory be to You, of course!)

and when he recited,

$$\text{سَبِّحِ ٱسْمَ رَبِّكَ ٱلْأَعْلَى}$$

"Glorify the name of your Lord Most High" (A'laa 87:1), he would say,

$$\text{سُبْحَانَ رَبِّيَ الْأَعْلَى}$$

(Glorified be my Lord Most High).[1]

The Permissibility of Reciting al-Faatihah only

Mu'aadh ibn Jabal used to pray 'Ishaa' [the last] with the Messenger of Allaah (sallallaahu 'alaihi wa sallam), and then return and lead his people in prayer. One night when he returned and prayed with them, a young man [called Sulaim, of the Banu Salamah] from his people prayed, but when it became too long for him, he [went away and] prayed [in the corner of the mosque], then came out, took the reins of his camel and departed. When Mu'aadh had prayed, this was mentioned to him, so he said: "He surely has some hypocrisy in him! I will surely tell the Messenger of Allaah (sallallaahu 'alaihi wa sallam) what he has done." The young man said: "And I will tell the Messenger of Allaah (sallallaahu 'alaihi wa sallam) what he has done." So in the morning they came to the Messenger of Allaah (sallallaahu 'alaihi wa sallam), and Mu'aadh informed him of what the young man had done. The young man said: "O Messenger of Allaah! He stays a long time with you, and then he returns and lengthens it for us." So the Messenger of Allaah (sallallaahu 'alaihi wa sallam) said: Are you one who causes great trouble, Mu'aadh?! and he said to the young man[2]: What do you do when you pray, son of my brother? He said: "I recite the opening chapter of the Book, then I ask Allaah for the Garden, and seek refuge with Him from the Fire. I know neither your dandanah[3]

---

[1] Abu Daawood & Baihaqi with a saheeh isnaad. This hadeeth is general, so it applies to both recitation during prayer, whether voluntary or obligatory, and outside it. Ibn Abi Shaibah (2/132/2) has transmitted from Abu Moosa al-Ash'ari and Mugheerah ibn Shu'bah that they used to say this in obligatory prayers, and from 'Umar and 'Ali without such specification.

[2] In the original, "the young man said".

[3] dandanah: when someone speaks some words such that their intonation is audible but they cannot be understood; it is a little bit more than murmuring. (Nihaayah)

27

nor the *dandanah* of Mu'aadh!" So the Messenger of Allaah (sallallaahu 'alaihi wa sallam) said: *I and Mu'aadh are similar in this.*

The narrator said: The young man said, "But Mu'aadh will know (about me) on going to the people when they will have been informed that the enemy has arrived." The narrator said: So the enemy came, and the young man attained *shahaadah* (martyrdom). So after that the Messenger of Allaah (sallallaahu 'alaihi wa sallam) said to Mu'aadh, *What did the one disputing with me and you do?* He said, "O Messenger of Allaah, he was true to Allaah, and I spoke falsely - he was martyred."[1]

Quiet and Loud Recitation in the Five Prayers and others

He (sallallaahu 'alaihi wa sallam) used to recite loudly in the morning prayer and in the first two rak'ahs of Maghrib and 'Ishaa', and quietly in Zuhr, 'Asr, the third rak'ah of Maghrib and the last two rak'ahs of Ishaa'.[2]

They could tell when he was reciting quietly from the movement of his beard[3], and because he would let them hear an aayah or so sometimes[4].

He also recited loudly in Friday prayer and the two 'Eid prayers[5], in the prayer for rain[6], and in the eclipse prayer[7].

---

[1] Ibn Khuzaimah in his saheeh (1634) & Baihaqi with a *saheeh* isnaad. It has a supporting narration in Abu Daawood (no. 758, *Saheeh Abi Dawood*) and the basic story is in Bukhaari and Muslim. The first addition is in one narration of Muslim, the second in Ahmad (5/74), and the third and fourth in Bukhaari . Also under this heading is the hadeeth on the authority of Ibn 'Abbaas: "that the Messenger of Allaah (sallallaahu 'alaihi wa sallam) prayed two rak'ahs in which he recited only al-Fatihah", transmitted by Ahmad (1/282), Haarith ibn Abi Usaamah in his musnad (p.38 of its zawaaid) and Baihaqi (2/62) with a *da'eef* isnaad. I used to declare this hadeeth hasan in previous works, until I realised that I had been mistaken, because this hadeeth depends on Hanzalah al-Dawsi, who is da'eef, and I do not know how this was unknown to me; maybe I thought he was someone else. Anyway, praise is due to Allaah who guided me to recognise my mistake, and that is why I hurried to correct it in print. Then Allaah compensated me with this better hadeeth of Mu'aadh which relates to what the hadeeth of Ibn 'Abbaas indicated. Praise be to Allaah by whose Grace good actions are completed.

[2] There is Ijmaa' (consensus of opinion) of the Muslims on this, with successors passing it on from the predecessors, along with authentic hadeeths which establish this, as Nawawi has said, and some of them follow. See also *Irwaa'* (345).

[3] Bukhaari & Abu Daawood.

[4] Bukhaari & Muslim.

[5] see the sections on his recitation in Friday prayer and the two 'Eid prayers.

[6] Bukhaari & Abu Daawood.

[7] Bukhaari & Muslim.

Quiet and Loud Recitation in the Night Prayer (Tahajjud)[1]

As for night prayer, he would sometimes recite quietly and sometimes loudly[2], and "he used to recite in his house such that he could be heard in the courtyard."[3]
"Occasionally he would raise his voice more than that until someone lying in bed could hear him"[4] (i.e. from outside the courtyard).

He ordered Abu Bakr and 'Umar (Allaah be pleased with them) likewise, when:

> "he came out at night to find Abu Bakr (Allaah be pleased with him) praying in a low voice, and he passed by 'Umar ibn al-Khattaab (Allaah be pleased with him) who was praying in a loud voice. Later, when they gathered around the Prophet (sallallaahu 'alaihi wa sallam) said: *O Abu Bakr, I passed by you and you were praying in a low voice?* He said: "I let Him whom I was consulting hear, O Messenger of Allaah." He said to 'Umar: *I passed by you and you were praying raising your voice?* So he said: "O Messenger of Allaah, I repel drowsiness and keep the devil away." The Prophet (sallallaahu 'alaihi wa sallam) said: *O Abu Bakr, raise your voice a little bit* and to 'Umar: *lower your voice a little bit.* [5]

He used to say: *The one who recites the Qur'aan loudly is like the one who gives charity loudly, and the one who recites the Qur'aan quietly is like the one who gives charity quietly.*[6]

What he (sallallaahu 'alaihi wa sallam) used to Recite in the Different Prayers

As for which soorahs and aayaat he (sallallaahu 'alaihi wa sallam) used to recite in prayer, this varied according to the different prayers. The details now follow, beginning with the first of the five prayers:

---

[1] 'Abdul Haqq said in *Tahajjud* (90/1):
"As for voluntary prayers during the day, there is nothing authentic from him (sallallaahu 'alaihi wa sallam) regarding either quiet or loud recitation, but it would seem that he used to recite quietly during them. It is reported from him (sallallaahu 'alaihi wa sallam) that once, during the daytime, he passed by 'Abdullaah ibn Hudhaafah who was praying and reciting loudly, so he said to him: O 'Abdullaah, let Allaah hear, not us. But this hadeeth is not strong."
[2] Muslim & Bukhaari in *Af'aal al-'Ibaad.*
[3] Abu Daawood & Tirmidhi in *Shamaa'il* with a hasan isnaad. The hadeeth means that he (sallallaahu 'alaihi wa sallam) used to moderate between quietness and loudness.
[4] Nasaa'i, Tirmidhi in *Shamaa'il* & Baihaqi in *Dalaa'il* with a hasan isnaad.
[5] Abu Daawood & Haakim , who declared it saheeh, and Dhahabi agreed.
[6] ibid.

He (sallallaahu 'alaihi wa sallam) used to recite the longer *mufassal*[1] surahs[2] hence "he (sometimes) recited al-Waaqi'ah (56:96) and similar surahs in two rak'ahs"[3].

He recited from soorah at-Toor (52:49) during the Farewell Pilgrimage.[4]

Sometimes "he would recite soorah Qaaf (50:45) or similar [in the first rak'ah]."[5]

Sometimes "he would recite the shorter *mufassal* surahs, such as **"When the sun is folded up"** (at-Takweer 81:29)."[6]

Once, he recited **"When the Earth is shaken..."** (Zilzaal 99:8) in both rak'ahs, so that the narrator said, "I do not know whether the Messenger of Allaah forgot or recited it on purpose."[7]

Once, on a journey, he recited **"Say: I seek refuge with the Lord of the Daybreak"** (Falaq 113:5) and **"Say: I seek refuge with the Lord of Mankind"** (Naas 114:6).[8] He also said to 'Uqbah ibn 'Aamir (may Allaah be pleased with him): *Recite the mu'awwadhatain[9] in your prayer, for no seeker of refuge has sought refuge by means of anything like them.*[10]

Sometimes he used to recite more than that: "he would recite sixty aayaat or more"[11] - one of the narrators said, "I do not know whether this was in each rak'ah or in total."

He used to recite soorah ar-Room (30:60)[12] and sometimes soorah Yaa Sin (36:83)[13].

---

[1] The last seventh of the Qur'aan, beginning with soorah Qaaf (no. 50) according to the soundest view, as before.

[2] Nasaa'i & Ahmad with a saheeh isnaad.

[3] Ahmad, Ibn Khuzaimah (1/69/1) & Haakim who declared it saheeh and Dhahabi agreeed.

[4] Bukhaari & Muslim.

[5] Muslim & Tirmidhi. It is given along with the next one in *Irwaa'* (345).

[6] Muslim & Abu Daawood.

[7] Abu Daawood & Baihaqi with a saheeh isnaad. And what is apparent is that he ('alaihis salaam) did it on purpose to establish its validity.

[8] Abu Daawood, Ibn Khuzaimah (1/76/1), Ibn Bushraan in *al-Amaali* & Ibn Abi Shaibah (12/176/1); Haakim declared it saheeh and Dhahabi agreed.

[9] lit. "the two by means of which refuge is sought", i.e. the last two surahs of the Qur'aan, both beginning "Say: I seek refuge ... "

[10] Abu Daawood & Ahmad with a saheeh isnaad.

[11] Bukhaari & Muslim.

[12] Nasaa'i, Ahmad & Bazzaar with a good isnaad.

[13] Ahmad with a saheeh isnaad.

Once, "he prayed the *Subh* [i.e. Fajr Prayer] in Makkah and started reciting soorah al-Mu'minoon (23:118) until, when he got to the mention of Moosaa and Haaroon or the mention of 'Isa[1] - one of the narrators was not sure - he started coughing and so made rukoo'."[2]

Sometimes, "he would lead them in Fajr with as-Saaffaat" (77:182).[3]

"In Fajr on Friday, he would recite as-Sajdah (32:30) [in the first rak'ah, and, in the second,] ad-Dahr" (76:31).[4]

He used to make the first rak'ah longer than the second.[5]

Recitation in the Sunnah prayer before Fajr

His recitation in the two rak'ahs of sunnah in Fajr used to be extremely short[6], so much so that 'Aa'ishah (may Allaah be pleased with her) used to say: "Has he recited soorah al-Faatihah or not ?"[7]

Sometimes, after al-Faatihah, he would recite the aayah **"Say: We believe in Allaah and the revelation given to us..."** (Baqarah 2:136) in the first rak'ah; in the second, the aayah **"Say: O People of the Book! Come to common terms as between us and you..."** (aal-'Imraan 3:64).[8] Occasionally, he would recite instead of the latter, **"When 'Isa found unbelief on their part..."** (aal-'Imraan 3:52).[9]

Sometimes he would recite soorah al-Kaafiroon (109:6) in the first rak'ah, and soorah al-Ikhlaas (112:4) in the second;[10] also, he used to say: *An excellent pair of soorahs they are!* [11]
He heard a man reciting the former soorah in the first rak'ah, so he said, *This is a slave who believes in his Lord.* Then the man recited the latter soorah in the second rak'ah, so he said, *This is a slave who knows his Lord.*[12]

---

[1] Moosaa is mentioned in aayah 45: **"Then We sent Moosaa and his brother Haaroon, with our signs and manifest authority. ;"** 'Isa is mentioned soon after in aayah 50: **"And We made the son of Maryam and his mother as a sign - we gave them both shelter on high ground, affording rest and security and furnished with springs. "**
[2] Muslim, & Bukhaari in ta'leeq.form. It is given in *Irwaa'* (397).
[3] Ahmad & Abu Ya'laa in their musnads, and Maqdisi in *al-Mukhtaarah*.
[4] Bukhaari & Muslim.
[5] ibid.
[6] Ahmad with a saheeh isnaad.
[7] Bukhaari & Muslim.
[8] Muslim, Ibn Khuzaimah & Haakim.
[9] Muslim & Abu Daawood.
[10] ibid.
[11] Ibn Maajah & Ibn Khuzaimah.
[12] Tahaawi, Ibn Hibbaan in his saheeh & Ibn Bushraan; Ibn Haajar declared it hasan in *al-Ahaadeeth al-'Aaliyaat* (no. 16).

2- Zuhr Prayer

"He (sallallaahu 'alaihi wa sallam) used to recite al-Faatihah and two soorahs in the first two rak'ahs, making the first one longer than the second."[1]

Sometimes he would make lengthen it to the extent that "the Zuhr prayer would have started, and someone could go to a plain: al-Baqi,' fulfil his need, [come back to his place,] make his ablution, and then come (to the mosque) while the Messenger of Allaah (sallallaahu 'alaihi wa sallam) was still in the first rak'ah, it was that long."[2]
Also, "they used to think that he did it so that the people could catch the first rak'ah."[3]

"He used to recite in each of these two rak'ah about thirty aayaat, such as al-Faatihah followed by soorah as-Sajdah (32:30)."[4]

Sometimes "he would recite **By the Sky and the Night-Visitant**" (Taariq, 86:17), **"By the Sky, (displaying) the Constellations"** (Burooj, 85:22), **"By the Night as it conceals"** (Layl, 92:21) and similar soorahs."[5]

Occasionally, he recited **"When the Sky is rent asunder"** (Inshiqaaq 84:25) and similar ones.[6]

"They could tell that he was reciting in Zuhr and 'Asr from the movement of his beard."[7]

Recitation of Aayaat after al-Faatihah in the last two Rak'ahs

"He used to make the last two rak'ahs about half as long as the first two, about fifteen aayaat[8], and sometimes he would recite only al-Faatihah in them."[9]

---

[1] Bukhaari & Muslim.

[2] Muslim, & Bukhaari in *Juz' al-Qiraa'ah* (Article on Recitation).

[3] Abu Daawood with a saheeh isnaad & Ibn Khuzaimah (1/165/1).

[4] Ahmad & Muslim.

[5] Abu Daawood, Tirmidhee& Ibn Khuzaimah (1/67/2); the latter two declared it saheeh.

[6] Ibn Khuzaimah in his saheeh (1/67/2).

[7] Bukhaari & Abu Daawood.

[8] Ahmad & Muslim. The hadeeth contains evidence that reciting more than al-Faatihah in the last two rak'ahs is a sunnah, and many Companions did so, among them Abu Bakr Siddeeq (may Allaah be pleased with him). It is also the view of Imaam Shaafi'i, whether in Zuhr or others, and of our later scholars, Abul Hasanaat al-Lucknowi took it in *Notes on Muhammad's al-Muwatta'* (p. 102) and said:
"Some of our companions take hold a very strange view in obligating a sajdah sahw (prostration for forgetfulness) for the recitation of a soorah in the last two rak'ahs, but the commentators on *al-Maniyyah*, Ibraaheem al-Halabi, Ibn Ameer Haajj and others, have refuted this view extremely
=

Sometimes "he would let them hear an aayah or so."[1]

"They would hear the tones of his recitation of "**Glorify the name of your Lord Most High**" (A'laa 87:19) and "**Has the story reached you of the Overwhelming ?**" (Ghaashiyah 88:26)."[2]

Sometimes "he would recite "**By the Sky and the Night-Visitant**" (Taariq 86:17), "**By the Sky, (displaying) the Constellations**" (Burooj 85:22), and similar soorahs."[3]

Sometimes "he would recite "**By the Night as it conceals**" (Layl 92:21) and similar soorahs."[4]

3- 'Asr prayer

"He (sallallaahu 'alaihi wa sallam) used to recite al-Faatihah and two (other) soorahs in the first two rak'ahs, making the first one longer than the second"[5], and "they used to think that he did it so that the people could catch the rak'ah."[6]

"He used to recite about fifteen aayaat in each of the first two rak'ahs, about half as much as he recited in each of the first two rak'ahs of Zuhr, and he used to make the last two rak'ahs about half as long the first two."[7]

"He used to recite al-Faatihah in the last two."[8]
"He would let them hear an aayah or so sometimes."[9]

He used to recite the surahs mentioned under "Zuhr prayer" above.

---

well. There is no doubt that those who said this were unaware of the hadeeth, and had it reached them they would not have said so."
[9] Bukhaari & Muslim.
[1] Ibn Khuzaimah in his saheeh (1/67/2) & Diyaa' al-Maqdisi in *al-Mukhtaarah* with a saheeh isnaad.
[2] Bukhaari in *Article on Recitation* & Tirmidhi, who declared it saheeh.
[3] Muslim & Tayaalisi.
[4] Bukhaari & Muslim.
[5] ibid.
[6] Abu Daawood with a saheeh isnaad & Ibn Khuzaimah.
[7] Ahmad & Muslim.
[8] Bukhaari & Muslim.
[9] ibid.

4- Maghrib prayer

"He (sallallaahu 'alaihi wa sallam) used to (sometimes) recite the short *mufassal* soorahs"[1], so that "when they had finished praying with him, they could go away and (it was possible to) shoot an arrow and see where it landed."[2]
Once, "while on a journey, he recited "By the Fig and the Olive" (Teen 95:8) in the second rak'ah."[3]

But sometimes he would recite the long or medium *mufassal* surahs, hence "he would recite "Those who disbelieve and hinder (men) from the Path of Allaah" (Muhammad 47:48);"[4]
or soorah at-Toor (52:49);[5]
or soorah al-Mursalaat (77:50), which he recited in the last prayer he prayed.[6]

Sometimes "he would recite the longer of the two long surahs[7] (A'raaf 7:206) [in two rak'ahs]."[8] Or he would recite al-Anfaal (8:75) in two rak'ahs.[9]

Recitation in the sunnah prayer after Maghrib

In this prayer, "he used to recite "Say: O you who reject faith" (Kaafiroon 109:6) and "Say: He is Allaah, the One and Only" (Ikhlaas 112:4)."[10]

5- 'Ishaa' prayer

He (sallallaahu 'alaihi wa sallam) would recite the medium *mufassal* surahs in the first two rak'ahs[11], hence "he used to recite "By the Sun and his splendour" (Shams 91:15) and surahs like it."[12]

Or "he would recite "When the Sky is rent asunder" (Inshiqaaq 84:25) and make sajdah during it."[13]

---

[1] ibid (Bukhaari & Muslim).
[2] Nasaa'i & Ahmad with a saheeh isnaad.
[3] Tayaalisi & Ahmad with a saheeh isnaad.
[4] Ibn Khuzaimah (1/166/2), Tabaraani & Maqdisi with a saheeh isnaad.
[5] Bukhaari & Muslim.
[6] ibid.
[7] called "at-toolayain": A'raaf (7) is agreed to be one; An'aam (6) is the other, according to the most correct saying, as in *Fath al-Baari*.
[8] Bukhaari, Abu Daawood, Ibn Khuzaimah (1/68/1), Ahmad, Siraaj & Mukhlis.
[9] Tabaraani in *Mu'jam al-Kabeer* with a saheeh isnaad.
[10] Ahmad, Maqdisi, Nasaa'ee Ibn Nasr & Tabaraani .
[11] Nasaa'i & Ahmad with a saheeh isnaad.
[12] Ahmad & Tirmidhi, who declared it hasan.
[13] Bukhaari, Muslim & Nasaai.

Also, "he once recited **"By the Fig and the Olive"** (Teen 95:8) [in the first rak'ah] while on a journey."[1]

He forbade prolonging of recitation in 'Ishaa', and that was when:

> Mu'aadh ibn Jabal led his people in 'Ishaa' prayer, and made it very long for them, so one of the Ansaar left and prayed (alone). When Mu'aadh was informed about this, he said: "He is surely a hypocrite". When the man heard of this, he went to the Messenger of Allaah (sallallaahu 'alaihi wa sallam) and told him what Mu'aadh had said, so the Prophet (sallallaahu 'alaihi wa sallam) said to him: "Do you want to be on who causes a lot of trouble, Mu'aadh?! When you lead the people, recite **"By the Sun and his splendour"** (Shams 91:15) or **"Glorify the Name of your Lord Most High"** (A'laa 77:19) or **"Read in the Name of your Lord"** ('Alaq 96:19) or **"By the Night as it conceals"** (Layl 92:21) [because the old, the weak and those who have a need to fulfil pray behind you]."[2]

6- Night prayer (Tahajjud)

He (sallallaahu 'alaihi wa sallam) would sometimes recite loudly in it and sometimes quietly,[3] He (sallallaahu 'alaihi wa sallam) would shorten his recitation in this sometimes and lengthen it sometimes, occasionally making it so exceedingly long that 'Abdullaah ibn Mas'ood (radi Allaahu 'anhu) once said:
> "I prayed with the Prophet (sallallaahu 'alaihi wa sallam) one night, and he carried on standing for so long that I was struck by a wrong idea." He was asked, "What was this idea?" He said: "I thought I would sit down and leave the Prophet (sallallaahu 'alaihi wa sallam)!"[4]

Also Hudhaifah ibn al-Yamaan said:
> "I prayed with the Prophet (sallallaahu 'alaihi wa sallam) that night when he started soorah al-Baqarah (2:286). So I said (to myself), "He will make rukoo' after one hundred aayaat". But he carried on after that, so I thought, "He will finish it (the soorah) in two rak'ahs". But he carried on, so I thought, "He will make rukoo' when he has finished it." Then he started soorah an-Nisaa' (4:176) and recited it all, then he started soorah aal-'Imraan (3:200)[5] and recited it all. He was reciting slowly; when he came to an aayah in which there was glorification of Allaah, he glorified Allaah; at an aayah which had something to be asked for, he asked for it; at

---

[1] ibid.
[2] ibid. It is also given in *Irwaa'* (295)
[3] Nasaai with Saheeh isnaad.
[4] Bukhaari & Muslim.
[5] The narration is like this, with Nisaa' (4) before aal-'Imraan (3), and thus it is evidence for (the permissibility of) departing from the order of surahs found in the 'Uthmaani copy of the Qur'aan in recitation. An example of this has already been seen.

mention of seeking refuge, he sought refuge (with Allaah). Then he made rukoo' ... " to the end of the hadeeth.[1]

Also, "one night when he was ill he recited the Seven Long surahs."[2]

Also, "he would (sometimes) recite one of these surahs in each rak'ah."[3]

"It was [totally] unknown for him to recite the whole Qur'aan in one night."[4] In fact, he did not recommend it for 'Abdullaah ibn 'Amr (may Allaah be pleased with him) when he said to him:
Recite the whole Qur'aan in each month. I said: "I have the power (to do more than that)." He said: Recite it in twenty nights. I said: "I have the power to do more". He said: Then recite it in seven days and do not go beyond that.[5]
Then "he allowed him to recite it in five days."[6]
Then "he allowed him to recite it in three days."[7]
Further, he forbade him from reciting it in less time than that[8], and he gave a reason for that by saying to him: Whoever recites the Qur'aan in less than three days does not understand it.[9] In another version: He does not understand, the one who recites the Qur'aan in less than three days.[10] Also when he said to him: For every worshipper has a (period of) keenness[11] and every (period of) keenness has a lapse[12], either towards a sunnah or towards a bid'ah (innovation); so he whose lapse is towards a sunnah has found guidance, and he whose lapse is towards other than that has been destroyed.[13]

---

[1] Muslim & Nasaa'i .

[2] Abu Ya'laa & Haakim, who declared it saheeh and Dhahabi agreed. Ibn al-Atheer says: "... the Seven Long surahs are Baqarah (2), aal-'Imraan (3), Nisaa' (4), Maa'idah (5), An'aam (6), A'raaf (7) and Tawbah (9)."

[3] Abu Daawood & Nasaa'i with a saheeh isnaad.

[4] Muslim & Abu Daawood.

[5] Bukhaari & Muslim.

[6] Nasaa'i & Tirmidhi, who declared it saheeh.

[7] Bukhaari & Ahmad.

[8] Daarimi & Sa'eed ibn Mansoor in his sunan with a saheeh isnaad.

[9] Ahmad with a saheeh isnaad.

[10] Daarimi & Tirmidhi, who declared it saheeh.

[11] Ar. shirrah: excitement, enthusiasm, keenness, energy. The shirrah of youth is his its beginning and its fervour/zeal. Imaam Tahaawi says:
"This is the zeal/fervour of the Muslims in their actions which bring them nearer to their Lord. However they are bound to fall short and leave some actions (which they began due to this zeal) so the most beloved of their actions to Allaah's Messenger (sallallaahu 'alaihi wa sallam) were those done otherwise (and kept up), so he ordered them to carry out righteous deeds which they are able to do continually and keep to until they meet their Lord-the Mighty and Majestic. It is narrated from him (sallallaahu 'alaihi wa sallam) to clarify this that he said: "The actions most loved by Allaah are those which are the most regular, even if they are little."
I say: this hadeeth which he prefixes with the words "it is narrated" is saheeh, agreed upon by Bukhaari & Muslim from the narration of 'Aa'ishah (Allaah be pleased with her).

[12] Ar. fatrah: interval, break, lapse; referring here to a period of reduced enthusiasm.

[13] Ahmad & Ibn Hibbaan in his saheeh.

For this reason, "he (sallallaahu 'alaihi wa sallam) would not recite the whole Qur'aan in less than three days."[1]

He used to say: *Whoever prays at night reciting two hundred aayaat will be written down as one of the sincere devotees.*[2] Also, "he used to recite soorah Bani Israa'eel (17:111) and soorah az-Zumar (39:75) every night."[3] He also used to say: *Whoever prays at night reciting a hundred aayaat will not be written down as one of the heedless.*[4] Sometimes "he would recite about fifty aayaat or more in each rak'ah"[5], or he "would recite about as much as soorah al-Muzzammil (73:20)."[6]

"He (sallallaahu 'alaihi wa sallam) would not pray all through the night"[7] except rarely, for once:

" 'Abdullaah ibn Khabbaab ibn al-Arat - who was present at (the Battle of) Badr with the Messenger of Allaah (sallallaahu 'alaihi wa sallam) - stayed up the whole night with the Messenger of Allaah (sallallaahu 'alaihi wa sallam) *(in another version: a night when he prayed throughout it)* until it was dawn. So when he finished his prayer, Khabbaab said to him: "O Messenger of Allaah, may my father and mother be sacrificed for you! Tonight, you have prayed a prayer the like of which I have never seen?" He said: *Yes, it was a prayer of hope and fear; [indeed] I asked my Lord, Mighty and Sublime, three things; He granted me two, but refused me one. I asked my Lord that He would not destroy us the way the nations before us were* (in another version: *that He would not destroy my ummah with famine) and He granted me this; I asked my Lord, Mighty and Sublime, that He would not impose on us an enemy from outside us, and*

---

[1] Ibn Sa'ad (1/376) & Abu ash-Shaikh in 'Akhlaaq Nabi (281).

[2] Daarimi & Haakim , who declared it saheeh and Dhahabi agreed.

[3] ibid.

[4] Ahmad & Ibn Nasr with a saheeh isnaad.

[5] Bukhaari & Abu Daawood.

[6] Ahmad & Abu Daawood with a saheeh isnaad.

[7] Muslim & Abu Daawood. This hadeeth and others make it disliked (makrooh) to stay awake the whole night, whether always or regularly, for it is against the example of the Prophet (sallallaahu 'alaihi wa sallam); for if staying up the whole night were better, he (sallallaahu 'alaihi wa sallam) would have done so, and the best guidance is the guidance of Muhammad. So do not be deceived by what is narrated from Abu Haneefah (rahimahullaah) that he prayed Fajr with the ablution of 'Ishaa' for forty years!! (translator's note: see *Tablighi Nisab: Virtues of Salaat* by Maulana Zakariyya Kandhalvi for examples of this type of claim) For this narration from him is totally baseless; in fact 'Allaamah al-Fairoozaabaadi says in *Ar-Radd 'alaa al-Mu'tarid* ((44/1):

"This narration is a clear lie and cannot be attributed to the Imaam, for there is nothing excellent about it, whereas it was the nature of the likes of the Imaam to do the better thing; there is no doubt that the renewal of purification for each prayer is more excellent, most complete, and best. This is even if it is correct that he stayed awake the length of the night for forty consecutive years! This story seems more like a fairy tale, and is an invention of some of the extremely ignorant fanatics, who say it about Abu Haneefah and others, and all of it is lies."

37

He granted me this; and I asked my Lord not to cover us with confusion in party strife, but He refused me this." "[1]

Also,

one night he stood (in prayer) repeating one aayah until it was dawn:

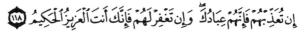

"If You do punish them, they are Your servants; if You do forgive them, You are indeed the Exalted in Power, the Wise." (Maa'idah 5:121) [with it he bowed, with it he prostrated, and with it he supplicated], [so in the morning Abu Dharr (radi Allaahu 'anhu) said to him: "O Messenger of Allaah, you did not stop reciting this aayah until it was morning; you bowed with it and you prostrated with it] [and you supplicated with it,] [whereas Allaah has taught you the whole Qur'aan;] [if one of us were to do this, we would be stern with him?] [He said: *Indeed I asked my Lord, the Mighty and Sublime, for intercession for my ummah: He granted me it, and it will be possible if Allaah wills for whoever does not associate any partners with Allaah.*[2]

A man said to him: "O Messenger of Allaah, I have a neighbour who stands (in prayer) at night and does not recite anything except **"Say: He is Allaah the One and Only"** (Ikhlaas 112:4), [repeating it,] [not adding anything else,] as if he considers it little." So the Prophet (sallallaahu 'alaihi wa sallam) said: *By Him in Whose Hand is my soul, it is worth a third of the Qur'aan.*[3]

7- Witr prayer

'He (sallallaahu 'alaihi wa sallam) used to recite **"Glorify the Name of Your Lord Most High"** (al-A'laa 87:19) in the first rak'ah, **"Say: O you who disbelieve"** (Kaafiroon 109:6) in the second, and **"Say: He is Allaah the One and Only"** (Ikhlaas 112:4) in the third.[4] Sometimes he would add on to the last one **"Say: I seek refuge with the Lord of Daybreak"** (Falaq 113:5) and **"Say: I seek refuge with the Lord of Mankind"** (Naas 114:6).[5]
Once, "he recited a hundred aayaat from soorah an-Nisaa' (4:176) in the third rak'ah."[6]

---

[1] Nasaa'i, Ahmad & Tabaraani (1/187/2); Tirmidhi declared it *saheeh*.

[2] Nasaa'i, Ibn Khuzaimah (1/70/1), Ahmad, Ibn Nasr & Haakim, who declared it *saheeh* and Dhahabi agreed.

[3] Ahmad & Bukhaari .

[4] Nasaa'i & Haakim, who declared it *saheeh*.

[5] Tirmidhi, Abul 'Abbaas al-Asamm in his *al-Hadeeth* (vol 2 no. 117) & Haakim, who declared it *saheeh* and Dhahabi agreed.

[6] Nasaa'i & Ahmad with a *saheeh* isnaad.

As for the two rak'ahs after witr[1], he used to recite "**When the earth is shaken...**" (Zilzaal 99:8) and "**Say: O you who disbelieve**" (Kaafiroon 109:6) in them.[2]

8- Friday Prayer

He (sallallaahu 'alaihi wa sallam) would sometimes recite soorah al-Jumu'ah (62:11) in the first rak'ah and "**When the hypocrites come to you**" (Munaafiqoon 63:11)[3] in the second, sometimes reciting "**Has the story reached you of the Overwhelming?**" (Ghaashiyah 88:26) instead of the latter.[4] Or sometimes "he would recite "**Glorify the Name of your Lord Most High**" (A'laa 87:19) in the first rak'ah and "**Has the story reached you...**" (Ghaashiyah 88:26) in the second."[5]

9- 'Eid Prayer

"He (sallallaahu 'alaihi wa sallam) would (sometimes) recite "**Glorify the Name of your Lord Most High**" (A'laa 87:19) in the first rak'ah and "**Has the story reached you...**" (Ghaashiyah 88:26) in the second."[6]
Or sometimes "he would recite in them "**Qaaaaf. By the Glorious Qur'aan.**" (Qaaf 50:45) and "**The Hour has drawn near**" (Qamar 54:55)."[7]

10- Funeral Prayer

"The Sunnah is to recite al-Faatihah[8] [and another soorah] in it."[9] Also, "he would be silent for a while, after the first takbeer."[10]

---

[1] The evidence for these two rak'ahs is found in Saheeh Muslim and others as a practice of the Prophet (sallallaahu 'alaihi wa sallam), but they oppose his saying: *Make the last of your prayer at night odd (witr)* transmitted by Bukhaari and Muslim. The scholars have differed in reconciling these two hadeeth, none of them being convincing to me, so the most cautious thing is to leave the two rak'ahs in compliance with the command of the Prophet (sallallaahu 'alaihi wa sallam). Allaah knows best.
Later I came across an authentic hadeeth which had a command for two rak'ahs after witr, so the order of the Prophet (sallallaahu 'alaihi wa sallam) agrees with his action, and the two rak'ahs are validated for everyone; the first command is thus one of recommendation, not negating the two rak'ahs. The latter hadeeth is given in *Silsilat al-ahaadeeth as-saheehah* (1993) - see Appendix 7.
[2] Ahmad & Ibn Nasr and Tahaawi (1/202) and Ibn Khuzaimah & Ibn Hibbaan with a *hasan saheeh* isnaad.
[3] Muslim & Abu Daawood. It is given in *Irwaa* (345).
[4] ibid.
[5] Muslim & Abu Daawood.
[6] ibid.
[7] ibid.
[8] This is the saying of Imaam Shaafi'i, Ahmad and Ishaaq, and some of the later Hanafis who researched took this view. As for the recitation of a soorah after it, this is the view of some of the Shaafi'ees and it is the correct view.
[9] Bukhaari , Abu Daawood, Nasaa'i & Ibn al-Jaarood. The addition is not *shaadhdh* (odd) as Tuwaijiri thinks.
[10] Nasaa'i & Tahaawi with a saheeh isnaad.

Tarteel (Recitation in slow, rhythmic tones), & Making the Voice Beautiful when Reciting

He (sallallaahu 'alaihi wa sallam) used to recite the Qur'aan in slow, measured rythmic tones as Allaah had instructed him, not racing or hurrying; rather, his was "a recitation clearly-distinguishing each letter"[1], so much so that "he would recite a soorah in such slow rhythmic tones that it would be longer than would seem possible."[2]

He also used to say: *It will be said to the reciter of the Qur'aan (on the Day of Judgment), 'Recite and ascend; recite slowly and rhythmically as you used to do in the previous world; your place will be at the last aayah you recite.*[3]

He "used to prolong his recitation (at a letter which can be prolonged), such as at *bismil-laah*, at *ar-rahmaan*, and at *ar-raheem*"[4], and at *"nadeed"* (Qaaf 50:10)[5] & their like.

He used to stop at the end of an aayah, as has already been explained.[6]

Sometimes "he would recite in an attractive vibrating tone[7], as he did on the Day of the Conquest of Makkah, when, while on his she-camel, he recited soorah al-Fath (48:29) [very softly][8], and 'Abdullaah ibn Mughaffal narrated this attractive tone thus : aaa."[9]

He used to command making one's voice beautiful when reciting the Qur'aan, saying

Beautify the Qur'aan with your voices [for a fine voice increases the Qur'aan in beauty][10] and

---

[1]Ibn al-Mubaarak in *az-Zuhd* (162/1 from *al-Kawaakib* 575), Abu Daawood & Ahmad with a saheeh isnaad.
[2]Muslim & Maalik.
[3]Abu Daawood & Tirmidhi, who declared it saheeh.
[4]Bukhaari & Abu Daawood.
[5]Bukhaari in *Af'aal al-'Ibaad* with a saheeh isnaad.
[6]In the section on "Recitation of one verse at a time".
[7]*Tarjee'* -explained as a vibrating tone by Ibn Hajar; Manaawi said: "It arises from a feeling of joy & happiness, which he (sallallaahu 'alaihi wa sallam) felt a good deal on the day of the conquest of Makkah."
[8]Bukhaari & Muslim.
[9]ibid. Ibn Hajar said in his commentary on"aaa (١ ١ ١)", "this is a hamzah with a fathah, followed by a silent alif, followed by another hamzah." Shaikh 'Ali al-Qaari quoted likewise from others and then said: "It is obvious that this is three prolonged alifs."
[10]Bukhaari as ta'leeq, Abu Daawood, Darimi, Haakim and Tammaam al-Raazi with two saheeh isnaads.
NOTE: This hadeeth was turned round by one of the narrators, who narrated it as "beautify your voices with the Qur'aan". This is a mistake in narration and understanding, and whoever declared it saheeh is submerged in error, for it contradicts the authentic explanatory narrations in this

Truly, the one who has one of the finest voices among the people for reciting the Qur'aan is the one whom you think fears Allaah when you hear him recite.[1]

He also used to command recitation of the Qur'aan in a pleasant tone, saying: *Study the Book of Allaah; recite it repeatedly; acquire (memorise) it; and recite it in a melodious tone, for by Him in whose Hand is my soul, it runs away quicker than camels from their tying ropes.*[2]

He also used to say, *He who does not recite the Qur'aan in a pleasant tone is not of us*[3] and

Allaah does not listen to anything as he listens (in some versions: *as he is listening*) *to a prophet* [*with a nice voice*, and in one version: *with a nice melody*] *who recites the Qur'aan in a pleasant tone*[4] [*loudly*].[5]

He said to Abu Moosaa al-Ash'ari (radi Allaahu 'anhu),

Had you seen me while I was listening to your recitation yesterday! You have surely been given one of the musical wind-instruments[6] *of the family of Daawood!* [So Abu Moosaa said: "Had I known you were there, I would have made my voice more pleasant and emotional for you].*"[7]

Correcting the Imaam

He (sallallaahu 'alaihi wa sallam) set the example of correcting the imaam when his recitation becomes mixed up, when once "he prayed, reciting loudly, and his recitation became mixed up, so when he finished, he said to Ubayy: *Did you pray with us?* He replied, 'Yes.' He said, *So what prevented you [from correcting me]?"*[8]

---

section. In fact, it is a prime example of a maqloob hadeeth, and the details of this brief note are in *Silsilah al-Ahaadeeth ad-Da'eefah* (no. 5328).

[1]A saheeh hadeeth transmitted by Ibn al Mubarak in *az-Zuhd* (162/1 from *al-Kawaakib* 575), Daarimi, Ibn Nasr, Tabaraani, Abu Nu'aim in *Akhbaar Isbahaan* and Diyaa' in *al-Mukhtaarah*.

[2]Daarimi & Ahmad with a saheeh isnaad.

[3]Abu Daawood and Haakim who declared it saheeh and Dhahabi agreed.

[4] Mundhiri said, "taghannnaa does mean to recite in a pleasant voice; Sufyaan bin 'Uyainah and others took the the view that it is to do with istighnaa (i.e. letting the Qur'aan make one dispense with worldly pleasures), but this is rejected."

[5]Bukhaari, Muslim, Tahaawi & Ibn Mandah in *Tawheed* (81/1).

[6]The scholars have said that musical instruments here means a beautiful voice and that the family of Daawood refers to Daawood himself; the family of so-and-so can be specifically for so-and-so only; Daawood ('alaihis salaam) had an extremely beautiful voice. This is mentioned by Nawawi in his commentary on Saheeh Muslim.

[7]'Abdur Razzaaq in *al-Amaali* (2/44/1), Bukhaari, Muslim, Ibn Nasr and Haakim.

[8] Abu Daawood, Ibn Hibbaan, Tabaraani, Ibn 'Asaakir (2/296/2) & Diyaa' in *al-Mukhtaarah* with a saheeh isnaad.

Seeking Refuge & Spitting Lightly during Prayer in order to Repel Temptation

'Uthmaan ibn Abi l-'Aas (radi Allaahu 'anhu) said to him, "O Messenger of Allaah! The devil comes between me and my prayer and confuses me in my recitation!" So the Messenger of Allaah (sallallaahu 'alaihi wa sallam) said, *That is a devil called Khinzab, so when you detect him, seek refuge with Allaah from him, and spit lightly[1] on your left three times.* He said, "So when I did that, Allaah caused him to go away from me."[2]

THE RUKOO' (BOWING)

After completing his recitation, he (sallallaahu 'alaihi wa sallam) would pause for a moment[3], then raise his hands[4] in the way described earlier under the "Opening Takbeer", say takbeer[5], and make rukoo'.[6]

He also ordered "the one who prayed badly" likewise, saying to him, *Indeed, the prayer of one of you is not complete until he makes an excellent ablution as Allaah has commanded him to ... then he celebrates Allaah's greatness, praises and glorifies Him, then recites the Qur'aan as much as is easy for him from what Allaah has taught him and allowed him, then says takbeer and makes rukoo' [and places his hands on his knees] until his joints are at ease and relaxed...*[7]

---

[1] Ar. *tafl*: to blow with a minimum amount of saliva - *Nihaayah*.

[2] Muslim & Ahmad. Nawawi (rahimahullaah) says, "This hadeeth contains a recommendation to seek refuge from the devil when he tempts, along with spitting to the left three times."

[3] Abu Daawood & Haakim, who declared it saheeh & Dhahabi agreed.

[4] Bukhaari & Muslim. This raising of the hands is reported as mutawaatir from him (sallallaahu 'alaihi wa sallam), as is the raising of the hands on straightening up after rukoo'. It is the madhhab of the three Imaams Maalik, Shaafi'i and Ahmad, and of the majority of scholars of hadeeth and fiqh. Imaam Maalik (rahimahullaah) practised it right up to his death, as reported by Ibn 'Asaakir (15/78/2). Some of the Hanafis chose to do it, among them 'Isaam bin Yusuf Abu 'Asamah al-Balkhi (d. 210), a student of Imaam Abu Yusuf (rahimahullaah), as has been explained in the Introduction. 'Abdullaah bin Ahmad reported from his father in his *Masaa'il* (p. 60), "It is related from 'Uqbah bin 'Aamir that he said about a man raising his hands during prayer, 'He earns ten good deeds for each such movement'." This is supported by the hadeeth qudsi, "... *he who intends a good deed and then does it, Allaah writes it down with Himself as from ten to seven hundred good deeds*", transmitted by Bukhaari & Muslim. See *Saheeh at-Targheeb*, no. 16.

[5] ibid.

[6] ibid.

[7] Abu Daawood & Nasaa'i. Haakim declared it saheeh & Dhahabi agreed.

The Rukoo' Described

"He (sallallaahu 'alaihi wa sallam) would place his palms on his knees"[1], and "would order them to do likewise"[2], as he ordered "the one who prayed badly" in the afore-mentioned hadeeth.

"He would put his hands firmly on his knees [as though he were grasping them]"[3], and "would space his fingers out"[4], ordering "the one who prayed badly" likewise, saying: *When you make rukoo', place your palms on your knees, then space your fingers out, then remain (like that) until every limb takes its (proper) place.*[5]

"He used to spread himself (i.e., not be in a compact position), and keep his elbows away from his sides."[6]

"When he made rukoo', he would spread his back and make it level"[7], "such that if water were poured on it, it (the water) would stay there (i.e., not run off)."[8] He also said to "the one who prayed badly", *When you make rukoo', put your palms on your knees, spread your back (flat) and hold firm in your rukoo'.*[9]

"He would neither let his head droop nor raise it (i.e. higher than his back)"[10], but it would be in between.[11]

The Obligation of Being at Ease in Rukoo'

He used to be at ease in his rukoo', and ordered "the one who prayed badly" to be so, as has been mentioned in the first section on rukoo'.

---

[1]Bukhaari & Abu Daawood.
[2]Bukhaari & Muslim.
[3] Bukhaari & Abu Daawood.
[4]Haakim , who declared it saheeh; Dhahabi & Tayaalisi agreed. It is given in *Saheeh Abi Daawood* (809).
[5]Ibn Khuzaimah & Ibn Hibbaan in their Saheehs.
[6] Tirmidhi, who declared it saheeh, & Ibn Khuzaimah.
[7]Bukhaari, and Baihaqi with a saheeh isnaad.
[8]Tabaraani in *Mu'jam al-Kabeer* and *Mu'jam al-Sagheer*, 'Abdullaah b. Ahmad in *Zawaa'id al-Musnad* & Ibn Maajah.
[9]Ahmad & Abu Daawood with a saheeh isnaad.
[10]Abu Daawood & Bukhaari in *Juz' al-Qiraa'ah* with a saheeh isnaad.
[11]Muslim & Abu 'Awaanah.

He used to say, *Complete the rukoo' and sujood, for by Him in whose Hand is my soul, I surely see you behind my back*[1] *when you make rukoo' and sujood.*[2]

"He saw a man praying not completing his rukoo' properly, and pecking in his sujood, so he said, *Were this man to die in this state, he would die on a faith other than that of Muhammad, [pecking in his prayer as a crow pecks at blood; he who does not make rukoo' completely and pecks in his sujood is like the hungry person who eats one or two dates, which are of no use to him at all.*[3]

Abu Hurairah (radi Allaahu 'anhu) said, "My close friend (sallallaahu 'alaihi wa sallam) forbade me from pecking in my prayer like a cockerel, from looking around like a fox, and from squatting like a monkey."[4]

The Messenger of Allaah (sallallaahu 'alaihi wa sallam) also used to say, *The worst thief among men is the one who steals from his prayer.* They said, "O Messenger of Allaah, how does he steal from his prayer?" He said, *He does not complete its rukoo' and sujood.*[5]

Once, "he was praying, when he glanced out of the corner of his eye at a man not settling his backbone in rukoo' and sujood. When he finished, he said, *O assembly of Muslims! Verily, the prayer is not valid of the one who does not settle his spine in rukoo' and sujood.*"[6]

He said in another hadeeth, *The prayer of a man does not count unless he straightens his back in rukoo' and sujood.*[7]

The *Adhkaar* of Rukoo'

He would say different types of remembrance of Allaah and supplication, any one of the following at a time:

1-

سُبْحَانَ رَبِّيَ الْعَظِيم

---

[1]This vision was physically real, and was one of his miracles; it was confined to during prayer: there is no evidence for it being of a general nature.

[2]Bukhaari & Muslim.

[3]Abu Ya'laa in his Musnad (340/3491/1), Aajuri in *al-Arba'een*, Baihaqi, Tabaraani (1/192/1), Diyaa' in *al-Muntaqaa* (276/1), Ibn 'Asaakir (2/226/2, 414/1, 8/14/1, 76/2) with a hasan isnaad, & Ibn Khuzaimah declared it saheeh (1/82/1). Ibn Battah has a supporting mursal narration for the first part of the hadeeth, minus the addition, in *al-Ibaanah* (5/43/1).

[4]Tayaalisi, Ahmad & Ibn Abi Shaibah; it is a hasan hadeeth, as I have explained in my footnotes on *al-Ahkaam* (1348) by 'Abdul Haqq Ishbeeli.

[5]Ibn Abi Shaibah (1/89/2), Tabaraani & Haakim , who declared it saheeh and Dhahabi agreed.

[6]Ibn Abi Shaibah (1/89/1), Ibn Maajah & Ahmad, with a saheeh isnaad.

[7]Abu 'Awaanah, Abu Daawood & Sahmi (61); Daaraqutni declared it saheeh.

How Perfect is my Lord, the Supreme!, three times.[1] But sometimes, he would repeat it more than that.[2]

Once, in night prayer, he repeated it so much that his rukoo' became nearly as long as his standing before it, in which he had recited three of the Long Soorahs: Baqarah, Nisaa' and aal-'Imraan. This prayer was full of supplication & seeking forgiveness, and the hadeeth has already been mentioned under *"Recitation in Night Prayer."*

2-

$$\text{سُبْحَانَ رَبِّيَ الْعَظِيم وَبِحَمْدِهِ}$$

How Perfect is my Lord, the Supreme, and Praised be He, three times.[3]

3-

$$\text{سُبُّوحٌ قُدُّوسٌ رَبُّ الْمَلَائِكَةِ وَالرُّوح}$$

Perfect, Blessed,[4] Lord of the Angels and the Spirit.[5]

4-

$$\text{سُبْحَانَكَ اَللَّهُمَّ وَبِحَمْدِكَ اَللَّهُمَّ اغْفِرْ لِي}$$

How Perfect You are O Allaah, and Praises are for You. O Allaah, forgive me. He would say it often in his rukoo' and sujood, implementing (the order of) the Qur'aan.[6]

5-

$$\text{اَللَّهُمَّ لَكَ رَكَعْتُ، وَبِكَ آمَنْتُ، وَلَكَ أَسْلَمْتُ، [أَنْتَ رَبِّي]، خَشَعَ لَكَ سَمْعِي وَبَصَرِي، وَمُخِّي وَعَظْمِي (وَفِي}$$
$$\text{رِوَايَةٍ: وَعِظَامِي) وَعَصَبِي، [وَمَا اسْتَقَلَّتْ بِهِ قَدَمِي لِلَّهِ رَبِّ الْعَالَمِينَ]}$$

---

[1]Ahmad, Abu Daawood, Ibn Maajah, Daaraqutni, Tahaawi, Bazzaar, & Tabaraani in *Mu'jam al-Kabeer*, on the authority of seven Companions. Hence this refutes those who did not accept the specification of the glorifications to three times, such as Ibn al-Qayyim and others.

[2]This can be deduced from the ahaadeeth which make it clear that he (sallallaahu 'alaihi wa sallam) used to make his standing, rukoo' and sujood equal in length, as mentioned after this section.

[3]A saheeh hadeeth, transmitted by Abu Daawood, Daaraqutni, Ahmad, Tabaraani & Baihaqi .

[4]Abu Ishaaq said: *subbooh* means "the one who is free of any defect", while *quddoos* means "the Blessed" or "the Pure". Ibn Saidah said: Glorified and Blessed are attributes of Allaah, Mighty and Sublime, because He is glorified and sanctified by others. (*Lisaan al-'Arab*)

[5]Muslim & Abu 'Awaanah.

[6]Bukhaari & Muslim. "Implementing the Qur'aan" refers to the saying of Allaah: **"Then glorify with the Praises of your Lord, and seek His Forgiveness, for He is Oft-Returning."** (Nasr 110:3)

O Allaah! To You I have bowed; in You I have believed; to You I have submitted; [You are my Lord]; humbled for You are my hearing, my seeing, my marrow, my bone (in one narration: my bones), my sinews, [and whatever my feet carry[1] (are humbled) for Allaah, Lord of the Worlds].[2]

6-

مَّ لَكَ رَكَعْتُ، وَبِكَ آمَنْتُ، وَلَكَ أَسْلَمْتُ، وَعَلَيْكَ تَوَكَّلْتُ، أَنْتَ رَبِّي، خَشَعَ سَمْعِي وَبَصَرِي وَدَمِي وَلَحْمِي لَمِي وَعَصَبِي لِلَّهِ رَبِّ الْعَالَمِين

O Allaah! to You I have bowed; in You I have believed; to You I have submitted; in You I have placed my trust; You are my Lord; my hearing, my seeing, my blood, my flesh, my bones, and my sinews are humbled for Allaah, Lord of the Worlds.[3]

7-

سُبْحَانَ ذِي الْجَبَرُوتِ وَالْمَلَكُوتِ وَالْكِبْرِيَاءِ وَالْعَظَمَةِ

How Perfect is He Who has all' Power, Kingdom, Magnificence and Supremity, which he used to say in night prayer.

Lengthening the Rukoo'

"He (sallallaahu 'alaihi wa sallam) used to make his rukoo', his standing after rukoo', his sujood, and his sitting in between the two sajdahs, nearly equal in length."[4]

---

[1]This is an example of use of a general phrase coming after mention of individual items.
[2]Muslim, Abu Awaanah, Tahaawi & Daaraqutni .
[3]Nasaa'i with a saheeh isnaad.

NOTE: Is there proof for combining two or more of these adhkaar in one rukoo', or not ? The scholars have differed about this. Ibn al-Qayyim was uncertain about this in *Zaad al-Ma'aad*. Nawawi chose the first possibility in *al-Adhkaar*, saying, "It is best to combine all of these adhkaar if possible, and similarly with the adhkaar of other postures." Abu al-Tayyib Siddeeq Hasan Khan disagreed with him, saying in *Nuzul al-Abraar* (84), "It is narrated with one of them here, another one there, but I see no evidence for combining. The Messenger of Allaah (sallallaahu 'alaihi wa sallam) would not combine them in one go, but he would say one of them sometimes, another one sometimes; to follow is better than to start something new." This latter view is the correct one, Allaah willing, but it is proved in the Sunnah to lengthen this posture, as well as others, until it is about the length of the standing: hence, if the worshipper wishes to follow the Prophet (sallallaahu alaihi wa sallam) in this sunnah, the only way is to combine adhkaar, as Nawawi said, and as Ibn Nasr has related it in *Qiyaam al-Layl* (76) from Ibn Juraij as done by 'Ataa , or to repeat one of the adhkaar for which there is text for repetition, and this is closer to the Sunnah. Allaah knows best.
[4]Bukhaari & Muslim. It is given in *Irwaa al-Ghaleel* (331).

Forbiddance of Reciting the Qur'aan in Rukoo'

"He used to forbid recitation of the Qur'aan in rukoo' and sujood."[1] Further, he used to say, *Verily, I have indeed been forbidden from reciting the Qur'aan in rukoo' or sujood. In the rukoo', therefore, glorify the Supremity of the Lord, Mighty and Sublime, in it; as for the sujood, exert yourselves in supplication in it, for it is most likely that you will be answered.*[2]

Straightening up from the Rukoo', & what is to be said then

Next, "he (sallallaahu 'alaihi wa sallam) would straighten up his back out of rukoo', saying,

$$\text{سَمِعَ اللّٰهُ لِمَنْ حَمِدَه}$$

(Allaah listens to the one who praises Him).[3]

He also ordered "the one who prayed badly" to do that, when he said to him: *No person's prayer is complete until ... he has said takbeer ... then made rukoo' ... then has said "Allaah listens to the one who praises Him" until he is standing straight."*[4] When he raised his head, he would stand straight until every vertebra returned to its place.[5]

Next, "he would say while standing:

$$\text{رَبَّنَا وَلَكَ الْحَمْدُ}$$

(Our Lord, [and] to You be all Praise).[6]

He has commanded all worshippers, whether behind an imaam or not, to do the above on rising from rukoo', by saying *Pray as you have seen me praying.*[7]

He also used to say, *The imaam is there to be followed ... when he has said 'Allaah listens to the one who praises Him' then say, '[O Allaah!] Our Lord, and to You be all Praise'; Allaah will listen to you, for indeed, Allaah, Blessed and*

---

[1]Muslim & Abu 'Awaanah. The forbiddance is general, hence covering both obligatory and voluntary prayers. The addition in Ibn 'Asaakir (17/299/1), "as for voluntary prayers, then there is no harm" is either shaaddh or munkar - Ibn 'Asaakir pointed out a defect in it - so it is not permissible to act according to it.
[2]ibid.
[3]Bukhaari & Muslim.
[4]Abu Daawood & Haakim , who declared it saheeh and Dhahabi agreed.
[5] Bukhaari & Abu Daawood; Ar. *faqaar*: vertebrae, "the bones making up the spine, from the base of the neck to the coccyx" according to *Qaamoos*; see also Fath al-Baari (2/308).
[6]Bukhaari & Ahmad.
[7]ibid.

Exalted, has said via the tongue of His Prophet (sallallaahu 'alaihi wa sallam): Allaah listens to the one who praises Him.'[1]

He also gave a reason for this command in another hadeeth, saying: *...for he whose saying coincides with that of the angels will have his past sins forgiven.*[2]

He used to raise his hands when straightening up[3], in the ways described under the Opening Takbeer.

While standing, he would say, as previously-mentioned,

1-

رَبَّنَا وَلَكَ الْحَمْدُ

Our Lord, and to You be all Praise[4]; or

2-

رَبَّنَا لَكَ الْحَمْدُ

Our Lord, to You be all Praise.[5]

Sometimes, he would add at the beginning of either of these:

3, 4-

اَللَّهُمَّ

O Allaah! ...[6]

---

[1]Muslim, Abu 'Awaanah, Ahmad & Abu Daawood.

*NB: This hadeeth does not prove that those following an imaam should not share with the imaam in saying: *Allaah listens to the one who praises Him,* just as it does not prove that the imaam does not share with those following him in saying: *Our Lord, to You be all Praise.* This is because the purpose of this hadeeth is not to set out exactly what the imaam and his followers should say in this position; rather, it explains that the followers' *tahmeed* should be said after the imaam's *tasmee'* This is supported by the fact that the Prophet (sallallaahu 'alaihi wa sallam) used to say the tahmeed when he was the imaam, and also because the generality of his saying, "Pray as you have seen me praying", dictates that the follower should say what the imaam says, e.g. tasmee', etc. Those respected brothers who referred to us in this issue should consider this, and perhaps what we have mentioned is satisfactory. Whoever would like further discussion on this issue should refer to the article by the Haafiz Suyooti on this matter in his book *al-Haawi lil Fataawi* (1/529).

[2]Bukhaari & Muslim; Tirmidhi declared it saheeh.

[3]Bukhaari & Muslim. The raising of the hands here is narrated in a mutawaatir way from the Messenger (sallallaahu 'alaihi wa sallam), and the majority of scholars have supported it, including some Hanafis. See the previous footnote under *Rukoo* .

[4]ibid.

[5]ibid.

[6]Bukhaari & Ahmad. Ibn al-Qayyim (rahimahullaah) erred on this point in *Zaad al-Ma'aad*, rejecting the combination of "O Allaah!" with "and", despite the fact that it is found in Saheeh al-Bukhaari, Musnad Ahmad, in Nasaa'i & Ahmad again via two routes of narration from Abu

He used to order others to do this, saying, "When the imaam says: *Allaah listens to the one who praises Him*, then say: *O Allaah! Our Lord, to You be all Praise*, for he whose saying coincides with that of the angels will have his past sins forgiven."[1]

Sometimes, he would add either:

5- مِلْءَ السَّمَاوَاتِ، وَمِلْءَ الْأَرْضِ، وَمِلْءَ مَا شِئْتَ مِنْ شَيْءٍ بَعْدُ

... *Filling the heavens, filling the earth, and filling whatever else You wish*[2], or

6- مِلْءَ السَّمَاوَاتِ، و[مِلْءَ] الْأَرْضِ [وَمَا بَيْنَهُمَا، وَمِلْءَ مَا شِئْتَ مِنْ شَيْءٍ بَعْدُ

... *Filling the heavens, [filling] the earth, whatever is between them, and filling whatever else You wish*.[3]

Sometimes, he would add even further:

7- أَهْلَ الثَّنَاءِ وَالْمَجْدِ، لَا مَانِعَ لِمَا أَعْطَيْتَ، وَلَا مُعْطِيَ لِمَا مَنَعْتَ، وَلَا يَنْفَعُ ذَا الْجَدِّ مِنْكَ الْجَدُّ

Lord of Glory & Majesty! None can withhold what You grant, and none can grant what You withhold; nor can the possessions of an owner benefit him in front of You.[4]

Or, sometimes, the addition would be:

8-

مِلْءَ السَّمَاوَاتِ، وَمِلْءَ الْأَرْضِ، وَمَا بَيْنَهُمَا وَمِلْءَ مَا شِئْتَ مِنْ شَيْءٍ بَعْدُ، أَهْلَ الثَّنَاءِ وَالْمَجْدِ، أَحَ
قَالَ الْعَبْدُ، وَكُلُّنَا لَكَ عَبْدٌ، [اَللَّهُمَّ] لَا مَانِعَ لِمَا أَعْطَيْتَ، [وَلَا مُعْطِيَ لِمَا مَنَعْتَ،]، وَلَا يَنْفَعُ ذَا الْجَدِّ
الْجَدُّ

Filling the heavens, filling the earth, and filling whatever else You wish. Lord of Glory and Majesty! - The truest thing a slave has said, and we are all slaves to

---

Hurairah, in Daarimi as a hadeeth of Ibn 'Umar, in Baihaqi from Abu Sa'eed al-Khudri, & in Nasaa'i again as a hadeeth of Abu Musa al-Ash'ari .

[1]Bukhaari & Muslim; Tirmidhi declared it *saheeh*.
[2]Muslim & Abu 'Awaanah.
[3]ibid.
[4] *jadd*: wealth, might, power; i.e., the one who has wealth, sons, might and power in this world will not benefit from them in front of You; his possessions will not save him from You: only righteous deeds will benefit or save anyone.

You. [O Allaah!] None can withhold what You grant, [and none can grant what You withhold,] nor can the possessions of an owner benefit him in front of You.[1]

Sometimes, he would say the following during night prayer:

9-

لِرَبِّيَ الْحَمْدُ، لِرَبِّيَ الْحَمْدُ

To my Lord be all Praise, to my Lord be all Praise, repeating it until his standing was about as long as his rukoo', which had been nearly as long as his first standing, in which he had recited soorah al-Baqarah.[2]

10-

رَبَّنَا وَلَكَ الْحَمْدُ، حَمْداً كَثِيراً طَيَّباً مُبَارَكاً فِيهِ [مُبَارَكاً عَلَيْهِ، كَمَا يُحِبُّ رَبُّنَا وَيَرْضَى]

Our Lord, and to You be all Praise, so much pure praise, inherently blessed, [externally blessed, as our Lord loves and is pleased with].[3]

A man praying behind him (sallallaahu 'alaihi wa sallam) said this after he (sallallaahu 'alaihi wa sallam) had raised his head from rukoo' and said: *Allaah listens to the one who praises Him.* ·When the Messenger of Allaah had finished his prayer, he said, *Who was the one speaking just now?* The man said, "It was I, O Messenger of Allaah." So the Messenger of Allaah (sallallaahu 'alaihi wa sallam) said, *I saw over thirty angels hurrying to be the first one to write it down.*[4]

Lengthening this Standing, & the Obligation to be at Ease in it

He (sallallaahu 'alaihi wa sallam) used to make this standing about as long as his rukoo', as has been mentioned; in fact, "he would stand (for so long) sometimes that one would say, 'He has forgotten', [because of his standing for so long.]"[5]

He used to instruct them to be at ease in it; hence, he said to "the one who prayed badly", ... *Next, raise your head until you are standing straight [and every bone has taken its proper place]* - in another narration, *When you rise, make your spine upright and raise your head, until the bones return to their joints.*[6]

---

[1]Muslim & Abu 'Awaanah.
[2]Muslim, Abu 'Awaanah & Abu Daawood.
[3]Abu Daawood & Nasaa'i with a *saheeh* isnaad. It is given in *Irwaa'* (335).
[4]Maalik, Bukhaari & Abu Daawood.
[5]Bukhaari , Muslim & Ahmad. It is given in *Irwaa'* (no. 307).
[6]Bukhaari & Muslim (first sentence only), Daarimi, Haakim, Shaafi'i & Ahmad. By 'bones' here is meant those of the spinal structure, the vertebrae, as has preceded in the main text.
*NB: The meaning of this hadeeth is clear and obvious: to be at ease in this standing. As for the usage of this hadeeth by our brothers from the Hijaaz and elsewhere as evidence to justify placing the right hand on the left in this standing, it is far-removed from the meaning of the multitude of

He also reminded him: *that no-one's prayer is complete unless he does that*, and used to say: *Allaah, Mighty and Sublime, does not look at the prayer of the slave who does not make his backbone upright in between his bowings and prostrations.*[1]

THE SUJOOD (PROSTRATION)

Next, "he (sallallaahu 'alaihi wa sallam) would say takbeer and go down into sajdah"[2], and he ordered "the one who prayed badly" to do so, saying to him, *No one's prayer is complete unless ... he says: Allaah listens to the one who praises Him and stands up straight, then says: Allaah is the Greatest and prostrates such that his joints are at rest.*[3]

Also, "when he wanted to perform sajdah, he would say takbeer, [separate his hands from his sides,] and then perform sajdah."[4]

---

narrations of this hadeeth. In fact it is a false argument, since the placing mentioned is not referred to with regard to the first standing in any of the narrations or wordings of the hadeeth; therefore, how can "the bones taking their proper places" mentioned in the hadeeth be interpreted as referring to the right hand taking hold of the left before rukoo'?! This would apply if all the versions of the hadeeth could be construed to mean this, so what about when they imply an obviously different meaning? In fact, this placing of theirs cannot be inferred from the hadeeth at all, since what is meant by "bones" is the bones of the spine, as confirmed by the Sunnah, "... he would stand straight until every vertebra returned to its place."

I, for one, am in no doubt that to place the hands on the chest in this standing is an innovation and a leading astray, for it is not mentioned in any of the ahaadeeth about prayer, despite their large number. Had this practice any foundation, it would have reached us by at least one narration. Further, not one of the Salaf practised it, nor has a single leading scholar of hadeeth mentioned it, as far as I know.

This is not inconsistent with what Shaikh Tuwaijiri has quoted in his article (pp. 18-19) from Imaam Ahmad (rahimahullaah), "if one wishes, he may leave his hands by his sides, or, if he wishes, he can place them on his chest", for Imaam Ahmad did not attribute this to the Prophet (sallallaahu 'alaihi wa sallam), but said it from his own *ijtihaad* and opinion, and opinion can be erroneous. When authentic evidence establishes the innovatory nature of any practice, such as this one, then the saying of an imaam in its favour does not negate its being an innovation, as Shaikh-ul-Islaam Ibn Taymiyyah (rahimahullaah) has written. In fact, I see in these words of his, an indication that Imaam Ahmad did not regard the above-mentioned placing as being proved in the Sunnah, for he allowed a choice between practising it and leaving it! - Does the respected shaikh think that the Imaam also allowed a similar choice regarding placing the hands before rukoo'? Thus, it is proved that the placing of the hands on the chest in the standing after rukoo' is not part of the Sunnah. This is a brief discussion of this issue, which could be dealt with in more detail and depth, but due to lack of space here, that is done instead in my Refutation against Shaikh Tuwaijiri.

[1] Ahmad & Tabaraani in *Mu'jam al-Kabeer* with a saheeh isnaad.
[2] Bukhaari & Muslim.
[3] Abu Daawood & Haakim, who declared it *saheeh* and Dhahabi agreed.
[4] Abu Ya'laa in his Musnad (284/2) with a good isnaad & Ibn Khuzaimah (1/79/2) with a different, *saheeh* isnaad.

Sometimes, "he would raise his hands when performing sajdah."[1]

Going Down into the Sajdah on the Hands

"He used to place his hands on the ground before his knees."[2]

He used to instruct likewise, saying, *When one of you performs sajdah, he should not kneel like a camel, but should place his hands before his knees.*[3]

He also used to say, *Verily, the hands prostrate as the face prostrates, so when one of you places his face (on the ground), he should place his hands, and when he raises it, he should raise them.*[4]

---

[1]Nasaa'i, Daaraqutni & Mukhlis in *al-Fawaa'id* (1/2/2) with two *saheeh* isnaads. This raising of the hands has been reported from ten Companions, and a number of the *Salaf* viewed it as correct, among them Ibn 'Umar, Ibn 'Abbas, Hasan Basri, Taawoos, his son 'Abdullaah, Naafi' the freed slave of Ibn 'Umar, Saalim the son of Ibn 'Umar, Qaasim bin Muhammad, 'Abdullaah bin Deenaar & 'Ataa'. Also, 'Abdur Rahmaan bin Mahdi said, "This is from the Sunnah", it was practised by the Imaam of the Sunnah, Ahmad bin Hanbal, and it has been quoted from Maalik & Shaafi'i .

[2]Ibn Khuzaimah (1/76/1), Daaraqutni & Haakim, who declared it *saheeh* and Dhahabi agreed. All the ahaadeeth which contradict this are inauthentic. This way has been endorsed by Maalik, and similar is reported from Ahmad in Ibn al-Jawzi's *al-Tahqeeq* (108/2). Also, al-Marwazi quoted with a *saheeh* isnaad, Imam al-Awzaa'i in his *Masaa'il* (1/147/1) as saying, "I found the people placing their hands before their knees."

[3]Abu Daawood, Tammaam in *al-Fawaa'id*, & Nasaa'i in *Sunan as-Sughraa* and *Sunan al-Kubraa* (47/1) with a *saheeh* isnaad. 'Abdul Haqq declared it *saheeh* in *al-Ahkaam* (54/1), and went on to say in *Kitaab al-Tahajjud* (56/1), "it has a sounder isnaad than the previous one", i.e. the hadeeth of Waa'il which is the other way round (knees before hands). In fact, the latter hadeeth, as well as being contradictory to this *saheeh* hadeeth and the preceding one, is neither authentic in isnaad nor in meaning, as I have explained in *Silsilah al-Ahaadeeth ad-Da'eefah* (no. 929) and *al-Irwaa'* (357).

It should be known that the way to differ from the camel is to place the hands before the knees, because the camel places its knees first; a camel's "knees" are in its forelegs, as defined in *Lisaan al-'Arab* and other books of the 'Arabic language, and as mentioned by Tahaawi in *Mushkil al-Aathaar* and *Sharh Ma'aani al-Aathaar*. Also, Imaam Qaasim al-Saraqusti (rahimahullaah) narrated in *Ghareeb al-Hadeeth* (2/70/1-2), with a *saheeh* isnaad, Abu Hurairah's statement, "No one should kneel the way a runaway camel does", and then added, "This is in sajdah. He is saying that one should not throw oneself down, as a runaway (or untamed) camel does, hurriedly and without calmness, but he should go down calmly, placing his hands first, followed by his knees, and an explanatory *marfoo'* hadeeth has been narrated in this regard." He then mentioned the hadeeth above.

As for Ibn al-Qayyim's extremely strange statement, "These words are incomprehensible, and not understood by the experts of the language", it is answered by the sources which we have mentioned, and also many others which can be consulted. I have also expanded on this in the refutation against Shaikh Tuwaijari, which may be published.

[4]Ibn Khuzaimah(1/79/2), Ahmad & Siraaj; Haakim declared it *saheeh* and Dhahabi agreed. It is given in *Irwaa'* (313).

The Sajdah Described

"He would support himself on his palms [and spread them]"[1], "put his fingers together"[2], and "point them towards the qiblah."[3]

Also, "he would put them (his palms) level with his shoulders"[4], and sometimes "level with his ears"[5]. "He would put his nose and forehead firmly on the ground."[6]

He said to "the one who prayed badly", *When you prostrate, then be firm in your prostration*[7]; in one narration: *When you prostrate, put your face and hands down firmly, until all of your bones are relaxed in their proper places.*[8]

He also used to say, "*There is no prayer for the one whose nose does not feel as much of the ground as the forehead.*"[9]

"He used to put his knees and toes down firmly"[10], "point with the front of the toes towards the qiblah"[11], "put his heels together"[12], "keep his feet upright"[13], and "ordered likewise."[14]

Hence, these are the seven limbs on which he (sallallaahu 'alaihi wa sallam) would prostrate: the palms, the knees, the feet, and the forehead and nose - counting the last two as one limb in prostration, as he (sallallaahu 'alaihi wa sallam) said: *I have been ordered to prostrate* (in one narration: *we have been ordered to prostrate*) *on seven bones: on the forehead* ..., and he indicated by

---

[1] Abu Daawood & Haakim, who declared it *saheeh* and Dhahabi agreed.

[2] Ibn Khuzaimah, Baihaqi & Haakim, who declared it *saheeh* and Dhahabi agreed.

[3] Baihaqi with a *saheeh* isnaad. Ibn Abi Shaibah (1/82/2) & Siraaj have related the pointing of the toes in a different narration.

[4] Abu Daawood & Tirmidhi, who declared it *saheeh*, as did Ibn al-Mulaqqin (27/2); it is given in *Irwaa'* (309).

[5] Abu Daawood & Nasaa'i with a *saheeh* isnaad.

[6] Abu Daawood & Tirmidhi, who declared it *saheeh*, as did Ibn al-Mulaqqin (27/2) it is given in *al-Irwaa*, (309).

[7] Abu Daawood & Ahmad with *saheeh* isnaad.

[8] Ibn Khuzaimah (1/10/1) with a *hasan* isnaad.

[9] Daaraqutni, Tabaraani (3/140/1) & Abu Nu'aim in *Akhbaar Isbahaan*.

[10] Baihaqi with a saheeh isnaad. Ibn Abi Shaibah (1/82/2) & Siraaj have related the pointing of the toes in a different narration.

[11] Bukhaari & Abu Daawood. Ibn Sa'd (4/157) related from Ibn 'Umar that he liked to point whatever of his body he could towards the *qiblah* when praying, even his thumbs.

[12] Tahaawi, Ibn Khuzaimah (no. 654) & Haakim, who declared it *saheeh* and Dhahabi agreed.

[13] Baihaqi with a *saheeh* isnaad.

[14] Tirmidhi & Siraaj; Haakim declared it *saheeh* and Dhahabi agreed.

moving his hand[1] around his nose, ... *the hands* (in one version: *the palms), the knees and the toes, and not to tuck up*[2] *the garments and hair.*[3]

He also used to say, *When a slave prostrates, seven limbs prostrate with him: his face, his palms, his knees and his feet.*[4]

He said about a man who was praying with his hair tied[5] behind him, *His example is surely like that of someone who prays with his hands bound (behind his back).*[6] He also said, *That is the saddle of the devil,* i.e. where the devil sits, referring to the knots in the hair.[7]

"He would not rest his fore-arms on the ground"[8], but "would raise them above the ground, and keep them away from his sides such that the whiteness of his armpits could be seen from behind"[9], and also "such that if a small lamb or kid wanted to pass under his arms, it would have been able to do so."[10]

He would do this to such an extent that one of his Companions said, "We used to feel sorry for the Messenger of Allaah (sallallaahu 'alaihi wa sallam) because of the way he kept his hands away from his sides."[11]

He used to order likewise, saying, *When you perform sajdah, place your palms (on the ground) and raise your elbows*[12], and *Be level in sujood, and none of you should spread his fore-arms like the spreading of a dog* (in one narration:

---

[1]This movement of the hand was deduced from the grammar of the 'Arabic text. (*Fath al-Baari*)

[2]i.e. to draw them in and prevent them from being scattered, meaning to gather the garment or hair with the hands for rukoo' and sujood. (*Nihaayah*). This forbiddance is not only during prayer; the majority of scholars include tucking in the hair and garments before prayer in the prohibition. This is further strengthened by his forbidding men to pray with their hair tied, which follows later.

[3]Bukhaari & Muslim. It is given in *al-Irwaa'* (310).

[4]Muslim, Abu 'Awaanah & Ibn Hibbaan.

[5]i.e. tied up or plaited.

[6]Muslim, Abu 'Awaanah & Ibn Hibbaan. Ibn al-Atheer says, "The meaning of this hadeeth is that were his hair loose, it would fall on the ground when in sajdah; hence, the man would be rewarded for the prostration of the hair. However, if the hair is tied, it is effectively as though it did not prostrate, for he compared him to someone whose hands are shackled together, since they would then not lie on the ground in sajdah."

It would seem that this instruction is limited to men and does not apply to women, as Shawkaani has quoted from Ibn al-'Arabi.

[7]Abu Daawood & Tirmidhi, who declared it hasan; Ibn Khuzaimah & Ibn Hibbaan declared it saheeh. See *Saheeh Abi Daawood* (653).

[8]Bukhaari & Abu Daawood.

[9]Bukhaari & Muslim. It is given in *Irwaa'* (359).

[10]Muslim, Abu 'Awaanah & Ibn Hibbaan.

[11]Abu Daawood & Ibn Maajah with a *hasan* isnaad.

[12]Muslim & Abu 'Awaanah.

54

...like a dog spreads them)[1]. In a separate hadeeth, *None of you should rest arms on the ground the way a dog rests them.*[2]

He also used to say, *Do not spread your arms [the way a beast of prey does], rest on your palms and keep your upper arms apart, for when you do all that, every one of your limbs prostrates with you.*[3]

The Obligation to be at Ease in Sujood

He (sallallaahu 'alaihi wa sallam) used to command the completion of rukoo' and sujood, comparing someone not doing so to the hungry man who eats one or two dates, which are of no use to him, and also saying about him, *he is indeed one of the worst thieves among the people.*

He also ruled that the prayer of one who does not straighten his spine fully in rukoo' and sujood is invalid, as has been mentioned under "Rukoo'", and ordered "the one who prayed badly" to be at ease in his sujood, as mentioned before.

The *Adhkaar* of Sujood

He (sallallaahu 'alaihi wa sallam) would say any one of the following remembrances of Allaah and supplications in this posture:

1-

سُبْحَانَ رَبِّيَ الْأَعْلَى

How Perfect is my Lord, the Most High, three times.[4]
Sometimes, "he would repeat it more times than that."[5]
Once, he repeated it so much that his sujood were nearly as long as his standing, in which he had recited three of the Long Soorahs: al-Baqarah, an-Nisaa' and aal-'Imraan. That prayer was full of supplication and seeking of forgiveness, as mentioned before under "Night Prayer".

2-

سُبْحَانَ رَبِّيَ الْأَعْلَى وَبِحَمْدِه

---

[1]Bukhaari, Muslim, Abu Daawood & Ahmad.
[2]Ahmad & Tirmidhi, who declared it *saheeh.*
[3]Ibn Khuzaimah (1/80/2), al-Maqdisi in *al-Mukhtaarah* & Haakim, who declared it saheeh and Dhahabi agreed.
[4]Ahmad, Abu Daawood, Ibn Maajah, Daaraqutni, Tahaawi, Bazzaar, & Tabaraani in *Mu'jam al-Kabeer* on the authority of seven different Companions. See also the note on this *dhikr* under "Rukoo'".
[5]See the previous note on this under "Rukoo'"also.

How Perfect is my Lord, the Most High, and Praised be He, three times.[1]

3-

سُبُّوحٌ قُدُّوسٌ رَبُّ الْمَلَائِكَةِ وَالرُّوحِ

Perfect, Blessed, Lord of the Angels and the Spirit.[2]

4-

سُبْحَانَكَ اَللَّهُمَّ رَبَّنَا وَبِحَمْدِكَ اَللَّهُمَّ اغْفِرْ لِي

How perfect You are O Allaah, our Lord, and Praised. O Allaah! Forgive me, which he would say often in his rukoo' and sujood, implementing the order of the Qur'aan.[3]

5-

اَللَّهُمَّ لَكَ سَجَدْتُ، وَبِكَ آمَنْتُ، وَلَكَ أَسْلَمْتُ، [وَأَنْتَ رَبِّي]، سَجَدَ وَجْهِيَ لِلَّذِي خَلَقَهُ وَصَوَّرَهُ، [فَأَحْسَنَ صُوَرَهُ]، وَشَقَّ سَمْعَهُ وَبَصَرَهُ، [فَـ] تَبَارَكَ اللَّهُ أَحْسَنُ الْخَالِقِين

O Allaah! For you I have prostrated; in You I have believed; to You I have submitted; [You are my Lord;] my face has prostrated for the One Who created it and shaped it , [shaped it excellently,] then brought forth its hearing and vision: [so] blessed be Allaah, the Best to Create![4]

6-

اَللَّهُمَّ اغْفِرْ لِي ذَنْبِي كُلَّهُ، وَدِقَّهُ وَجِلَّهُ، وَأَوَّلَهُ وَآخِرَهُ، وَعَلَانِيَتَهُ وَسِرَّهُ

O Allaah! Forgive me all my sins: the minor and the major, the first and the last, the open and the hidden.[5]

7-

سَجَدَ لَكَ سَوَادِي وَخَيَالِي، وَآمَنَ بِكَ فُؤَادِي، أَبُوءُ بِنِعْمَتِكَ عَلَيَّ، هَذِي يَدَيَّ وَمَا جَنَيْتُ عَلَى نَفْسِي

My person and my shadow have prostrated to You; my heart has believed in You; I acknowledge Your favours towards me: here are my hands and whatever I have earned against myself.[6]

8-

سُبْحَانَ ذِي الْجَبَرُوتِ وَالْمَلَكُوتِ وَالْكِبْرِيَاءِ وَالْعَظَمَةِ

---

[1] *Saheeh*, transmitted by Abu Daawood, Daaraqutni, Ahmad, Tabaraani & Baihaqi.
[2] Muslim & Abu 'Awaanah.
[3] Bukhaari & Muslim.
[4] Muslim, Abu 'Awaanah, Tahaawi & Daaraqutni.
[5] Muslim & Abu 'Awaanah.
[6] Ibn Nasr, Bazzaar & Haakim, who declared it saheeh but Dhahabi disagreed, however, it has a support which is mentioned in the manuscript version.

How Perfect is He Who has all Power, Kingdom, Magnificence and Supremity[1], which he would say in night prayer, as with the following ones:

9-

$$سُبْحَانَك [اَللَّهُمَّ] وَبِحَمْدِكَ، لاَ إِلهَ إِلاَّ أَنْتَ$$

How perfect You are [O Allaah] and Praised. None has the right to be worshipped except you.[2]

10-

$$اَللَّهُمَّ اغْفِرْ لِي مَا أَسْرَرْتُ، وَمَا أَعْلَنْتُ$$

O Allaah! Forgive me what (sins) I have concealed and what (sins) I have done openly.[3]

11-

$$اَللَّهُمَّ اجْعَلْ فِي قَلْبِي نُوراً، [وَفِي لِسَانِي نُوراً]، وَاجْعَلْ فِي سَمْعِي نُوراً، وَاجْعَلْ فِي بَصَرِي نُوراً، وَاجْعَلْ مِنْ تَحْتِي نُوراً، وَاجْعَلْ مِنْ فَوْقِي نُوراً، وَعَنْ يَمِينِي نُوراً، وَعَنْ يَسَارِي نُوراً، وَاجْعَلْ أَمَامِي نُوراً، وَاجْعَلْ خَلْفِي نُوراً، [وَاجْعَلْ فِي نَفْسِي نُوراً]، وَأَعْظِمْ لِي نُوراً،$$

O Allaah! Place light in my heart; [and light in my tongue;] and place light in my hearing; and place light in my seeing; and place light from below me; and place light from above me, and light on my right, and light on my left; and place light ahead of me; and place light behind me; [and place light in my self;] and make the light greater for me.[4]

12-

$$[اَللَّهُمَّ] [إِنِّي] أَعُوذُ بِرِضَاكَ مِنْ سَخَطِكَ، وَ[أَعُوذُ] بِمُعَافَاتِكَ مِنْ عُقُوبَتِكَ، وَأَعُوذُ بِكَ مِنْكَ، لَا أُحْصِي ثَنَاءً عَلَيْكَ، أَنْتَ كَمَا أَثْنَيْتَ عَلَى نَفْسِكَ$$

[O Allaah!] [Indeed] I seek refuge with Your Pleasure from Your Anger; [I seek refuge] with Your Pardons from Your Punishment; I seek refuge with You from You. I cannot count all exultations upon You; You are as You have extolled Yourself.[5]

---

[1] Abu Daawood & Nasaa'i, with a *saheeh* isnaad.
[2] Muslim, Abu 'Awaanah, Nasaa'i & Ibn Nasr.
[3] Ibn Abi Shaibah (62/112/1) & Nasaa'i ; Haakim declared it *saheeh* and Dhahabi agreed.
[4] Muslim, Abu 'Awaanah & Ibn Abi Shaibah (12/106/2, 112/1).
[5] ibid.

57

Forbiddance of Reciting the Qur'aan in Sujood

He (sallallaahu 'alaihi wa sallam) used to forbid recitation of the Qur'aan in rukoo' and sujood, and commanded striving in, and a lot of, supplication in this posture, as explained previously under "Rukoo'". He also used to say, *The slave is closest to his Lord when he is prostrating, so increase supplication [in it].*[1]

Lengthening the Sajdah

He (sallallaahu 'alaihi wa sallam) would make his sujood about as long as his rukoo', and sometimes he would make it extremely long due to the circumstances, as one of his Companions said:

"The Messenger of Allaah (sallallaahu 'alaihi wa sallam) came out to us for one of the two later prayers, [Zuhr or 'Asr,] carrying Hasan or Husain. The Prophet (sallallaahu 'alaihi wa sallam) then came to the front and put him down [next to his right foot], said takbeer for the prayer and commenced praying. During the prayer, he performed a very long prostration, so I raised my head [from among the people], and there was the child, on the back of the Messenger of Allaah (sallallaahu 'alaihi wa sallam), who was in prostration. I then returned to my prostration. When the Messenger of Allaah (sallallaahu 'alaihi wa sallam) had offered the prayer, the people said, 'O Messenger of Allaah! In the middle of [this] your prayer, you performed a prostration and lengthened it so much that we thought either something had happened, or that you were receiving revelation!' He said, *Neither of those was the case: actually, my son made me his mount, so I did not want to hurry him until he had satisfied his wish.*"[2]

In another hadeeth, "He (sallallaahu 'alaihi wa sallam) was praying. When he performed sajdah, al-Hasan and al-Husain jumped onto his back. When the people tried to stop them, he gestured to them to leave the two alone. After offering his prayer, he placed them in his lap and said, *Whoever loves me should love these two.*"[3]

The Excellence of the Sajdah

He (sallallaahu 'alaihi wa sallam) used to say, *There is no one among my ummah whom I will not recognise on the Day of Resurrection.* They said, "How

---

[1]Muslim, Abu 'Awaanah & Baihaqi . It is given in *Irwaa* (456).

[2]Nasaa'i, Ibn 'Asaakir (4/257/1-2) & Haakim, who declared it *saheeh* and Dhahabi agreed.

[3]Ibn Khuzaimah in his Saheeh, with a *hasan* isnaad from Ibn Mas'ood (887) & Baihaqi in *mursal* form. Ibn Khuzaimah prefixed it with, "Chapter: evidence that gesturing which is understood during prayer neither invalidates nor spoils the prayer" - this action is one which the People of Opinion have prohibited! In this regard, there are also ahaadeeth in Bukhaari, Muslim and others.

will you recognise them, O Messenger of Allaah, among the multitude of created beings?" He said, *Do you not see that were one of you to enter an enclosure in which there was a jet black[1] steed and a horse with a white forehead and legs[2], would you not recognise the latter from the former?* They said, "Of course." He said, *Thus, my ummah on that day will surely have white faces[3] because of sujood, and white arms and feet[4] because of ablution.*[5]

He would also say, *When Allaah intends to have mercy on whomsoever he wishes of the people of the Fire, He will order the angels to bring out whoever used to worship Allaah; so they will bring them out, recognising them from the marks of sujood, for Allaah has prohibited the Fire from devouring the marks of sujood. Thus, they will be brought out from the Fire, for the Fire devours all of a son of Aadam except the marks of sujood.*[6]

Sajdah on the Ground, and on Mats [7]

He would often prostrate on the (bare) ground.[8]

"His Companions would pray with him in the intense heat, so when one of them could not press his forehead against the ground, he would spread his robe and prostrate on that."[9]

He also used to say, *...the whole earth has been made a place of worship (masjid) and a purification for me and my ummah; so wherever prayer becomes due on someone of my ummah, he has his place of worship (masjid) and his purification next to him. Those before me used to think that this was too much: indeed, they would only pray in their churches and synagogues.*[10]

Sometimes, he would prostrate in mud and water, and that happened to him once at dawn on the twenty-first night of Ramadaan, when it rained and the roof

---

[1]i.e. its colour is pure black, with no other colours mixed with it. (*Nihaayah*)
[2]the whiteness refers to that part of the horse where chains and bangles are put, including the lower legs but not the knees.
[3]i.e. the shining of the face due to the light of sujood.
[4]i.e. the shining of the parts covered in ablution: the face, hands and feet. The shining marks of ablution on the face, hands and legs of humans is compared to the whiteness of a horse's face and legs.
[5]Ahmad, with a *saheeh* isnaad. Tirmidhi related a part of it and declared it *saheeh*. It is given in *Silsilah al-Ahaadeeth as-Saheehah*.
[6]Bukhaari & Muslim; the hadeeth shows that the sinful from among those regular at Prayer, will not remain the Fire forever; in fact, even those given to missing prayers out of laziness will not remain in the Fire forever, this is authentic - see *as-Saheehah* (2054).
[7] Ar. *haseer*: a mat made of date-palm leaves or straw, etc.
[8]This was because his mosque was not covered with mats, etc. This is evident from a great many ahaadeeth, such as the next one and the one of Abu Sa'eed later.
[9]Muslim & Abu 'Awaanah.
[10]Ahmad, Siraaj & Baihaqi, with a saheeh isnaad.

of the mosque, which was made of palm-branches, was washed away. So he (sallallaahu 'alaihi wa sallam) prostrated in mud and water; Abu Sa'eed al-Khudri said, "So I saw, with my own eyes, the Messenger of Allaah (sallallaahu 'alaihi wa sallam), with traces of mud and water on his forehead and nose."[1]

Also, "he would pray on a *khumrah*"[2] sometimes, or "on a mat"[3] sometimes, and "he prayed on it once when it had become blackened due to prolonged use."[4]

Rising from Sajdah

Next, "he (sallallaahu 'alaihi wa sallam) would raise his head from prostration while saying takbeer"[5], and he ordered "the one who prayed badly" to do that, saying, *The prayer of any person is not complete until ... he prostrates until his limbs are at rest, then he says, 'Allah is the Greatest' and raises his head until he is sitting straight.*[6] Also, "he would raise his hands with this takbeer" sometimes.[7]

To sit *muftarishan* between the Two Sajdahs

Next, "he would lay his left foot along the ground and sit on it [relaxed]"[8], and he ordered "the one who prayed badly" thus, saying to him, *When you prostrate, prostrate firmly, then when you rise, sit on your left thigh*[9]

---

[1]Bukhaari & Muslim.
[2]ibid. A *khumrah* is a piece of matting, palm-fibre, or other material which is big enough for a man to place his face on it in sajdah; the term does not apply to larger pieces.
[3]ibid.
[4]Muslim & Abu 'Awaanah. Ar. *labisa* usually means 'to wear', but here it is used to mean 'to use', i.e. to sit on; hence 'wearing' includes 'sitting on', so this indicates that it is prohibited (haraam) to sit on silk, because of the prohibition on wearing it established in the Saheehs of Bukhaari and Muslim, and others. In fact, a clear forbiddance of sitting on silk is related in these, so do not be confused by the fact that some leading scholars allow it.
[5]Bukhaari & Muslim.
[6]Abu Daawood & Haakim who declared it *saheeh* and Dhahabi agreed.
[7]Bukhaari in his *Juz' Raf' al-Yadain*, Abu Daawood with a *saheeh* isnaad, Muslim & Abu 'Awaanah. It is given in *Irwaa'* (316).

To raise the hands here, and with every takbeer, was a view voiced by Ahmad, as in Ibn al-Qayyim's *Badaa'i'* (3/89): "Athram quoted from him (Imaam Ahmad) that on being asked about raising the hands, he said: With every movement down and up. Athram said: I saw Abu 'Abdullaah (i.e. Imaam Ahmad) raising his hands in prayer with every movement down and up."

This was also the opinion of Ibn al-Mundhir & Abu 'Ali of the Shaafi'is, and also a view of Maalik and Shaafi'i themselves, as in *Tarh at-Tathreeb*. The raising of the hands here is also authentically-reported from Anas bin Maalik, Ibn 'Umar, Naafi', Taawoos, Hasan Basri, Ibn Seereen & Ayyoob as-Sikhtiaani, as in *Musannaf Ibn Abi Shaibah* (1/106) with saheeh narrations from them.
[8]Ahmad & Abu Daawood with a good isnaad.
[9]Bukhaari & Baihaqi .

"He would have his right foot upright"[1], and "point its toes towards the qiblah."[2]

Iq'aa' Between the Two Sajdahs

"He would sometimes practise iq'aa' [resting on both his heels and (all) his toes]."[3]

The Obligation of Being at Ease between the Two Sajdahs

"He (sallallaahu 'alaihi wa sallam) would be relaxed until every bone returned to its (proper) position"[4], and he ordered "the one who prayed badly" likewise, and said to him, *The prayer of any of you is not complete until he does this.*[5]

Lengthening the Sitting between the Two Sajdahs

Also, "he would lengthen it until it was about almost as long as his sajdah"[6], and sometimes, "he would remain (in this position) until one would say: He has forgotten."[7]

---

[1]Nasaa'i with a saheeh isnaad.

[2]Muslim, Abu 'Awaanah, Abu Shaikh in *Maa Rawaahu Abu az-Zubair 'an Ghair Jaabir* (nos. 104-6) & Baihaqi .

[3]ibid. Ibn al-Qayyim (rahimahullaah) overlooked this, so after mentioning the Prophet's (sallallaahu 'alaihi wa sallam) iftiraash between the two sajdahs, he said, "No other way of sitting here is preserved from him" ! How can this be correct, when iq'aa' has reached us via: the hadeeth of Ibn 'Abbaas in Muslim, Abu Daawood & Tirmidhi, who declared it saheeh, and others (see *Silsilah al-Ahaadeeth as-Saheehah* 383); the hadeeth of Ibn 'Umar with a hasan isnaad in Baihaqi, declared saheeh by Ibn Hajar. Also, Abu Ishaaq al-Harbi related in *Ghareeb al-Hadeeth* (5/12/1) from Taawoos, who saw Ibn 'Umar and Ibn 'Abbaas practising iq'aa'; its sanad is saheeh. May Allaah shower His Mercy on Imaam Maalik, who said, "Every one of us can refute and be refuted, except the occupant of this grave", and he pointed to the grave of the Prophet (sallallaahu 'alaihi wa sallam). This sunnah was practised by several Companions, Successors and others, and I have expanded on this in *al-Asl*.

Of course, this iq'aa' is different to the one which is forbidden, and follows under "Tashahhud".

[4]Abu Daawood & Baihaqi with a saheeh isnaad.

[5]Abu Daawood & Haakim , who declared it saheeh and Dhahabi agreed.

[6]Bukhaari & Muslim.

[7]ibid. Ibn al-Qayyim said, "This sunnah was abandoned by the people after the time of the Companions. But as for the one who abides by the Sunnah, and does not glance sideways towards whatever contradicts it, he is unworried by anything opposing this guidance."

The *Adhkaar* between the Two Sajdahs

In this sitting, he (sallallaahu 'alaihi wa sallam) would say:

1- اَللَّهُمَّ (وَفِي لَفْظٍ: رَبِّ) اغْفِرْ لِي، وَارْحَمْنِي، [وَاجْبُرْنِي]، [وَارْفَعْنِي]، وَاهْدِنِي،
[وَعَافِنِي]، وَارْزُقْنِي

*O Allaah! (in one version: O my Lord!) Forgive me; have mercy on me;
[strengthen me;] [raise my rank;] guide me; [pardon me;] sustain me.*[1]

Or sometimes, he would say:

2- رَبِّ اغْفِرْ لِي اغْفِرْ لِي

O my Lord! Forgive me, forgive me.[2]

He would say the above two in night prayer also.[3]

The Second Sajdah

Next, "he would say takbeer and prostrate for the second time."[4] He also ordered
"the one who prayed badly" to do so, saying to him after he had ordered him to
be at ease between sajdahs, *then say 'Allaah is the Greatest' and prostrate until
your joints are relaxed [and do that in all your prayer].*[5] He would perform this
sajdah exactly as he performed the first one. Also, "he would raise his hands
with this takbeer" sometimes.[6]

Next, "he would raise his head while saying takbeer"[7], and he ordered "the one
who prayed badly" to do likewise, saying to him after ordering him to prostrate

---

[1]Abu Daawood, Tirmidhi, Ibn Maajah & Haakim , who declared it saheeh and Dhahabi agreed.

[2]Ibn Maajah with a hasan sanad. Imaam Ahmad chose to supplicate with this one; Ishaaq bin
Raahawaih said, "If he wishes, he can say this three times, or he can say O Allaah! Forgive me
..., because both of them have been reported from the Prophet (sallallaahu 'alaihi wa sallam)
between the two sajdahs." (*Masaa'il of Imaam Ahmad & Ishaaq bin Raahawaih as related by
Ishaaq al-Marwazi, p. 19*).

[3]This does not negate the validity of the expressions in the obligatory prayers due to the absence of
anything to differentiate between those and voluntary prayers. This is the view of Shaafi'i,
Ahmad & Ishaaq, who held that this was allowed in compulsory and voluntary prayers, as
Tirmidhi has narrated. Imaam Tahaawi has also taken this view in *Mushkil al-Aathaar*. Proper
analysis supports this argument, for there is no position in prayer where a dhikr is not valid, and so
it is fitting that this should be the case here.

[4]Bukhaari & Muslim.

[5]Abu Daawood & Haakim , who declared it saheeh and Dhahabi agreed; the addition is from
Bukhaari & Muslim.

[6]Abu 'Awaanah & Abu Daawood with two saheeh sanads. this raising of the hands has supported
by Ahmad, Maalik & Shaafi'i in narrations from them. See the previous note under *Sujood*.

[7]Bukhaari & Muslim.

for the second time, *"then raise your head and say takbeer"*[1]. He also said to him, *"[then do that in all your bowings and prostrations,] for if you do that, your prayer will be complete, and if you fall short in any of this, you will be deficient in your prayer."*[2] Also, *"he would raise his hands"*[3] sometimes with this takbeer.

The Sitting of Rest

Next, *"he would sit straight [on his left foot, upright, until every bone returned to its position]."*[4]

Supporting Oneself with the Hands on Rising for the Next Rak'ah

Next, *"he (sallallaahu 'alaihi wa sallam) would get up for the second rak'ah, supporting himself on the ground."*[5] Also, *"he would clench his fists[6] during prayer: supporting himself with his hands when getting up."*[7]

THE SECOND RAK'AH

"When he (sallallaahu 'alaihi wa sallam) got up for the second rak'ah, he would commence with All Praise be to Allaah (Faatihah 1:1), without pausing."[8]

---

[1] Abu Daawood & Haakim , who declared it saheeh and Dhahabi agreed.

[2] Ahmad & Tirmidhi, who declared it ṣaheeh.

[3] see the fourth last note.

[4] Bukhaari & Abu Daawood. This sitting is known as *jalsah al-istiraahah* (the sitting of rest) by the scholars of fiqh. Shaafi'i supported it, as did Ahmad in *Tahqeeq* (111/1) and favoured it more strongly, as is well-known of him that he would insist on following a sunnah which had nothing to contradict it. Ibn Haani said in his *Masaa'il of Imaam Ahmad* (p. 42), "I saw Abu 'Abdullaah (i.e. Imaam Ahmad) sometimes leaning on his hands when standing up for the next rak'ah, and sometimes sitting straight and then getting up." It was also the preference of Imaam Ishaaq bin Raahawaih, who said in Marwazi's *Masaa'il* (1/147/2), "The example was set by the Prophet (sallallaahu 'alaihi wa sallam) of supporting himself with his hands when getting up, whether he was old or young." See also *Irwaa'* (2/82-3).

[5] Bukhaari & Shaafi'i .

[6] literally, "as one who kneads dough".

[7] Abu Ishaaq al-Harbi with a faultless sanad, and its meaning is found in Baihaqi with a saheeh sanad. As for the hadeeth, "He used to get up like an arrow, not supporting himself with his hands", it is mawdoo' (fabricated), and all narrations of similar meaning are weak, not authentic, and I have explained this in *Silsilah al-Ahaadeeth ad-Da'eefah* (562, 929, 968).

[8] Muslim & Abu 'Awaanah. The pause negated in this hadeeth could be a pause for reciting an opening supplication, and not include a pause for reciting the *isti'aadhah*, or it could be wider in meaning than that; I find the former possibility more convincing. There are two views among the scholars regarding the isti'aadhah, and we regard the correct one as being that it is to be said in every rak'ah; the details of all this are given in *al-Asl*.

He would perform this rak'ah exactly as he performed the first, except that he would make it shorter than the first, as before.

The Obligation of Reciting Soorah al-Faatihah in Every Rak'ah

He ordered "the one who prayed badly" to recite al-Faatihah in every rak'ah, when he said to him after ordering him to recite it in the first rak'ah[1], *then do that throughout your prayer*[2] (in one narration: *in every rak'ah*).[3] He also used to say, *There is recitation in every rak'ah.*[4]

THE FIRST TASHAHHUD

Next, he (sallallaahu 'alaihi wa sallam) would sit for tashahhud after finishing the second rak'ah. In a two-rak'ah prayer such as Fajr, "he would sit *muftarishan*"[5], as he used to sit between the two sajdahs, and "he would sit in the first tashahhud similarly"[6] in a three- or four-rak'ah prayer.

He also ordered "the one who prayed badly" thus, saying to him, *When you sit in the middle of the prayer, then be calm, spread your left thigh and perform tashahhud.*[7]

Abu Hurairah (radi Allaahu 'anhu) said, "My friend (sallallaahu 'alaihi wa sallam) forbade me from squatting (*iq'aa'*) like a dog"[8]; in another hadeeth, "he used to forbid the squatting of the devil."[9]

"When he sat in tashahhud, he would place his right palm on his right thigh (*in one narration*: knee), and his left palm on his left thigh (in one narration: knee,

---

[1]Abu Daawood & Ahmad with a strong sanad.
[2]Bukhaari & Muslim.
[3]Ahmad with a good isnaad.
[4]Ibn Maajah, Ibn Hibbaan in his Saheeh & Ahmad in Ibn Haani's *Masaa'il* (1/52). Jaabir bin 'Abdullaah (radi Allaahu 'anhu) said, "He who prays a rak'ah in which he does not recite the Mother of the Qur'aan has not prayed, except behind an imaam" - related by Maalik in *Muwatta'*.
[5]Nasaa'i (1/173) with a saheeh isnaad.
[6]Bukhaari & Abu Daawood.
[7]Abu Daawood & Baihaqi with a good sanad.
[8]Tayaalisi, Ahmad & Ibn Abi Shaibah. About iq'aa', Abu 'Ubaidah and others said, "It is when a man presses his buttocks against the ground, keeps his shins upright, and leans his hands on the ground, the way a dog does." This is different to the iq'aa' between sajdahs, which is approved in the Sunnah, as covered previously.
[9]Muslim, Abu 'Awaanah & others. It is given in *Irwaa'* (316).

spreading it upon it)"[1]; and "he would put the end of his right elbow on his right thigh."[2]

Also, "he forbade a man who was sitting in prayer resting on his left hand, and said: *Verily, that is the prayer of the Jews*[3]; in one wording, *Do not sit like this, for indeed this is the way of sitting of those who are punished*[4]; in another hadeeth, *It is the sitting posture of those who incurred (Allaah's) anger.*[5]

Moving the Finger in Tashahhud

"He (sallallaahu 'alaihi wa sallam) would spread his left palm on his left knee, clench all the fingers of his right hand, point with the finger adjacent to the thumb towards the qiblah, and fix his sight on it (i.e. the finger)."[6]

Also, "when he pointed with his finger, he would put his thumb on his middle finger"[7], and sometimes "he would make a circle with these two."[8]

"When he raised his finger, he would move it, supplicating with it"[9], and he used to say, "It is surely more powerful against the devil than iron, meaning the forefinger."[10]

---

[1]Muslim & Abu 'Awaanah.

[2]Abu Daawood & Nasaa'i with a saheeh sanad. It is as though the meaning is that he would not separate his elbows from his side, as Ibn al-Qayyim has elucidated in *Zaad al-Ma'aad.*

[3]Baihaqi & Haakim , who declared it saheeh and Dhahabi agreed. It is given, as well as the next one, in Irwaa' (380).

[4]Ahmad & Abu Daawood with a good isnaad.

[5]'Abdur Razzaaq; 'Abdul Haqq declared it saheeh in his *Ahkaam* (no. 1284 - with my checking).

[6]Muslim, Abu 'Awaanah & Ibn Khuzaimah. Humaidi (13/1) and Abu Ya'laa (275/2) added with a saheeh sanad on the authority of Ibn 'Umar: "and this is the shooting of the devil; no-one will forget when he does this", and Humaidi raised his finger. Humaidi also said that Muslim bin Abi Maryam said, "A man related to me that in a church in Syria, he saw images of Prophets depicted like this", and Humaidi raised his finger. This is an extremely strange remark, but its sanad up to "the man" is saheeh.

[7]Muslim & Abu 'Awaanah.

[8]Abu Daawood, Nasaa'i, Ibn al-Jaarood in *al-Muntaqaa* (208), Ibn Khuzaimah (1/86/1-2) & Ibn Hibbaan in his Saheeh (485) with a saheeh sanad. Ibn al-Mulaqqin also declared it saheeh (28/2), and it has a supporting narration in Ibn 'Adi (287/1).

[9]ibid. About "supplicating with it", Imaam Tahaawi said, "This is evidence that it was at the end of the prayer." Hence, there is evidence in this that the Sunnah is to continue pointing and moving the finger until the tasleem, for the supplication is until then. This is the view of Maalik and others. Imaam Ahmad was asked, "Should a man point with his finger during prayer?" He replied, "Yes, vigorously." (Mentioned by Ibn Haani in his *Masaa'il of Imaam Ahmad*, 1/80). From this, it is clear that moving the finger in tashahhud is a proven sunnah of the Prophet (sallallaahu 'alaihi wa sallam), and it was practised by Ahmad and other imaams of the Sunnah. Therefore, those who think that it is pointless and irrelevant and has nothing to do with the Prayer, should fear Allaah, since because of this, they do not move their fingers although they know it to be an established sunnah; and they take great pains to interpret it in a way which is inconsistent with the 'Arabic way of expression and contrary to the understanding of the imaams with regard to it.

Also, "the Companions of the Prophet (sallallaahu 'alaihi wa sallam) used to remind each other, that is, about pointing with the finger when supplicating."[1]

Once, "he saw a man supplicating with two fingers, so he said, *Make it one, [make it one,]*" and indicated with his forefinger."[2]

"He (sallallaahu 'alaihi wa sallam) would do this in both tashahhuds."[3]

The Obligation of the First Tashahhud, & the Validity of Supplication during it

"He (sallallaahu 'alaihi wa sallam) would recite the *Tahiyyah* after every two rak'ahs"[4]; "the first thing he would say in this sitting would be: *All compliments be to Allaah.*"[5]

"When he forgot to perform the tashahhud after the first two rak'ahs, he would prostrate (twice) for forgetfulness."[6]

He used to order them to perform tashahhud, saying, *When you sit after every two rak'ahs, then say: All compliments ... and then each of you should select the*

The amazing thing is that some of them will defend an imaam on other issues, even if his opinion conflicts with the Sunnah, with the argument that to point out the imaam's mistakes inevitably means to taunt and disrespect him. They then forget this and reject this established sunnah, at the same time mocking at those who practise it. Whether or not they realise it, their mockery also includes those imaams whom they often defend wrongly, and who are correct about the Sunnah this time! In fact, they are deriding the Prophet (sallallaahu 'alaihi wa sallam) himself, for he is the one who brought us this sunnah, and so jeering at it is equivalent to jeering at him. << But what is the reward for those among you who behave like this except ... >>

As for putting the finger down after pointing, or limiting the movement to the affirmation (saying *laa ilaaha*: 'there is no god ...') and negation (saying: *illallaahu*: '... except Allaah'), all of that has no basis in the Sunnah; in fact, it is contrary to the Sunnah, as this hadeeth proves.

Further, the hadeeth that he would not move his finger does not have an authentic isnaad, as I have explained in *Da'eef Abi Daawood* (175). Even if it were authentic, it is negatory, while the hadeeth above is affirmatory: the affirmatory takes precedence over the negatory, as is well-known among the scholars.

[10]Ahmad, Bazzaar, Abu Ja'far al-Bukhteeri in *al-Amaali* (60/1), 'Abdul Ghani al-Maqdisi in his Sunan (12/2) with a hasan sanad, Rooyaani in his Musnad (249/2) & Baihaqi .

[1]Ibn Abi Shaibah (2/123/2) with a hasan sanad.

[2]Ibn Abi Shaibah (12/40/1, 2/123/2) & Nasaa'i . Haakim declared it saheeh and Dhahabi agreed, and there is a supporting narration for it in Ibn Abi Shaibah.

[3]Nasaa'i & Baihaqi with a saheeh sanad.

[4]Muslim & Abu 'Awaanah.

[5]Baihaqi transmitted it as a narration from 'Aa'ishah with a good isnaad, as verified by Ibn al-Mulaqqin (28/2).

[6]Bukhaari & Muslim. It is given in *Irwaa' al-Ghaleel* (338).

supplication he likes best and supplicate Allaah, Mighty and Sublime, [with it][1]; in another version: Say, All compliments ... in every sitting[2], and he also ordered "the one who prayed badly" to do so, as has been mentioned.

"He (sallallaahu 'alaihi wa sallam) would teach them the tashahhud the way he taught them Soorahs of the Qur'aan"[3], and "the Sunnah is to say it quietly."[4]

The Manner of Tashahhud

He taught several ways of tashahhud:

1- The tashahhud of Ibn Mas'ood, who said, "The Messenger of Allaah (sallallaahu 'alaihi wa sallam) taught me the tashahhud, [with] my palm between his palms, the way he taught me Soorahs of the Qur'aan:

اَلتَّحِيَّاتُ لِلَّهِ، وَالصَّلَوَاتُ وَالطَّيِّبَاتُ، اَلسَّلَامُ عَلَيْكَ أَيُّهَا النَّبِيُّ وَرَحْمَةُ اللّهِ وَبَرَكَاتُهُ اَلسَّلَامُ عَلَيْنَا وَعَلَى
اللّهِ الصَّالِحِين أَشْهَدُ أَنْ لَا إِلهَ إِلاَّ اللّهُ، وأَشْهَدُ أَنْ مُحَمَّداً عَبْدُهُ وَرَسُولُهُ

All compliments[5], prayers[6] and pure words[7] are due to Allaah. Peace[8] be on you, O Prophet, and also the mercy of Allaah and His blessings[9]. Peace be on us, and on the righteous slaves of Allaah. [For when one says that, it includes every righteous slave in the heaven and the earth.] I bear witness that none has the right to be worshipped except Allaah, and I bear witness that Muhammad is His slave and messenger.

[This was while he was among us, but after he was taken, we would say:

اَلسَّلَامُ عَلَى النَّبِيِّ

---

[1]Nasaa'i, Ahmad & Tabaraani in Mu'jam al-Kabeer (3/25/1) with a saheeh sanad. The literal meaning of the hadeeth is evidence for the validity of supplication in every tashahhud, even the one not adjacent to the tasleem, and this is the view of Ibn Hazm (rahimahullaah).
[2]Nasaa'i with a saheeh sanad.
[3]Bukhaari & Muslim.
[4]Abu Daawood & Haakim , who declared it saheeh and Dhahabi agreed.
[5]Ar. tahiyyaat, i.e. "all words which imply peace, sovereignty and eternity, are due to Allaah." (Nihaayah)
[6]Ar. salawaat, i.e. "all supplications which are used to glorigy the majesty of Allaah, for He is fully entitled to them, and none but Him is worthy of them." (Nihaayah)
[7]Ar. tayyibaat, i.e. "all good and pure words suitable for praising Allaah, not those ones incompatible with his attributes with which kings were greeted." (Fath al-Baari)
[8]meaning seeking of refuge with Allaah and being strengthened by him, since as-Salaam (Peace) is actually a name of Allaah. Hence, the greeting effectively means: Allaah be a watcher and safeguard over you. Similarly, it is said, "Allaah be with you", i.e. in His safeguarding, help and favour.
[9]A term for all the good continuously emanating from Allaah.

Peace be on the Prophet]."[1]

2- The tashahhud of Ibn 'Abbaas: "The Messenger of Allaah (sallallaahu 'alaihi wa sallam) used to teach us the tashahhud the way he taught us [soorahs of] the Qur'aan; he used to say,

التَّحِيَّاتُ الْمُبَارَكَاتُ الصَّلَوَاتُ الطَّيِّبَاتُ لِلَّهِ، [الـ]سَلَامُ عَلَيْكَ أَيُّهَا النَّبِيُّ وَرَحْمَةُ اللَّهِ وَبَرَكَاتُهُ، [الـ]سَلَامُ عَلَيْنَا وَعَلَى عِبَادِ اللَّهِ الصَّالِحِينَ، أَشْهَدُ أَنْ لَا إِلَهَ إِلاَّ اللَّهُ، وَ[أَشْهَدُ] أَنَّ مُحَمَّداً رَسُولُ اللَّهِ، (وفي رواية: عَبْدُهُ وَرَسُولُهُ)

All compliments, blessed words, prayers, pure words are due to Allaah. Peace be on you, O Prophet, and also the mercy of Allaah and His blessings. Peace be on us

---

[1]Bukhaari, Muslim, Ibn Abi Shaibah (1/90/2), Siraaj & Abu Ya'laa in his Musnad (258/2). It is given in *Irwaa'* (321).

Ibn Mas'ood's statement, "We said: Peace be on the Prophet" clarifies that the Companions (radi Allaahu 'anhum) used to say, "Peace be on you, O Prophet" in tashahhud while the Prophet (sallallaahu 'alaihi wa sallam) was alive, but when he died, they ceased to do that, instead saying, "Peace be on the Prophet". Undoubtedly, this was with the endorsement of the Prophet (sallallaahu 'alaihi wa sallam); this is supported by the fact that 'Aa'ishah (radi Allaahu 'anhaa) would similarly teach the tashahhud in prayer with "Peace be on the Prophet", as transmitted by Siraaj in his Musnad (9/1/2) & Mukhlis in *al-Fawaa'id* (11/54/1) with two saheeh isnaads from her.

Ibn Hajar says, "This addition shows clearly that they used to say 'Peace be on you, O Prophet', addressing him directly during his life, but when the Prophet (sallallaahu 'alaihi wa sallam) died, they stopped addressing him and mentioned him in the third person instead, saying 'Peace be on the Prophet'." He also says in a different place, "Subki said in *Sharh al-Minhaaj*, after mentioning this narration from Abu 'Awaanah only, 'If this is authentically-reported from the Companions, it proves that after his time, it is not compulsory to address the Prophet (sallallaahu 'alaihi wa sallam) directly in the greeting of peace, so one says: Peace be on the Prophet.' (Ibn Hajar continues:) This is authentic without doubt (i.e. because it is established in Sahih al-Bukhaari), and I have also found strong support for it:- 'Abdur Razzaaq said: Ibn Juraij informed me: 'Ataa' informed me that the Companions used to say 'Peace be on you, O Prophet' while the Prophet (sallallaahu 'alaihi wa sallam) was alive, but after he died, they would say 'Peace be on the Prophet', and this is a saheeh isnaad. As for Sa'eed bin Mansoor's narration from Abu 'Ubaidah bin 'Abdullaah bin Mas'ood, who reported from his father that the Prophet (sallallaahu 'alaihi wa sallam) taught them the tashahhud, and then he ('Abdullaah bin Mas'ood) said it (the tashahhud); Ibn 'Abbaas said: We used to say 'Peace be on you, O Prophet' only while he was alive, to which Ibn Mas'ood replied, 'This is how we were taught, and this is how we teach it', it would appear that Ibn 'Abbaas said this as a matter of discussion but Ibn Mas'ood did not accept. However, the narration of Abu Ma'mar (i.e. the narration of Bukhaari) is more authentic, since Abu 'Ubaidah did not hear (ahaadeeth) from his father, and furthermore, the isnaad up to Abu 'Ubaidah is weak." (End of quote from Ibn Hajar)

These words of Ibn Hajar have been quoted by several scholars in their analysis, e.g. Qastalaani, Zarqaani, Lucknowi, etc. They all chose to give his words without commenting further. This discussion is treated more fully in *al-Asl*.

and on the righteous slaves of Allaah. I bear witness that none has the right to be worshipped except Allaah, and [I bear witness] that Muhammad is the Messenger of Allaah (in one narration: ... is His slave and messenger)."[1]

3- The tashahhud of Ibn 'Umar, who reported the Messenger of Allaah (sallallaahu 'alaihi wa sallam) as saying in the tashahhud:

$$
اَلتَّحِيَّاتُ لِلَّهِ، [وَ] الصَّلَوَاتُ [وَ] الطَّيِّبَاتُ، اَلسَّلَامُ عَلَيْكَ أَيُّهَا النَّبِيُّ وَرَحْمَةُ اللَّهِ
$$

$$
– وَبَرَكَاتُهُ – اَلسَّلَامُ عَلَيْنَا وَعَلَى عِبَادِ اللَّهِ الصَّالِحِينَ، أَشْهَدُ أَنْ لَا إِلَهَ إِلاَّ اللَّهُ
$$

$$
– وَحْدَهُ لَا شَرِيكَ لَهُ – وَأَشْهَدُ أَنَّ مُحَمَّداً عَبْدُهُ وَرَسُولُهُ
$$

All compliments, prayers and good words are due to Allaah. Peace be on you, O Prophet, and also the mercy of Allaah - Ibn 'Umar said, "I add:"[2] ... and His blessings. - Peace be on us and on the righteous slaves of Allaah. I bear witness that none has the right to be worshipped except Allaah - Ibn 'Umar said, "I add:"[3] ... alone, He has no partner, - and I bear witness that Muhammad is His slave and messenger.[4]

4- The tashahhud of Abu Moosaa al-Ash'ari, who said that the Messenger of Allaah (sallallaahu 'alaihi wa sallam) said, ... when you are sitting, the first thing each of you says should be:

$$
اَلتَّحِيَّاتُ الطَّيِّبَاتُ الصَّلَوَاتُ لِلَّهِ، اَلسَّلَامُ عَلَيْكَ أَيُّهَا النَّبِيُّ وَرَحْمَةُ اللَّهِ وَبَرَكَاتُهُ، اَلسَّلَامُ عَلَيْنَا وَعَلَى عِبَا
$$

$$
اللَّهِ الصَّالِحِينَ، أَشْهَدُ أَنْ لَا إِلَهَ إِلاَّ اللَّهُ [وَحْدَهُ لَا شَرِيكَ لَهُ]، وَأَشْهَدُ أَنَّ مُحَمَّداً عَبْدُهُ وَرَسُولُهُ
$$

All compliments, good words and prayers are due to Allaah. Peace be on you, O Prophet, and also the mercy of Allaah and His blessings. Peace be on us, and on the righteous slaves of Allaah. I bear witness that none has the right to be worshipped except Allaah [alone, He has no partner], and I bear witness that Muhammad is His slave and messenger - seven phrases, and they are the greetings in the prayer."[5]

---

[1]Muslim, Abu 'Awaanah, Shaafi'i & Nasaa'i .
[2]see next note.
[3]These two additions have been proved to be part of the tashahhud from the Prophet (sallallaahu 'alaihi wa sallam). Ibn 'Umar did not add them of his own accord (far is he above such a thing!); in fact, he learnt them from other Companions who reported them from the Prophet (sallallaahu 'alaihi wa sallam), and he then added them to the tashahhud which he heard from the Prophet (sallallaahu 'alaihi wa sallam) directly.
[4]Abu Daawood & Daaraqutni, who declared it saheeh.
[5]Muslim, Abu 'Awaanah, Abu Daawood & Ibn Maajah.

5- The tashahhud of 'Umar ibn al-Khattaab, who would teach the people the tashahhud while on the pulpit, saying, "Say:

اَلتَّحِيَّاتُ لِلَّهِ، اَلزَّاكِيَاتُ لِلَّهِ، اَلطَّيِّبَاتُ [لِلَّهِ]، اَلصَّلَوَاتُ لِلَّهِ، اَلسَّلَامُ عَلَيْكَ أَيُّهَا النَّبِيُّ وَرَحْمَةُ اللَّهِ وَبَرَكَاتُهُ

اَلسَّلَامُ عَلَيْنَا وَعَلَى عِبَادِ اللَّهِ الصَّالِحِينَ أَشْهَدُ أَنْ لَا إِلَهَ إِلَّا اللَّهُ، وَأَشْهَدُ أَنَّ مُحَمَّداً عَبْدُهُ وَرَسُولُهُ

All compliments are due to Allaah; all pure titles are due to Allaah; all good words [are due to Allaah]; all prayers are due to Allaah. Peace be on you, O Prophet, and also the mercy of Allaah and His blessings. Peace be on us and on the righteous slaves of Allaah. I bear witness that none has the right to be worshipped except Allaah, and I bear witness that Muhammad is His slave and messenger.[1]

As-Salaah 'alaa an-Nabiyy (Sending Prayers on the Prophet) - Its Place & Manner

He (sallallaahu 'alaihi wa sallam) used to send prayers on himself in the first tashahhud as well as the other.[2] He also established it for his ummah, ordering them to send prayers on him after sending peace on him[3], and he taught them several ways of doing so:

---

[1]Maalik & Baihaqi with saheeh isnaads. Although this hadeeth is *mawqoof*, it is effectively *marfoo'*, for it is known that this sort of thing is not said from personal opinion, since it were so, would be no better than any other sayings of *dhikr*, as Ibn 'Abdul Barr has said.

*NB: In none of the types of tashahhud is there the addition: *wa maghfiratuhu* (... "and His forgiveness"), so one should not be accustomed to it. Hence some of the Salaf rebuked it, as the following narrations show:

Tabaraani (3/56/1) reported with a saheeh isnaad from Talhah bin Musarrif, who said: Rabee' bin Khaitham added during tashahhud, "... and His blessings, *and His forgiveness*"! So 'Alqamah said, "We stop where we were taught: Peace be upon you, O Prophet, and also the mercy of Allaah and His blessings"; 'Alqamah was actually following the example of his teacher 'Abdullaah bin Mas'ood (radi Allaahu 'anhu), from whom it is authentically-reported that he was teaching a man the tashahhud: when he got to "I bear witness that there is no (true) god except Allaah ...", the man said: "alone, He has no partner", to which 'Abdullaah said, "He is so, but we stop where we were taught." (Transmitted by Tabaraani in *Mu'jam al-Awsat*, no. 2848, with a saheeh isnaad.)

[2]Abu 'Awaanah in his Saheeh (2/324) & Nasaa'i .
[3]They had said, "O Messenger of Allaah, we have been taught how to send peace on you (i.e. in tashahhud), but how do we send prayers on you? He said, "Say: O Allaah! send prayers on Muhammad ..." etc. Thus he did not specify one tashahhud to the exclusion of another, so there is evidence here to establish sending prayers on him in the first tashahhud also. This is the way of Imaam Shaafi'i, as in the text of his book *al-Umm*, and it is held to be correct by his companions, as Nawawi has explained in *al-Majmoo'* (3/460) and supported in *Rawdah Taalibeen* (1/263). It is also the view of Wazeer bin Hubairah al-Hanbali in al-Ifsaah, as Ibn Rajab ha quoted and strongly supported in *Dhail Tabaqaat* (1/280). Many ahaadeeth exist about sending prayers on

1-

اَللَّهُمَّ صَلِّ عَلَى مُحَمَّدٍ، وَعَلَى أَهْلِ بَيْتِهِ، وَعَلَى أَزْوَاجِهِ وَذُرِّيَّتِهِ، كَمَا صَلَّيْتَ عَلَى آلِ إِبْرَاهِيمَ، إِنَّكَ حَمِيـ
مَجِيدٌ، وَبَارِكْ عَلَى مُحَمَّدٍ، وَعَلَى آلِ بَيْتِهِ، وَعَلَى أَزْوَاجِهِ وَذُرِّيَّتِهِ، كَمَا بَارَكْتَ عَلَى آلِ إِبْرَاهِيمَ، إِنَّكَ حَمـ
مَجِيدٌ

O Allaah! send prayers on Muhammad[1], and on his household, and on his wives and progeny, as you sent prayers on the family of Ibraaheem; You are indeed Worthy of Praise, Full of Glory. And send blessings on Muhammad[2], and his household, and his wives and progeny, as you sent blessings on the family of Ibraaheem; You are indeed Worthy of Praise, Full of Glory.

This supplication he would use himself.[3]

2-

اَللَّهُمَّ صَلِّ عَلَى مُحَمَّدٍ، وَعَلَى آلِ مُحَمَّدٍ، كَمَا صَلَّيْتَ عَلَى [إِبْرَاهِيمَ، وَعَلَى] آلِ إِبْرَاهِيمَ، إِنَّكَ حَمِيدٌ
مَجِيدٌ، اَللَّهُمَّ بَارِكْ عَلَى مُحَمَّدٍ، وَعَلَى آلِ مُحَمَّدٍ، كَمَا بَارَكْتَ عَلَى [إِبْرَاهِيمَ، وَعَلَى] آلِ إِبْرَاهِيمَ، إِنَّكَ
حَمِيدٌ مَجِيدٌ

O Allaah! send prayers on Muhammad, and on the family of Muhammad, as you sent prayers on [Ibraaheem, and on][4] the family of Ibraaheem; You are

---

him (sallallaahu 'alaihi wa sallam) in tashahhud; in none of them is there any such specification mentioned. In fact, these ahaadeeth are general, hence including every tashahhud, and I have given them in al-Asl as ta'leeq, but not in the main text, for they do not satisfy our conditions for authenticity. However, they do support each other in meaning, and those who reject and oppose this have no authentic evidence to use as proof, as I have detailed in al-Asl. Similarly, to say that adding anything to "O Allaah! send prayers on Muhammad" is makrooh has no basis in the Sunnah, nor is there any convincing proof for it. In fact, we see that whoever says this does not implement the previous instruction of the Prophet (sallallaahu 'alaihi wa sallam), "Say: O Allaah! send prayers on Muhammad, and on the family of Muhammad ..." ; there is more to this discussion in al-Asl.

[1]One of the earliest views about the meaning of "sending prayers on the Prophet (sallallaahu 'alaihi wa sallam)" is that of Abu al-'Aaliyah (with reference to Surah al-Ahzaab, 33:56), "Allaah's sending prayers on his Prophet means His exalting him and raising his rank; the angels' and others' sending prayers means their seeking this from Allaah, and here it is meant asking the prayers to be increased, not asking for the original prayer in itself." Ibn Hajar quoted this in Fath al-Baari, and went on to refute the widespread notion that the Lord's prayer on someone is His Mercy; Ibn al-Qayyim also clarified this in Jalaa' al-Afhaam, leaving little scope for further comment.

[2]from barakah: growth, increase. Hence this supplication secures for Muhammad the good which Allaah granted to the family of Ibraaheem, continual, established good, as well as its multiplying and increase.

[3]Ahmad & Tahaawi with a saheeh sanad.

[4]see next note.

indeed Worthy of Praise, Full of Glory. O Allaah! send blessings on Muhammad, and on the family of Muhammad, as you sent blessings on [Ibraaheem, and on]¹ the family of Ibraaheem; You are indeed Worthy of Praise, Full of Glory.²

3-

اَللّٰهُمَّ صَلِّ عَلَى مُحَمَّدٍ، وَعَلَى آلِ مُحَمَّدٍ، كَمَا صَلَّيْتَ عَلَى إِبْرَاهِيمَ [وَآلِ إِبْرَاهِيمَ]، إِنَّكَ حَمِيدٌ مَجِيدٌ، وَبَارِكْ عَلَى مُحَمَّدٍ، وَعَلَى آلِ مُحَمَّدٍ، كَمَا بَارَكْتَ عَلَى [إِبْرَاهِيمَ وَ] آلِ إِبْرَاهِيمَ، إِنَّكَ حَمِيدٌ مَجِيدٌ

O Allaah! send prayers on Muhammad, and on the family of Muhammad, as you sent prayers on Ibraaheem, [and the family of Ibraaheem]; You are indeed Worthy of Praise, Full of Glory. And send blessings on Muhammad, and on the family of Muhammad, as you sent blessings on [Ibraaheem, and] the family of Ibraaheem; You are indeed Worthy of Praise, Full of Glory.³

4-

اَللّٰهُمَّ صَلِّ عَلَى مُحَمَّدٍ [النَّبِيِّ الْأُمِّيِّ]، وَعَلَى آلِ مُحَمَّدٍ، كَمَا صَلَّيْتَ عَلَى [آلِ] إِبْرَاهِيمَ، وَبَارِكْ عَلَى مُحَمَّدٍ [النَّبِيِّ الْأُمِّيِّ]، وَعَلَى آلِ مُحَمَّدٍ، كَمَا بَارَكْتَ عَلَى [آلِ] إِبْرَاهِيمَ فِي الْعَالَمِينَ، إِنَّكَ حَمِيدٌ مَجِيدٌ

O Allaah! send prayers on Muhammad [the Unlettered Prophet], and on the family of Muhammad, as you sent prayers on [the family of] Ibraaheem; and send blessings on Muhammad [the Unlettered Prophet] and the family of Muhammad, as you sent blessings on [the family of] Ibraaheem among the nations; You are indeed Worthy of Praise, Full of Glory.⁴

5-

اَللّٰهُمَّ صَلِّ عَلَى مُحَمَّدٍ عَبْدِكَ وَرَسُولِكَ، كَمَا صَلَّيْتَ عَلَى [آلِ] إِبْرَاهِيمَ، وَبَارِكْ عَلَى مُحَمَّدٍ [عَبْدِكَ وَرَسُولِكَ]، [وَعَلَى آلِ مُحَمَّدٍ]، كَمَا بَارَكْتَ عَلَى إِبْرَاهِيمَ [وَعَلَى آلِ إِبْرَاهِيمَ]

O Allaah! send prayers on Muhammad, Your slave and messenger, as You sent prayers on [the family of] Ibraaheem. And send blessings on Muhammad [Your

---

¹These two additions are conclusively found in Bukhaari, Tahaawi, Baihaqi, Ahmad & Nasaa'i . They also exist via different routes of narration in other types of this supplication (see nos. 3,7), and so do not be confused by Ibn al-Qayyim's view in *Jalaa' al-Afhaam* (p. 198), following in the footsteps of his great teacher Ibn Taymiyyah in *al-Fataawaa* (1/16), "There is no authentic hadeeth with the phrases 'Ibraaheem' and 'the family of Ibraaheem' together"; here, we have shown you such authentic ahaadeeth. Ibn al-Qayyim's error is further established by the fact that he himself declared no. 7 saheeh, which contains what he denied above!

²Bukhaari, Muslim, Humaidi (138/1) & Ibn Mandah (68/2), who said, "There is consensus on this hadeeth being authentic."

³Ahmad, Nasaa'i & Abu Ya'laa in his Musnad (44/2) with a saheeh sanad.

⁴Muslim, Abu 'Awaanah, Ibn Abi Shaibah (2/132/1) & Abu Daawood; Haakim declared it saheeh.

slave and messenger], *[and the family of Muhammad,]* *as you sent blessings on Ibraaheem [and on the famly of Ibraaheem].*[1]

6-

$$اَللّٰهُمَّ صَلِّ عَلَى مُحَمَّدٍ، وَ[عَلَى] أَزْوَاجِهِ وَذُرِّيَّتِهِ، كَمَا صَلَّيْتَ عَلَى [آلِ] إِبْرَاهِيمَ، وَبَارِكْ عَلَى مُحَمَّدٍ وَ[عَلَى] أَزْوَاجِهِ وَذُرِّيَّتِهِ، كَمَا بَارَكْتَ عَلَى [آلِ] إِبْرَاهِيمَ، إِنَّكَ حَمِيدٌ مَجِيدٌ$$

O Allaah! send prayers on Muhammad and [on] his wives and progeny, as You sent prayers on [the family of Ibraaheem]. And send blessings on Muhammad, and [on] his wives and progeny, as You sent blessings on [the family of] Ibraaheem; You are indeed Worthy of Praise, Full of Glory.[2]

7-

$$اَللّٰهُمَّ صَلِّ عَلَى مُحَمَّدٍ، وَعَلَى آلِ مُحَمَّدٍ، وَبَارِكْ عَلَى مُحَمَّدٍ، وَعَلَى آلِ مُحَمَّدٍ، كَمَا صَلَّيْتَ وَبَارَكْتَ عَلَى إِبْرَاهِيمَ وَآلِ إِبْرَاهِيمَ إِنَّكَ حَمِيدٌ مَجِيدٌ$$

O Allaah! send prayers on Muhammad, and on the family of Muhammad, and send blessings on Muhammad, and on the family of Muhammad, as you sent prayers and sent blessings on Ibraaheem and the family of Ibraaheem; You are indeed Worthy of Praise, Full of Glory.[3]

---

[1] Bukhaari, Nasaa'i, Tahaawi, Ahmad & Ismaa'eel al-Qaadi in *Fadl as-Salaah 'alaa Nabi sallallaahu 'alaihi wa sallam* (p. 28 1st ed., p. 62 2nd ed. with my checking).

[2] Bukhaari, Muslim & Nasaa'i.

[3] Nasaa'i, Tahaawi, Abu Sa'eed bin al-'Arabi in *al-Mu'jam* (79/2) with a saheeh sanad. Ibn al-Qayyim gave its source as Muhammad bin Ishaaq as-Siraaj in *Jalaa' al-Afhaam* (pp. 14-15) and then declared it saheeh. This wording includes both 'Ibraaheem' and 'the family of Ibraaheem', something overlooked by both Ibn al-Qayyim & his teacher Ibn Taymiyyah, as explained above.

Important Notes about *as-Salaah 'alaa an-Nabiyy* - Sending Prayers on the Prophet of the Ummah

1) It can be seen that in most of these ways of sending prayers on the Prophet (sallallaahu 'alaihi wa sallam), there is no mention of Ibraaheem separate from his family, the wording being, "... as you have sent prayers on *the family of Ibraaheem.*" The reason for this is that in 'Arabic, the family of a man includes the man as well as his dependants, e.g. in the words of the Exalted,

$$ إِنَّ ٱللَّهَ ٱصْطَفَىٰٓ ءَادَمَ وَنُوحًا وَءَالَ إِبْرَٰهِيمَ وَءَالَ عِمْرَٰنَ عَلَى ٱلْعَٰلَمِينَ $$

"Allaah has chosen Aadam, Nooh, the family of Ibraaheem and the family of 'Imraan above all people" (aal-'Imraan 3:33);

$$ إِنَّآ أَرْسَلْنَا عَلَيْهِمْ حَاصِبًا إِلَّآ ءَالَ لُوطٍ نَّجَّيْنَٰهُم بِسَحَرٍ $$

"We sent against them a violent tornado with showers of stones, except the family of Loot - We delivered them by early dawn" (Qamar 54:34); similar is his saying (sallallaahu 'alaihi wa sallam), *O Allaah! send prayers on the family of Abu Awfaa.* The phrase *Ahl al-Bayt* (people of the house) is also like this, e.g.

$$ رَحْمَتُ ٱللَّهِ وَبَرَكَٰتُهُۥ عَلَيْكُمْ أَهْلَ ٱلْبَيْتِ $$

"Allaah's grace and His blessings be on you, O people of the house" (Houd 11:73). Hence, Ibraaheem is included in "the family of Ibraaheem"

Shaikh-ul-Islaam Ibn Taymiyyah says,

> "Most of the versions have, 'as you sent prayers on the family of Ibraaheem' and 'as you sent blessings on the family of Ibraaheem'; some have 'Ibraaheem' himself. This is because he is the cause of all prayers and purifications on them; the rest of his family are secondary recipients of all that. To show these two points, both wordings have been employed separately."

Further, there is a well-known question among the people of knowledge: about the nature of the comparison in his statement, "as you sent prayers on ...", for it is true that the model for comparison is normally superior to the one being compared; here, the opposite is the case, since Muhammad (sallallaahu 'alaihi wa sallam) is greater than Ibraaheem, and so his superiority dictates that the prayers requested are more excellent than any prayers received or to be received by anyone else. The people of knowledge have provided many answers to this, and these can be found in *Fath al-Baari* and *Jalaa' al-Ifhaam*. They amount to about ten views, all of which are unsubstantiated, some weaker than others, except one, a well-supported view, and adopted by Shaikh-ul-Islaam Ibn Taymiyyah and Ibn al-Qayyim. This view is: "The family of Ibraaheem includes many prophets; none like them is found in the family of Muhammad. Therefore, when prayers on the Prophet (sallallaahu 'alaihi wa sallam) and his family are sought similar to that bestowed on Ibraaheem and his family, which includes prophets, the family of Muhammad receives out of that what is appropriate for them. Since the family of Muhammad does not reach the rank of the prophets, the extra blessings and benefit given to the prophets, including Ibraaheem, are left for Muhammad (sallallaahu 'alaihi wa sallam). Thus he gains a distinguished position which others cannot reach."

Ibn al-Qayyim says,

"This is the best of all the previous views: that Muhammad (sallallaahu 'alaihi wa sallam) is one of the family of Ibraaheem; in fact, he is the best of the family of Ibraaheem, as 'Ali ibn Talhah has related from Ibn 'Abbaas (radi Allaahu 'anhu) about the saying of the Exalted, **"Allaah has chosen Aadam, Nooh, the family of Ibraaheem and the family of 'Imraan above all people"** (aal-'Imraan 3:33); Ibn 'Abbaas said, "Muhammad is among the family of Ibraaheem". This is text for the fact that if other prophets descended from Ibraaheem are included in his family, then the inclusion of the Messenger of Allaah (sallallaahu 'alaihi wa sallam) is more fitting. Hence our saying, "... as you sent prayers on the family of Ibraaheem", includes the prayers sent on him and on the rest of the prophets descended from Ibraaheem. Allaah has then ordered us to specifically send prayers on Muhammad and his family, as much as we send prayers on him, along with the rest of Ibraaheem's family generally. Therefore, the Prophet's family receives out of that what is appropriate for them, leaving all of the remainder to him (sallallaahu 'alaihi wa sallam).

There is no doubt that the total amount of prayers received by Ibraaheem's family, with the Messenger of Allaah (sallallaahu 'alaihi wa sallam) among them, is greater than that received by the Prophet (sallallaahu 'alaihi wa sallam) alone. Therefore, what is sought for him is such a great favour, definitely superior than that sought for Ibraaheem.

Hence, the nature of the comparison and its consistency become clear. The prayers sought for him with these words are greater than those requested any other way, since what is requested with the supplication is that it be as much as the model of comparison, and that the Prophet (sallallaahu 'alaihi wa sallam) receive a large portion: the comparison dictates that what is requested is more than what was given to Ibraaheem and others.

Thus, the excellence and nobility of Muhammad (sallallaahu 'alaihi wa sallam), over and above Ibraaheem and his family, which includes many prophets, is evident, and is as he deserves. This sending of prayers on the Prophet (sallallaahu 'alaihi wa sallam) becomes evidence for this excellence of his, and this is no more than he deserves. So, may Allaah send prayers on him and on his family, and send peace on them, many greetings of peace, and reward him from our supplications better than He has rewarded any prophet from his people. O Allaah! send prayers on Muhammad, and on the family of Muhammad, as you sent prayers on the family of Ibraaheem; You are indeed Worthy of Praise, Full of Glory. And send blessings on Muhammad, and on the family of Muhammad, as you sent blessings on the family of Ibraaheem; You are indeed Worthy of Praise, Full of Glory."

2) The reader will see that this part of the Prayer, with all its different types, is always a sending of prayers on the family of the Prophet (sallallaahu 'alaihi wa sallam): on his wives and children as well as himself. Therefore, it is neither from the Sunnah, nor carrying out the Prophet's command, to leave it at "O Allaah! send prayers on Muhammad" only. Rather, one of these complete types of supplication must be used, as is reported from his action (sallallaahu 'alaihi wa sallam), whether in the first or the last tashahhud. There is text about this from Imaam Shaafi'i in al-Umm: "The tashahhud in the first and second instance is the same thing; by 'tashahhud', I mean the bearing of witness and the sending of prayers on the Prophet (sallallaahu 'alaihi wa sallam): neither will suffice without the other."

In fact, one of the most amazing things to arise from this age and its intellectual anarchy is that one person, Muhammad Is'aaf Nashaasheebi, in his book *al-Islaam as-Saheeh* ("The Correct Islaam"), has the audacity to reject the sending of prayers on the family of the Prophet (sallallaahu 'alaihi wa sallam) when sending prayers on him, despite it being firmly established in the Saheehs of al-Bukhaari and Muslim, and elsewhere, on the authority of several Companions, e.g. Ka'b ibn 'Ujrah, Abu Humaid as-Saa'idi, Abu Sa'eed al-Khudri, Abu Mas'ood al-Ansaari, Abu Hurairah and Talhah ibn 'Ubaidullaah! In their ahaadeeth, it is found that they asked the Prophet (sallallaahu 'alaihi wa sallam), "How do we send prayers on you?", so he taught them this way of doing so. Nashaasheebi's argument for his view is that Allaah the Exalted did not mention anyone else with the Prophet (sallallaahu 'alaihi wa sallam) in His saying:

$$\text{يَـٰٓأَيُّهَا ٱلَّذِينَ ءَامَنُوا۟ صَلُّوا۟ عَلَيْهِ وَسَلِّمُوا۟ تَسْلِيمًا}$$

"O you who believe! Send prayers on him, and salute him with all respect." (Ahzaab 33:56) He then goes on to say in his refutation that the Companions asked him (sallallaahu 'alaihi wa sallam) that question because the meaning of "salaah" was known to them as "supplication", so they were asking: "How can we supplicate to you?"!

This is a clear deception, for their question was not about the *meaning* of "salaah" on him, in which case he would have a point, but it was about the manner of doing the salaah on him, as is found in the narrations to which we have referred. Thus it all fits, for they asked him about the *way* of doing it according to the Sharee'ah, something which they could not possibly find out except from the guidance of the All-Knowing, All-Wise, Giver of the Sharee'ah. Similarly, they could also ask him about the way of performing the Salaah made obligatory by words of the Exalted such as **"Establish the *Salaah* (Prayer)"**; for their knowledge of the literal meaning of "Salaah" could not remove their need to ask about its manner according to the Sharee'ah, and this is crystal clear.

As for Nashaasheebi's argument referred to, it is of no consequence, for it is well-known among the Muslims that the Prophet (sallallaahu 'alaihi wa sallam) is the expounder of the words of the Lord of the Worlds, as He says:

$$\text{وَأَنزَلْنَا إِلَيْكَ ٱلذِّكْرَ لِتُبَيِّنَ لِلنَّاسِ مَا نُزِّلَ إِلَيْهِمْ}$$

"And We have sent down to you the Message that you may explain clearly to the people what is sent for them" (Nahl 16:44). Hence, the Prophet (sallallaahu 'alaihi wa sallam) explained the way of doing salaah on him, and it included mention of his family, so it is compulsory to accept that from him, due to Allaah's saying:

$$\text{وَمَا ءَاتَىٰكُمُ ٱلرَّسُولُ فَخُذُوهُ}$$

So take what the Messenger gives you (Hashr 59:7), and the well-known authentic hadeeth, *Verily, I have been given the Qur'aan and something similar to it.*[1]

I really wonder what Nashaasheebi and those taken in by his pompous words would say if someone were to reject the tashahhud in prayer altogether, or reject the menstruating woman's abstaining from prayer and fasting, all with the argument that Allaah the Exalted did not mention the tashahhud in the Qur'aan; He only mentioned bowing and prostration, and He did not exempt a menstruating woman from prayer and fasting in the Qur'aan!! So, do they agree with such arguments, which are along the lines of his original one, or not? If they do, and we hope not, then they have strayed far, far away from guidance, and have left the mainstream of the Muslims; if they do not, then they are correct in agreeing with us, and their reasons for rejecting those arguments are exactly the same as our reasons for rejecting Nashaasheebi's original pronouncement, which we have explained clearly.

Therefore beware, O Muslims, of attempting to understand the Qur'aan without recourse to the Sunnah, for you will never be able to do that, even if you were the Seebawaih[2] of the age, the expert of the age in the 'Arabic language. Here is an example in front of you, for this Nashaasheebi is one of the leading scholars of the 'Arabic language of this period; you have seen how he has strayed, after being deceived by his knowledge of the language, by not seeking the aid of the Sunnah in understanding the Qur'aan; in fact he has rejected this aid, as you know. There are many other examples of this - there is not enough room here to mention them, but what we have mentioned will suffice, and Allaah is the Granter of all capability.

3) The reader will also see that in none of these types of salaah on the Prophet (sallallaahu 'alaihi wa sallam) is there the word sayyid (chief, leader). The later scholars have differed about the validity of its inclusion in the Ibraaheemee

---

[1] Abu Daawood & Ahmad with a saheeh isnaad.
[2] a famous grammarian and scholar of the 'Arabic language of the second century AH.

salaah. Due to lack of space we will not go into the details of that nor make mention of those who rejected its validity in keeping with the Prophet (sallallaahu 'alaihi wa sallam)'s complete teaching to his ummah when he instructed, "Say: O Allaah! send prayers on Muhammad ..." on being asked about the manner of salaah on him, but we will quote the Haafidh Ibn Hajr al-'Asqalaani on this, bearing in mind his position as one of the great Shaafi'i scholars of both hadeeth and fiqh, for contradiction of this teaching of the Prophet (sallallaahu 'alaihi wa sallam) has become widespread among Shaafi'i scholars!

Haafiz Muhammad ibn Muhammad ibn Muhammad al-Ghuraabeeli (790-835 AH), a companion of Ibn Hajr, said, and I quote from his manuscript[1]:

> He (i.e. Ibn Hajr), may Allaah benefit us with his life, was asked about the features of salaah on the Prophet (sallallaahu 'alaihi wa sallam), whether during prayer or outside it, compulsory or recommended: Is one of its conditions that the Prophet (sallallaahu 'alaihi wa sallam) be attributed with sayaadah (leadership), e.g. 'O Allaah! send prayers on sayyidinaa (our leader) Muhammad ...' or 'the foremost of creation', or 'the leader of the children of Aadam' etc.? Or should one stick to 'O Allaah! send prayers on Muhammad'? Which of these two is the better approach: including the word sayyid, due to it being an established attribute of the Prophet (sallallaahu 'alaihi wa sallam), or leaving it out due to the absence of it in the narrations?

He (Ibn Hajr), may Allaah be pleased with him, replied:

> "Yes, to follow the narrated wording is superior. It cannot be said, "Maybe the Prophet (sallallaahu 'alaihi wa sallam) himself did not say it out of modesty, just as he did not say (sallallaahu 'alaihi wa sallam) on mention of his name, although his ummah has been encouraged to do so" - for we say that if that were superior, it would have been quoted from the Companions and then from the Successors, but we do not come across it in any narrations from any Companion or Successor. This is despite the volume of quotations from them. We have Imaam Shaafi'i, may Allaah exalt his rank, one of the foremost among men in his respect for the Prophet (sallallaahu 'alaihi wa sallam), saying in the preface to his book which is a base for the people of his madhhab: "O Allaah! send prayers on Muhammad ..." etc. until the end of what his judgment dictated, "... every time one of the rememberers remembers him, and every time one of the heedless fails to remember him", which he seems to have deduced from the authentic hadeeth which has in it that the Prophet (sallallaahu 'alaihi wa sallam) saw the Mother of the Believers engaging in long and numerous glorifications, so he said to her, "You have said words which, if weighed against the following, would be balanced: Glorified be Allaah, as many times as the number of His creation"; he (sallallaahu 'alaihi wa

[1]which is preserved in the Zaahiriyyah Library in Damascus.

sallam) used to like supplications which were concise, but exhaustive in meaning.

Qaadi 'Iyaad set out a chapter about salaah on the Prophet (sallallaahu 'alaihi wa sallam) in his book *ash-Shifaa'* (The Book of Cure), quoting in it narrations from the Prophet (sallallaahu 'alaihi wa sallam) on the authority of several Companions and Successors; in none of these is the word sayyid reported:

a) The hadith of 'Ali, that he used to teach them the manner of salaah on the Prophet (sallallaahu 'alaihi wa sallam) by saying, *O Allaah, Spreader of Plains, Originator of Heights, send the foremost of Your prayers, the most fertile of Your blessings, and any remaining compliments, on Muhammad, Your slave and messenger, the opener of what is closed.*

b) Again from 'Ali, that he used to say, "The prayers of Allaah, the Beneficent, the Merciful, of the Angels nearest (to Allaah), of the Prophets, of the Sincere ones, of the Witnesses, of the Righteous, and of whatever glorifies You, O Lord of the Worlds, be on Muhammad son of 'Abdullaah, Seal of the Prophets, Imaam of the Godfearers, ... etc."

c) On the authority of 'Abdullaah ibn Mas'ood, that he used to say, "O Allaah! send Your prayers, Your blessings and Your mercy, on Muhammad, Your slave and messenger, the imaam of goodness, the messenger of mercy, ..." etc.

d) From al-Hasan al-Basri, that he used to say, "Whoever wants to drink from the cup which quenches, from the fount of the al-Mustafaa, should say: O Allaah! send prayers on Muhammad, and on his family, his Companions, his wives, his children, his descendants, his household, his in-laws, his helpers, his followers, and all those who love him."

This is what he (Qaadi 'Iyaad) has written in *ash-Shifaa'*, regarding the manner of salaah on the Prophet, on the authority of the Companions and those who succeeded them, and he also mentioned other things in it.

Yes, it is related in a hadeeth of Ibn Mas'ood that in his salaah on the Prophet (sallallaahu 'alaihi wa sallam), he would say, "O Allaah! send the best of Your prayers, mercy and blessings on the leader (sayyid) of the messengers ..." etc., transmitted by Ibn Maajah, but its isnaad is weak, so the hadeeth of 'Ali, transmitted by Tabaraani with a acceptable isnaad, takes precedence. This hadeeth has difficult words, which I have reported and explained in the book *Fadl an-Nabi* (Excellence of the Prophet (sallallaahu 'alaihi wa sallam)") by Abul Hasan ibn al-Faaris. Some Shaafi'is have said that if a man took an oath to send the best salaah on the Prophet (sallallaahu 'alaihi wa sallam), the way to fulfil his oath would be to say, "O Allaah! send prayers on Muhammad every time the rememberers remember him or the heedless fail to remember him"; Nawawi said, "The one which is most fitting to be designated as correct is that one should say: O Allaah! send prayers on Muhammad, and on the family of Muhammad, as you sent prayers on Ibraaheem ..."

Several of the later scholars have replied to this by saying that in neither of the two ways mentioned above is there anything to prove which is superior as regards narration, but as regards the meaning, then the former is clearly superior.

This issue is well-known in the books of fiqh, and of all the scholars of fiqh who addressed this issue, without exception, in none of their words does the word *sayyid* appear. Had this additional word been commendable, it would not have escaped all of them, leaving them ignorant of it. All good is in following what is narrated, and Allaah knows best."

Ibn Hajr's view of the unacceptability of describing the Prophet (sallallaahu 'alaihi wa sallam) as *sayyid* during the salaah on him in accordance with the Qur'aanic order, is also that of the Hanafi scholars. It is the view which must be adhered to, for it is a true indication of love for him, (sallallaahu 'alaihi wa sallam);

$$\text{قُلۡ إِن كُنتُمۡ تُحِبُّونَ ٱللَّهَ فَٱتَّبِعُونِي يُحۡبِبۡكُمُ ٱللَّهُ}$$

"Say: If you do love Allaah, then follow me: Allaah will love you." (aal-'Imraan 3:31)

Because of this, Imaam Nawawi said in *Rawdah at-Taalibeen* (1/265), "The most complete salaah on the Prophet (sallallaahu 'alaihi wa sallam) is: O Allaah! send your prayers on Muhammad ..." etc., corresponding to type no. 3 given, in which there is no mention of *sayyid*!

4) It should be known that types nos. 1 and 4 are the ones which the Messenger of Allaah (sallallaahu 'alaihi wa sallam) taught his Companions when they asked about the manner of salaah on him, so this has been used as evidence that these are the best ways of doing the salaah on him, for he would not choose anything for them or himself except the best and noblest. Imaam Nawawi, as mentioned, endorsed (in *Rawdah at-Taalibeen*) that if a man were to take an oath to do the best possible salaah on the Prophet (sallallaahu 'alaihi wa sallam), this could not be fulfilled except in these ways.

Subki has given another reason: whoever does salaah with those types has made salaah on the Prophet (sallallaahu 'alaihi wa sallam) with certainty, and whoever does so with other words is in doubt whether or not he has performed the prayers as requested. This is because they said, "How do we send prayers on you?" and he replied, "Say: ...", thus defining their salaah on him as their saying such-and-such. This was mentioned by Haitami in *ad-Darr al-Mandood* (25/2); he then said (27/1) that the objective is achieved with all the types which have occurred in authentic ahaadeeth.

5) It should be known that it is not valid to combine all these way into one way of salaah, and the same goes for the different tashahhuds given previously. In

fact, that would be an innovation in the religion; the Sunnah is to say different ones at different times, as Shaikh-ul-Islaam Ibn Taymiyyah has explained in his discussion of the takbeers of the two 'Eids (*Majmoo' al-Fataawaa* 29/253/1).

6) 'Allaamah Siddeeq Hasan Khaan says in his book *Nuzul al-Abraar bil 'Ilm al-Ma'thoor min al-Ad'iyah wal-Adhkaar*, after giving many ahaadeeth about the excellence of repeated salaah on the Prophet (sallallaahu 'alaihi wa sallam) (p. 161):

"There is no doubt that the foremost among the Muslims in sending salaah on him (sall-Allaahu 'alaihi wa sallam) are the People of Hadeeth and the narrators of the purified Sunnah, for it is one of their duties in this noble branch of learning to make salaah on him before every hadeeth, and so their tongues are always engaged in his mention, may Allah grant him mercy and peace. There is no book of Sunnah or collection of hadeeth, be it a *jaami'*, *musnad*, *mu'jam*, *juz'*, etc., except that it comprises thousands of ahaadeeth; even one of the least bulky ones, Suyooti's *al-Jaami' as-Sagheer*, contains ten thousand ahaadeeth, and the rest of the collections are no different. So this is the Saved Sect: the body of the People of Hadeeth, who will be the closest among men to the Messenger of Allaah (sallallaahu 'alaihi wa sallam) on the Day of Resurrection, and the most likely to be rewarded by his intercession (sallallaahu 'alaihi wa sallam), may my mother and father be sacrificed for him! This excellence of the People of Hadeeth cannot be surpassed by anyone unless he does more than what they do, something which is well-nigh impossible. Therefore, O desirer of good, seeker of salvation, no matter what, you should either be a muhaddith, or be close to the muhaddatheen; do not be otherwise ... for apart from that there is nothing which will benefit you."

I ask Allaah, Blessed and Exalted, to make me one of these People of Hadeeth, who are the closest among men to the Messenger of Allaah (sallallaahu 'alaihi wa sallam); perhaps this book will be a testimony to that. May Allaah shower His mercy on Imaam Ahmad, who recited:

The religion of Muhammad is in narrations,
    The best mounts for a young man are the traditions;
Turn not away from Hadeeth and its people,
    For Opinion is night, while Hadeeth is day,
A young man can be ignorant of the guidance ...
    Although the sun is shining in all its splendour !

Du'aa' in the First Tashahhud

He (sallallaahu 'alaihi wa sallam) also set the guidance of du'aa in this tashahhud as well, saying, *When you sit after every two rak'ahs, then say: All compliments are due to Allaah ...* (till the end of that supplication, and then said:) ... *then he should select of the supplications what is most pleasing to him.*[1]

Standing up for the Third, and then the Fourth, Rak'ah

Next, he (sallallaahu 'alaihi wa sallam) would get up for the third rak'ah with takbeer[2], and he ordered "the one who prayed badly" to do so: *Then do that in every rak'ah*, as before.

"When he (sallallaahu 'alaihi wa sallam) stood from the sitting position, he would say takbeer, and then stand up"[3]; and "he (sallallaahu 'alaihi wa sallam) would raise his hands"[4] with this takbeer sometimes.

"When he wanted to stand up for the fourth rak'ah, he would say: *Allaah is the Greatest*"[5], and he ordered "the one who prayed badly" likewise, as before, and "he (sallallaahu 'alaihi wa sallam) would raise his hands"[6] with this takbeer sometimes.

"He would sit up straight on his left foot, at ease, until every bone returned to its proper place, then stand up, supporting himself on the ground; and he would clench his fists[7]: supporting himself with his hands when standing up."[8]

He would recite *al-Faatihah* in both these rak'ahs, and he ordered "the one who prayed badly" to do that. In Zuhr prayer, he would sometimes add a few aayaat to this, as has been explained under "Recitation in Zuhr Prayer".

---

[1] Nasaa'i, Ahmad & Tabaraani with various isnaads from Ibn Mas'ood - the details are given in *as-Saheehah* (878) - and there is a supporting hadeeth of Ibn az-Zubair in *Majma' az-Zawaa'id* (2/142).

[2] Bukhaari & Muslim.

[3] Abu Ya'laa in his Musnad (284/2) with a good isnaad. It is given in *Silsilah al-Ahaadeeth as-Saheehah* (604).

[4] Bukhaari & Abu Daawood.

[5] ibid.

[6] Abu 'Awaanah & Nasaa'i with a saheeh sanad.

[7] literally, "as one who kneads dough."

[8] Harbi in *Ghareeb al-Hadeeth*; its meaning is found in Bukhaari and Abu Daawood. As for the hadeeth, he forbade that a man should support himself with his hand when getting up during prayer", it is *munkar* and not authentic, as I have explained in *Silsilah al-Ahaadeeth ad-Da'eefah* (967).

Qunoot in the Five Prayers because of a Calamity

"When he (sallallaahu 'alaihi wa sallam) wanted to supplicate against someone, or supplicate for someone, he would perform qunoot[1] in the last rak'ah, after rukoo'; after having said: *Allaah listens to the one who praises Him*.[2] "He would supplicate loudly"[3], "raise his hands"[4], and "those behind him would say: aameen"[5].

"He was known to perform qunoot in all five prayers"[6], although "he would only perform qunoot in them when he supplicated for a people or supplicated against a people"[7]. For example, he once said, *O Allaah! rescue al-Waleed ibn al-Waleed, and Salamah ibn Hishaam, and 'Ayyaash ibn Abi Rabee'ah. O Allaah! harden Your penalty on (the tribe of) Mudar, and cause for it years (of famine) like the years of Yoosuf. [O Allaah! curse Lahyaan, and Ru'l, and Dhakwaan, and 'Usayyah, who disobeyed Allaah and His Messenger!]*[8]

Then, "he would say: *Allaah is the Greatest* when he had finished qunoot and prostrate."[9]

Qunoot in Witr Prayer

"He (sallallaahu 'alaihi wa sallam) used to perform qunoot in the (odd) rak'ah of the Witr prayer"[10] sometimes[11], and "he would perform it before rukoo'."[12]

---

[1]*Qunoot*: carries several meanings, e.g. humility, devotion. What is meant here is the special supplication while standing during prayer.
[2]Bukhaari & Ahmad.
[3]ibid.
[4]Ahmad & Tabaraani with a saheeh sanad. To raise the hands in qunoot is the madhhab of Ahmad and also Ishaaq bin Raahawaih, cf. Marwazi's *Masaa'il* (p. 23). As for wiping the face with the hands, it is not reported in this position, and is thus an innovation; as for outside of prayer, it is not authentically-reported: all that has been transmitted in this regard is either weak or very weak, as I have shown in *Da'eef Abi Daawood* (262) & *Silsilah al-Ahaadeeth as-Saheehah* (597). This is why 'Izz bin 'Abd as-Salaam said in one of his fatwas, "Only an ignorant person does it." See Appendix 8.
[5]Abu Daawood & Siraaj ; Haakim declared it saheeh, and Dhahabi & others agreed.
[6]Abu Daawood, Siraaj & Daaraqutni with two hasan sanads.
[7]Ibn Khuzaimah in his Saheeh (1/78/2) & Khateeb in *Kitaab al-Qunoot* with a saheeh sanad.
[8]Bukhaari & Ahmad; the addition is in Muslim.
[9]Nasaa'i, Ahmad, Siraaj (109/1) & Abu Ya'laa in his Musnad with a good sanad.
[10]Ibn Nasr & Daaraqutni with a saheeh sanad.
[11]We have said, "... sometimes" because the Companions who narrated the Witr prayer did not mention the qunoot in it, whereas had the Prophet (sallallaahu 'alaihi wa sallam) done so always, they would have all mentioned it. However, Ubayy ibn Ka'b alone narrated the qunoot in Witr, so this shows that he used to do it sometimes. Hence, this is evidence that qunoot in Witr is not obligatory (waajib), and this is the opinion of the majority of scholars. For this reason, the researching Hanafi scholar, Ibn al-Humaam, recognised in *Fath at-Qadeer* (1/306,359,360) that the view of it being obligatory is feeble and not substantiated by evidence. This shows his fairness and lack of party-spirit, for this view which he has supported is contrary to his madhhab !

He taught al-Hasan ibn 'Ali (radi Allaahu 'anhu) to say [after finishing his recitation in Witr]:

اللّهُمَّ أهْدِني فِيمَنْ هَدَيْتَ، وَعَافِني فِيمَنْ عَافَيْتَ، وَتَوَلَّني فِيمَنْ تَوَلَّيْتَ، وَبَارِكْ لِي فِيمَا أعْطَيْتَ؛ وَقِني شَرَّ قَضَيْتَ، [فَ] إنَّكَ تَقْضِي وَلاَ يُقْضى عَلَيْكَ، [وَ] إنَّهُ لاَ يَذِلُّ مَنْ وَالَيْتَ، [وَلاَ يَعِزُّ مَنْ عَادَيْتَ]، تَبَارَكْتَ رَبَّنَا وَتَعَالَيْتَ. [لاَ مَنْجَا مِنْكَ إلاَّ إلَيْكَ]

"O Allaah! guide me among those whom You have guided; and pardon me among those who You have pardoned; and turn on me in friendship among those on whom You have turned in friendship; and bless me in what You have bestowed; and save me from the evil of what You have decreed; [for] indeed You decree, and none can influence You; [and] he is not humiliated whom You have befriended; [nor is he honoured who is Your enemy.] Blessed are You, O Lord, and Exalted. [There is no place of safety from You except towards You.]"[1]

[12]Ibn Abi Shaibah (12/41/1), Abu Daawood, Nasaa'i in *Sunan al-Kubraa* (218/1-2), Ahmad, Tabaraani, Baihaqi & Ibn 'Asaakir (4/244/2) narrated this, along with the supplication after it, with a *saheeh* sanad. Ibn Mandah narrated the supplication only in *Tawheed* (70/2) with a different, hasan sanad. Its *takhreej* is also given in *Irwaa'* (426).

[1]Ibn Khuzaimah (1/119/2) & also Ibn Abi Shaibah etc., as for the last hadeeth.

*NB: Nasaa'i adds at the end of the qunoot: *wa sall-Allaahu 'ala-n-Nabiyy al-Ummiyy* ("may Allaah send prayers on the Unlettered Prophet"), related with a weak isnaad; among those who declared it da'eef are Ibn Hajar al-'Asqalaani & Zurqaani. Therefore, we have not included it in our system of combining acceptable narrations. 'Izz bin 'Abd as-Salaam said in *al-Fataawaa* (66/1,1962), "To send prayers on the Messenger of Allaah (sallallaahu 'alaihi wa sallam) in qunoot is not authentic, nor is it fitting to add to the Messenger of Allaah (sallallaahu 'alaihi wa sallam)'s prayer in any way." This view of his shows that he did not widen the argument by including the idea of bid'ah hasanah ("good" innovation), as some of the later scholars are prone to doing !

However, it is proved in the hadeeth about Ubayy bin Ka'b leading the people during the Ramadaan night prayers that he used to send prayers on the Prophet (sallallaahu 'alaihi wa sallam) at the end of the qunoot, and that was during the reign of 'Umar (radi Allaahu 'anhu) - transmitted by Ibn Khuzaimah in his Saheeh (1097). Similarly is proved from Abu Haleemah Mu'aadh al-Ansaari, who also used to lead them during 'Umar's rule - transmitted by Ismaa'eel al-Qaadi (no. 107) & others, so this addition is justified by the practice of the Salaf, and it is thus not fitting to categorically state that this addition is an innovation. Allaah knows best.

THE FINAL TASHAHHUD

The Obligation of this Tashahhud

Next, after completing the fourth rak'ah, he (sallallaahu 'alaihi wa sallam) would sit for the last tashahhud. He would instruct regarding it, and do in it, just as he did in the first tashahhud, except that "he would sit *mutawarrikan*"[1], "with his left upper thigh on the ground, and both his feet protruding from one (i.e. the right) side."[2] "He would have his left foot under his (right) thigh and shin"[3], "his right foot upright"[4] or occasionally "he would lay it along the ground."[5] "His left palm would cover his (left) knee, leaning heavily on it."[6]

He set the example of sending prayers on him (sallallaahu 'alaihi wa sallam) in this tashahhud, as in the first tashahhud; the ways of sending prayer on him (sallallaahu 'alaihi wa sallam) narrated have been given in that section.

The Obligation of Sending Prayers on the Prophet (sallallaahu 'alaihi wa sallam) in this Tashahhud

Once, "he (sallallaahu 'alaihi wa sallam) heard a man supplicating in his prayer without glorifying the majesty of Allaah Exalted, nor sending prayers on the Prophet (sallallaahu 'alaihi wa sallam), so he said: *This man has been hasty.*" He then called him and said to him and others, "*When one of you prays, he should begin with the praise of his Lord, Sublime and Mighty, and his exultation, and then send prayers* (in one narration: *he should send prayers*) *on the Prophet (sallallaahu 'alaihi wa sallam), and then supplicate as he wishes.*"[7]

Also, "he heard a man glorifying and praising Allaah, and sending prayers on the Prophet (sallallaahu 'alaihi wa sallam) in prayer, so the Messenger of Allaah

---

[1]Bukhaari .
[2]ibid. As for two-rak'ah prayers such as Fajr, the Sunnah is to sit *muftarishan*. This difference in detail is documented from Imaam Ahmad, cf. Ibn Hani's *Masaa'il of Imaam Ahmad* (p. 79).
[3]Abu Daawood & Baihaqi with a saheeh sanad.
[4]Muslim & Abu 'Awaanah.
[5]ibid.
[6]ibid.
[7]Ahmad, Abu Daawood, Ibn Khuzaimah (1/83/2) & al-Haakim   , who declared it saheeh and Dhahabi agreed.

It should be known that this hadeeth proves that salaah (sending prayers) on the Prophet (sallallaahu 'alaihi wa sallam) in this tashahhud is obligatory, due to the command about it. This opinion was taken by Imaam Shaafi'i and by Imaam Ahmad in the later of the two narrations from him, and before them by several Companions, as well as other people of knowledge. Because of this, Aajuri said in *Sharee'ah* (p. 415): "He who does not send prayers on the Prophet (sallallaahu 'alaihi wa sallam) in the final tashahhud must repeat the prayer." Hence, those who label Imaam Shaafi'i as being alone and odd in his opinion on this, are not being just, as the faqeeh Haitami has explained in *Darr al-Mandood* (sections 13-16).

(sallallaahu 'alaihi wa sallam) said to him: *Supplicate, and you will be answered; ask, and you will be given."*[1]

The Obligation to Seek Refuge from Four Things before Supplicating

He (sallallaahu 'alaihi wa sallam) used to say, "*When one of you has finished the [last] tashahhud, he should seek refuge with Allaah from four things; [saying:*

اَللّٰهُمَّ إِنِّي أَعُوذُ بِكَ مِنْ عَذَابِ جَهَنَّمَ، وَمِنْ عَذَابِ الْقَبْرِ، وَمِنْ فِتْنَةِ الْمَحْيَا وَالْمَمَاتِ، وَمِنْ شَرِّ [فِتْنَةِ] الْمَسِيحِ الدَّجَّالِ

O Allaah! I truly seek refuge with You] from the punishment of Hellfire, and from the punishment of the grave, and from the trials of living and dying, and from the evil [trials] of the False Christ. [Then he should supplicate for himself with what occurs to him.]"[2] - "He (sallallaahu 'alaihi wa sallam) would supplicate with it in his own tashahhud."[3]

Also, "he used to teach the Companions (radi Allaahu 'anhum) this the way he taught them Soorahs of the Qur'aan."[4]

Supplication before the *Salaam*, & its various types

He (sallallaahu 'alaihi wa sallam) used to use different supplications in his prayer[5], supplicating with different ones at different times; he also endorsed other supplications, and "ordered the worshipper to select of them what he wishes."[6] They are:

---

[1]Nasaa'i with a saheeh sanad.
[2]Muslim, Abu 'Awaanah, Nasaa'i & Ibn al-Jaarood in *al-Muntaqaa* (27). It is given in Irwaa' (350).
[3]Abu Daawood & Ahmad with a saheeh sanad.
[4]Muslim & Abu 'Awaanah.
[5]We have not said, "... in his tashahhud" because the text is "... in his prayer", not specifying either tashahhud or anything else. Hence, it covers all positions suitable for supplication, e.g. prostration and tashahhud; the instruction to supplicate in these two postures has been mentioned.
[6]Bukhaari & Muslim. Athram said, "I asked Ahmad: 'With what (words) should I supplicate after tashahhud ?' He said, 'As has been narrated.' I said, 'Didn't the Messenger of Allaah (sallallaahu 'alaihi wa sallam) say, "Then he should select whichever supplication he likes" ?' He said, 'He should select out of what has been narrated.' I repeated the question: he said, 'From what has been narrated'." This was quoted by Ibn Taymiyyah (*Majmoo' al-Fataawaa* 69/218/1), who endorsed it, adding, "Hence, 'whichever supplication' refers to the supplications which Allaah loves, not to any supplication ..."; later he said, "Hence, it is best to say: (one should supplicate) with the approved, established supplications, and these are what have been narrated and those that are beneficial." This is so, but to recognise which supplications are indeed beneficial depends on authentic knowledge, and this is rarely found among the people, so it is best to stick to the supplications quoted, especially when they include what the worshipper wishes to request. Allaah knows best.

1-

اَللَّهُمَّ إِنِّي أَعُوذُ بِكَ مِنْ عَذَابِ الْقَبْرِ، وأَعُوذُ بِكَ مِنْ فِتْنَةِ الْمَسِيحِ الدَّجَّالِ، وأَعُوذُ بِكَ مِنْ فِتْنَةِ الْمَحْيَا وَالْمَمَاتِ، اَللَّهُمَّ إِنِّي أَعُوذُ بِكَ مِنَ الْمَأْثَمِ وَالْمَغْرَمِ

"O Allaah! truly I seek refuge with You from the punishment of the grave, and I seek refuge with you from the trials of the False Christ, and I seek refuge with You from the trials of living and dying. O Allaah! truly I seek refuge with You from sin[1] and burden[2]."[3]

2-

اَللَّهُمَّ إِنِّي أَعُوذُ بِكَ مِنْ شَرِّ مَا عَمِلْتُ، وَمِنْ شَرِّ مَا لَمْ أَعْمَلْ [بَعْدُ]

"O Allaah! truly I seek refuge with You from the evil of what I have done, and from the evil of what I have not done[4] [yet]."[5]

3-

اَللَّهُمَّ حَاسِبْنِي حِسَاباً يَسِيراً

"O Allaah! call me to account with an easy reckoning."[6]

4-

اَللَّهُمَّ بِعِلْمِكَ الْغَيْبَ، وَقُدْرَتِكَ عَلَى الْخَلْقِ، أَحْيِنِي مَا عَلِمْتَ الْحَيَاةَ خَيْراً لِي، وَتَوَفَّنِي إِذَا كَانَتِ الْوَفَاةُ خَيْرٌ لِي، اَللَّهُمَّ وَأَسْأَلُكَ خَشْيَتَكَ فِي الْغَيْبِ وَالشَّهَادَةِ، وَأَسْأَلُكَ كَلِمَةَ الْحَقِّ (وفي رواية: الحُكْمِ)، وَالْعَدْلَ فِي الْغَضَبِ وَالرِّضَى، وَأَسْأَلُكَ الْقَصْدَ فِي الْفَقْرِ وَالْغِنَى، وَأَسْأَلُكَ نَعِيماً لاَ يَبِيدُ، وَأَسْأَلُكَ قُرَّةَ عَيْنٍ [لاَ تَنْفَذُ، وَ] لاَ تَنْقَطِعُ، وَأَسْأَلُكَ الرِّضَى بَعْدَ الْقَضَاءِ، وَأَسْأَلُكَ بَرْدَ الْعَيْشِ بَعْدَ الْمَوْتِ، وَأَسْأَلُكَ لَذَّةَ النَّظَرِ إِلَى وَجْهِكَ، وَ[أَسْأَلُكَ] الشَّوْقَ إِلَى لِقَائِكَ، فِي غَيْرِ ضَرَّاءَ مُضِرَّةٍ، وَلاَ فِتْنَةٍ مُضِلَّةٍ، اَللَّهُمَّ زَيِّنَّا بِزِينَةِ الْأِيمَانِ، وَاجْعَلْنَا هُدَاةً مُهْتَدِينَ

---

[1]ma'tham: what causes a man to sin, or the sin itself.
[2]maghram: burden; here it means debt, as proved by the rest of the hadeeth, in which 'Aa'ishah said, "Someone said to him, 'Why do you seek refuge from maghram, so often, O Messenger of Allaah ?' He replied, *Truly, when a man becomes indebted, he speaks and lies, and he promises and breaks his promise.*
[3]Bukhaari & Muslim.
[4]i.e. from the evil of the bad actions I have done, and from the evil of not doing good actions.
[5]Nasaa'i with a saheeh sanad & Ibn Abi 'Aasim in his *as-Sunnah* (no. 370 - with my checking); the addition is from the latter.
[6]Ahmad & Haakim who declared it saheeh and Dhahabi agreed.

"O Allaah! [I ask you], by Your knowledge of the Unseen, and Your control over the creation: give me life as long as You know that life is best for me, and take me when death is best for me. O Allaah! I also ask of You fear of You, in secret and in open; I ask of You the word of Truth (in one narration: Wisdom) and justice in anger and in pleasure; I ask of You moderation in poverty and affluence; I ask of You joy which does not fade; I ask of You pleasure [which does not pass away, nor that] which ceases; I ask of You contentment with Your decree; I ask of You coolness of life after death; I ask of You the delight of looking towards Your Face; and [I ask of You] eagerness towards meeting You, not in harmful adversity, nor in misleading afflictions. O Allaah! adorn us with the decoration of eemaan, and make us those who guide and are guided.[1]

5- He taught Abu Bakr as-Siddeeq (radi Allaahu 'anhu) to say:

اللَّهُمَّ إِنِّي ظَلَمْتُ نَفْسِي ظُلْماً كَثِيراً، وَلاَ يَغْفِرُ الذُّنُوبَ إِلاَّ أَنْتَ، فَاغْفِرْ لِي مَغْفِرَةً مِنْ عِنْدِكَ، وَارْحَمْنِي نَّكَ أَنْتَ الْغَفُورُ الرَّحِيمُ

"O Allaah! indeed I have wronged myself greatly, and none can forgive sins except You, so forgive me out of Your forgiveness, and have mercy on me. Truly, You are the Oft-Forgiving, the Most Merciful."[2]

6- He instructed 'Aa'ishah (radi Allaahu 'anhaa) to say:

اللَّهُمَّ إِنِّي أَسْأَلُكَ مِنَ الْخَيْرِ كُلِّهِ [عَاجِلِهِ وَآجِلِهِ] مَا عَلِمْتُ مِنْهُ وَمَا لَمْ أَعْلَمْ، وَأَعُوذُ بِكَ مِنَ الشَّرِّ كُلِّهِ، عَاجِلِهِ وَآجِلِهِ] مَا عَلِمْتُ مِنْهُ وَمَا لَمْ أَعْلَمْ، وَأَسْأَلُكَ (وَفِي رِوَايَةٍ: اَللَّهُمَّ إِنِّي أَسْأَلُكَ) الْجَنَّةَ وَمَا قَرَّبَ إِلَيْهَا نْ قَوْلٍ أَوْ عَمَلٍ، وَأَعُوذُ بِكَ مِنَ النَّارِ وَمَا قَرَّبَ إِلَيْهَا مِنْ قَوْلٍ أَوْ عَمَلٍ، وَأَسْأَلُكَ (وَفِي رِوَايَةٍ: اَللَّهُمَّ إِنِّي سْأَلُكَ) مِنْ [الـ] خَيْرِ مَا سَأَلَكَ عَبْدُكَ وَرَسُولُكَ [مُحَمَّدٌ، وَأَعُوذُ بِكَ مِنْ شَرِّ مَا اسْتَعَاذَكَ مِنْهُ عَبْدُكَ رَسُولُكَ مُحَمَّدٌ صَلَّى اللَّهُ عَلَيْهِ وَسَلَّمَ]، [وَأَسْأَلُكَ] مَا قَضَيْتَ لِي مِنْ أَمْرٍ أَنْ تَجْعَلَ عَاقِبَتَهُ [إِلِي] رُشْداً

"O Allaah! indeed I ask of You all Good, [the imminent and the far-off,] that of it which I know and that which I do not know. I seek refuge with You from all Evil, [the imminent and the far-off,] that of it which I know and that which I do not know. I ask of You (in one narration: O Allaah! indeed I ask of You) the Garden, and whatever saying or deed which brings one near to it; I seek refuge with You from the Fire, and (from) whatever saying or deed which brings one near to it. I ask of You (in one narration: O Allaah! indeed I ask of You) [the] good of what was asked of You by Your slave and messenger [Muhammad; and I seek refuge with You from evil of what Your slave and messenger Muhammad

---

[1] Nasaa'i & al-Haakim who declared it saheeh and Dhahabi agreed.
[2] Bukhaari & Muslim.

(sallallaahu 'alaihi wa sallam) sought refuge with You]. [I ask of You] that whatever You have decreed for me, its result [for me] be beneficial.[1]

7- He said to a man, *What do you say during the prayer?* He replied, "I bear witness (i.e. do the tashahhud), then I ask Allaah for the Garden, and I seek refuge with Him from the Fire. However, by Allaah, there is no murmuring[2] as good as yours or that of Mu'aadh." So he said, *Our murmuring is like yours.*[3]

8- He heard a man saying in his tashahhud:

اَللّٰهُمَّ إِنِّي أَسْأَلُكَ يَا اَللّٰهُ (وفي رواية: بِاللّٰهِ) [اَلْوَاحِدُ] الأَحَدُ الصَّمَدُ الَّذِي لَمْ يَلِدْ وَلَمْ يُولَدْ وَلَمْ يَكُنْ كُفُواً أَحَدٌ – أَنْ تَغْفِرَ لِي ذُنُوبِي إِنَّكَ أَنْتَ الْغَفُورُ الرَّحِيمُ.

"O Allaah! indeed I ask of You, O Allaah (in one narration: by Allaah), the One, the Only, the Absolute, Who begets not and nor is He begotten, and there is none like Him, that You forgive me my sins; indeed You are the Oft-Forgiving, Most Merciful.

On this, he (sallallaahu 'alaihi wa sallam) said, *He has been forgiven, he has been forgiven.*[4]

9- He heard another man say in his tashahhud:

اَللّٰهُمَّ إِنِّي أَسْأَلُكَ بِأَنَّ لَكَ الْحَمْدُ، لاَ إِلٰهَ إِلاَّ أَنْتَ [وَحْدَكَ لاَ شَرِيكَ لَكَ]، [اَلْمَنَّانُ]، [يَا] بَدِيعَ السَّمَاوَاتِ وَالأَرْضِ، يَا ذَا الْجَلاَلِ وَالاِكْرَامِ، يَا حَيُّ يَا قَيُّومُ [إِنِّي أَسْأَلُكَ] [الْجَنَّةَ وَأَعُوذُ بِكَ مِنَ النَّارِ]

"O Allaah! Indeed, I ask of You, by the fact that to You belongs all Praise; there is no (true) god except You, [You alone, You have no partners;] the Bestower of Favours; [O] Originator of the Heavens and the Earth; O One that is Full of Majesty and Honour; O Living One, O Eternal One; [indeed I ask of You] [the Garden, and I seek refuge with You from the Fire]. [So the Prophet (sallallaahu 'alaihi wa sallam) said to his Companions, *Do you know with what he has supplicated?* They said, "Allaah and His Messenger know best." He said, *By Him in Whose Hand is my soul,*] he has supplicated Allaah with His Mighty (in one

---

[1] Ahmad, Tayaalisi, Bukhaari in *al-Adab al-Mufrad*, Ibn Maajah & Haakim who declared it saheeh and Dhahabi agreed. I have given its takhreej in *Silsilah al-Ahaadeeth as-Saheehah* (1542).
[2] *dandanah*: to speak such the intonation is audible, but the words are incomprehensible - in the case, the quiet words of supplication. The final statement means, "Our words are like yours."
[3] Abu Daawood, Ibn Maajah & Ibn Khuzaimah (1/87/1) with a saheeh isnaad.
[4] Abu Daawood, Nasaa'i, Ahmad & Ibn Khuzaimah; Haakim declared it saheeh and Dhahabi agreed.

narration: Mightiest) name[1], with which if He is supplicated, He answers, and with which if He is asked, He gives.[2]

10- One of the last things he would say between the tashahhud and the tasleem would be:

اَللّٰهُمَّ اغْفِرْ لِي مَا قَدَّمْتُ، وَمَا أَخَّرْتُ، وَمَا أَسْرَرْتُ، وَمَا أَعْلَنْتُ، وَمَا أَسْرَفْتُ، وَمَا أَنْتَ أَعْلَمُ بِهِ مِنِّي، أَنْتَ الْمُقَدِّمُ، وَأَنْتَ الْمُؤَخِّرُ، لَا إِلهَ إِلاَّ أَنْتَ

"O Allaah! Forgive me what I have done in the past, and what I will do in the future, and what I have concealed, and what I have done openly, and what I have exceeded in, whatever You know about more know than I. You are the Bringer-Forward, and You are the Delayer, there is no (true) god except You."[3]

THE *TASLEEM* (SALUTATION OF PEACE)

Next, "he (sallallaahu 'alaihi wa sallam) would salute to his right:

اَلسَّلَامُ عَلَيْكُمْ وَرَحْمَةُ اللّٰه

Peace and Allaah's Mercy be on you [such that the whiteness of his right cheek was visible,], and on his left:

اَلسَّلَامُ عَلَيْكُمْ وَرَحْمَةُ اللّٰه

---

[1]This is *tawassul* (a seeking of approach) to Allaah through His most beautiful names and attributes, and this is what Allaah the Exalted commands: **"To Allaah belong the most beautiful names, so call on Him by them."** (A'raaf 7:180). As for seeking to approaching Allaah through other things, e.g. for so-and-so's sake, or by so-and-so's right, status, dignity, etc., there is text from Imaam Abu Haneefah (rahimahullaah) and his companions that such a practice is at least disliked (makrooh); in general it is prohibited (haraam). Therefore, it is a pity that one sees most of the people, among them many shaikhs, totally neglecting the approved tawassul, - you will never hear them approaching Allaah this way - but they are well-versed in innovated forms of tawassul, which are at the very least debatable, as though no other way is allowed! Shaikh-ul-Islaam Ibn Taymiyyah has composed an extremely good essay on this subject entitled *Tawassul and Waseelah* ("Approaching Allaah, and the Means of doing so"), which should be consulted, for it is very important, and there is little to compare with it in its coverage. There is also my article *Tawassul - its types and its rules*, which is also important in its subject-matter and format, and also refutes some of the latest misconceptions advanced by contemporary doctors of religion. May Allaah guide us and them.
[2]Abu Daawood, Nasaa'i, Ahmad, Bukhaari in *al-Adab al-Mufrad*, Tabaraani & Ibn Mandah in *Tawheed* (44/2, 67/1, 70/1-2) with saheeh isnaads.
[3]Muslim & Abu 'Awaanah.

Peace and Allaah's Mercy be on you [such that the whiteness of his left cheek was visible]."1

Sometimes, he would add to the greeting on the right:

وَبَرَكَاتُهُ

*... and His blessings (be on you).*2

"When he said:

اَلسَّلَامُ عَلَيْكُمْ وَرَحْمَةُ اللَّهِ

Peace and Allaah's Mercy be on you to his right, he would sometimes shorten the greeting on his left to:

اَلسَّلَامُ عَلَيْكُمْ

*Peace be on you.*3

Sometimes, "he would salute once only, [اَلسَّلَامُ عَلَيْكُمْ

Peace be on you] [in front of his face, turning to his right side a bit,] [or a little]."4

"They used to gesture with their hands when saluting to the right and left; when the Messenger of Allaah (sallallaahu 'alaihi wa sallam) saw them, he said, '*What is the matter with you, gesturing with your hands as if they are the tails of wild horses?! When one of you salutes, he should look towards his companion and not indicate with his hand.*' [So when they prayed with him, they did not gesture.] (In one narration: *It is enough for each of you to place his hand on his thigh, and then salute his brothers who are on his right and left*).5

1Abu Daawood, Nasaa'i & Tirmidhi, who declared it saheeh.
2Abu Daawood & Ibn Khuzaimah (1/87/2) with a saheeh sanad. 'Abdul Haqq also declared it saheeh in his *Ahkaam* (56/2), as did Nawawi & Ibn Hajar. It was also transmitted via another route by 'Abdur Razzaaq in his Musannaf (2/219), Abu Ya'laa in his Musnad (3/1253), Tabaraani in *Mu'jam al-Kabeer* (3/67/2) and *Mu'jam al-Awsat* (no. 4476 - my numbering) & Daaraqutni .
3Nasaa'i, Ahmad & Siraaj with a saheeh sanad.
4Ibn Khuzaimah, Baihaqi, Diyaa' in *al-Mukhtaarah* & 'Abdul Ghani al-Maqdisi in his Sunan (243/1) with a saheeh isnaad; Ahmad, Tabaraani in *Mu'jam al-Awsat* (32/2), Baihaqi, Ibn al-Mulaqqin (29/1) and Haakim, who declared it saheeh and Dhahabi agreed. Its takhreej is given in *Irwaa'* al-Ghaleel under hadeeth no. 327.
5Muslim, Abu 'Awaanah, Siraaj, Ibn Khuzaimah & Tabaraani.

*NB: The Ibaadiyyah have distorted this hadeeth: their scholar Rabee' has related it in his unreliable Musnad with a different wording to justify their view that raising the hands with takbeer invalidates the Prayer! That wording is false, as I have explained in *ad-Da'eefah* (6044).

The Obligation of the *Tasleem*

He (sallallaahu 'alaihi wa sallam) used to say, ... *it (the prayer) is exited by the tasleem.*[1]

* * *

This is the last of what has been possible to compile regarding the description of the Prophet's prayer (sallallaahu 'alaihi wa sallam) from the takbeer to the tasleem: I hope that Allaah will make it sincerely for His Face, Full of Honour, and a guide to the Sunnah of His kind and merciful Prophet.

سُبْحَانَ اللهِ وَبِحَمْدِهِ، سُبْحَانَكَ اَللَّهُمَّ وَبِحَمْدِكَ، أَشْهَدُ أَنْ لاَ إِلهَ إِلاَّ أَنْتَ، أَسْتَغْفِرُكَ وَأَتُوبُ إِلَيْكَ

اَللَّهُمَّ صَلِّ عَلَى مُحَمَّدٍ، وَعَلَى آلِ مُحَمَّدٍ، وَبَارِكْ عَلَى مُحَمَّدٍ، وَعَلَى آلِ مُحَمَّدٍ، كَمَا صَلَّيْتَ وَبَارَكْتَ عَلَى

إِبْرَاهِيمَ، وَآلِ إِبْرَاهِيمَ، إِنَّكَ حَمِيدٌ مَجِيدٌ

Glorified be Allaah, and Praised. Glorified be You, O Allaah, and Praised. I bear witness that there is no true god except You. I seek forgiveness from You and repent to You.

O Allaah! send prayers on Muhammad, and on the family of Muhammad, and send blessings on Muhammad, and on the family of Muhammad, as You sent prayers on Ibraaheem and the family of Ibraaheem; You are indeed Worthy of Praise, Full of Glory.[2]

---

[1]Haakim & Dhahabi declared it saheeh; it has already been given in full under the opening "Takbeer".

[2] The first supplication is the fullest form of the du'aa' known as *kaffaarah al-majlis* (expiation of the gathering); "he who says it in a gathering of Remembrance (of Allaah), it will be like a seal to stamp it with, and he who says it in a gathering of vain talk, it will be an expiation for it" - authentically related by Haakim and Tabaraan. The second supplication is, of course, from the Sunnah of sending peace and mercy on the Messenger. These two supplications are thus the best way of implementing the following Islamic guideline: "No people sit in a gathering in which they do not mention Allaah, nor send prayers on the Prophet, without it being a source of regret for them; if Allaah wishes, He will punish them, or if He wishes, he will forgive them" - authentically related by Tirmidhi, Haakim & Ahmad. See Shaykh Albaani's *Silsilah al-Ahaadeeth as-Saheehah* (74-81) for details.

ADDENDUM

All that has been mentioned of the description of the Prophet's prayer (sallallaahu 'alaihi wa sallam) applies equally to men and women, for there is nothing in the Sunnah to necessitate the exception of women from any of these descriptions; in fact, the generality of his statement (sallallaahu 'alaihi wa sallam), *"Pray as you have seen me praying"*, includes women.

This is the view of Ibraaheem an-Nakh'i, who said, "A woman's actions in the prayer are the same as a man's" - transmitted by Ibn Abi Shaibah (1/75/2), with a saheeh sanad from him.

Also, Bukhaari reported in *at-Taareekh as-Sagheer* (p. 95) with a saheeh sanad from Umm ad-Dardaa', "that she used to sit in her prayer just as a man sits, and she was a woman of understanding."

The hadeeth about the *indimaam* (tucking up) of a woman in prostration, and that she is in that regard not like a man, is *mursal* and not authentic. Abu Daawood transmitted it in *al-Maraaseel* on the authority of Yazeed ibn Abi Habeeb.

As for what Imaam Ahmad has reported, as in his son 'Abdullaah's *Masaa'il*, from Ibn 'Umar, that he used to instruct his wives to sit cross-legged in prayer, its sanad is not authentic, for it contains 'Abdullaah ibn 'Umar al-'Amri, who is a *da'eef* (weak) narrator.

APPENDIX 1

The Weakness of the Ahaadeeth endorsing
ikhtilaaf (disagreement, differing)

from: Silsilah al-Ahaadeeth ad-Da'eefah wa'l-Mawdoo'ah (58-62) by Shaykh al-Albaani

1) "The disagreement among my ummah is a mercy."

a) **Laa Asla Lahu (Baseless).** The muhadditheen have tried to find an isnaad for it but have not found one, to the extent that Suyooti said in his *al-Jaami' as-Sagheer*, "Perhaps it was collected in one of the books of the huffaadh which did not reach us"!
This suggestion is very far-fetched, since it would mean that some of the sayings of the Prophet (sallallaahu 'alaihi wa sallam) have been lost to the ummah forever, something which is not permissible for a Muslim to believe.

Manaawi quoted Subki as saying, "It (i.e. the saying) is not known to the muhadditheen and I cannot find any isnaad for it, whether saheeh, da'eef or mawdoo'", and this was endorsed by Shaykh Zakareeyyah al-Ansaari in his notes on *Tafseer al-Baidaawi* [92/2].

Further, the meaning of this hadeeth is also incorrect as shown by the verifying scholars, hence Ibn Hazm says in *al-Ihkaam fi Usool al-Ahkaam* [5/64] after indicating that it is not a hadeeth,

"This is one of the most incorrect sayings possible, since if ikhtilaaf were a mercy, then agreement would be a punishment, something which no Muslim would say, because there can only be agreement or disagreement, and there can only be mercy or punishment."

More of Ibn Hazm's words are quoted below.

b) **It contradicts the Qur'aan**, which has condemned *ikhtilaaf* in many places.

2) "My Companions are like the stars: whichever of them you follow, you will be rightly-guided."

Mawdoo' (Fabricated). Related by Ibn 'Abdul-Barr in *Jaami' Bayaan al-'Ilm* [2/91] & Ibn Hazm in *al-Ihkaam* [6/82] via the route:

Sallaam ibn Sulaim, who said: al-Haarith ibn Ghisseen narrated to us from al-A'mash from Abu Sufyaan from Jaabir from the Prophet (sallallaahu 'alaihi wa sallam).

Ibn 'Abdul-Barr said, "Proof cannot be established with this isnaad because al-Haarith ibn Ghisseen is *majhool* (unknown)"; Ibn Hazm said, "This is a fallen narration. Abu Sufyaan is weak; al-Haarith ibn Ghisseen is Abu Wahb ath-Thaqafee; Sallaam ibn Sulaimaan narrated fabricated ahaadeeth - this is one of them without a doubt."

To judge this hadeeth on Sallaam ibn Sulaim - also known as Sallaam ibn Sulaimaan - is better, for he is agreed to be da'eef; in fact, Ibn Khiraash said about him, "An utter liar" and Ibn Hibbaan said, "He narrated fabricated ahaadeeth."

As for Abu Sufyaan, he is not weak as Ibn Hazm said, but rather he is reliable as Ibn Hajar has said in *at-Taqreeb*, and Muslim narrates from him in his *Saheeh*.

Al-Haarith ibn Ghisseen is unknown as Ibn Hazm said, as did Ibn 'Abdul Barr, even though Ibn Hibbaan does mention him in *ath-Thiqaat (The Reliable Narrators)*

Hence, Ahmad said, "This hadeeth is not authentic", as quoted in *al-Muntakhab* [10/199/2] of Ibn Qudaamah.

As for the saying of Sha'raani in *al-Meezaan* [1/28], "This hadeeth, although debatable in the eyes of the muhaddtheen, is nevertheless authentic in the eyes of the people of Kashf", it is completely false and whimsical, and is not to be given any significance! This is because authenticating ahaadeeth by way of Kashf ("unveiling", while in a state of trance) is a wicked innovation of the Sufis, and depending upon it leads to the authentication of false, baseless ahaadeeth such as this one. This is because, even at the best of times, Kashf is like opinion, which is sometimes correct and sometimes wrong - and that is if no personal desires enter into it! We ask Allaah to save us from it and from everything He is not pleased with.

Similar narrations to the above are as follows:

2.1) "The example of my Companions is that of the stars: he who follows any of them will be rightly-guided."

Mawdoo' (Fabricated). Related by Qudaa'i (109/2) via:

Ja'far ibn 'Abdul Waahid, who said: Wahb ibn Jareer ibn Haazim informed us from his father from al-A'mash from Abu Salih from Abu Hurairah from The Prophet (sallallaahu 'alaihi wa sallam).

One of the muhadditheen, either Ibn al-Muhibb or Dhahabi, wrote in the margin, "This hadeeth is not at all authentic", i.e. it is fabricated: the flaw in it is Ja'far here, about whom Daaraqutni said, "He used to fabricate ahaadeeth"; Abu Zur'ah said, "He narrated baseless ahaadeeth"; Dhahabi gave some hadeeth because of which he disparaged him, among them being this one, and then said, "This is one of his calamities!"

2.2) "Whatever you are given from the Book of Allaah is to be acted upon; there is no excuse for anyone to leave it. If it is not in the Book of Allaah, then (act upon) a previous example (sunnah) of mine. If there is no previous example (sunnah) of mine, then (act upon) what my Companions say: verily, my Companions are of the station of the stars in the sky, so whichever of them you take, you will be guided, and the disagreement of my Companions is a mercy for you."

Mawdoo' (Fabricated). Collected by Khateeb in al-Kifaayah fi 'Ilm ar-Riwaayah [p.48] and also by Abul-'Abbaas al-Asamm in the his Hadeeth (no. 142), & Ibn 'Asaakir [7/315/2] by way of:

Sulaimaan ibn Abi Kareemah from Juwaibir from ad-Dahhaak from Ibn 'Abbaas from The Prophet (sallallaahu 'alaihi wa sallam).

This isnaad is da'eef jiddan (very weak).

About Sulaimaan ibn Abi Kareemah, Ibn Abi Haatim [2/1/138] reported from his father about him, "He is weak in hadeeth."

Juwaibir is Ibn Sa'eed al-Azadee, and is matrook (abandoned) as Daaraqutnee, Nasaa'i and others have said, and Ibn al-Madeeni declared him to be very weak.

Dahhaak is Ibn Muzaahim al-Hilaalee, and he did not meet Ibn 'Abbaas.

'Iraaqi quoted the last part of the hadeeth in his Takhreej of Ghazaali's Ihyaa' 'Uloom ad-Deen [1/25] and then said, "Its isnaad is da'eef."

The isnaad is actually very weak due to what we have mentioned about Juwaibir, as Sakhaawi said in al-Maqaasid . In meaning, however, the hadeeth is fabricated, as is clear from what has preceeded and what will follow.

Suyooti quoted the hadeeth in its entirety at the begining of his treatise Jazeel al-Mawaahib fi Ikhtilaaf al-Madhaahib from the narration of Bayhaqi in al-Madkhal, and Dailami related it from this route, as occurs in al-Mawdoo'aat of 'Ali al-Qaari [p.19]. Once you know this, then the saying of Suyooti in his aforementioned treatise is very strange: "... and this hadeeth contains several points to note; among them his (sallallaahu 'alaihi wa sallam) informing of the disagreements between the madhaahib in non-fundamental matters, and that is one of his miracles, since it is information about the Unseen; also, his being

96

pleased with that and approving of it, since he described it as a mercy, and that the burdened person may choose whichever of them he wishes."

It could be said to him: first establish the throne, and then sit. What he has mentioned about the choice is false: it is not possible for the Muslim to cling to it and act upon its generality, since it leads to breaking away from the restrictions of the Sharee'ah, as is not hard to see. See also the discussion under 2.4 below.

2.3) "I asked my Lord about that which my Companions would disagri about after me, so Allaah inspired me: O Muhammad! Your Companions are to Me of the station of the stars in the sky - some are brighter than others; so whoever takes from any of them in those matters where they have differed, then to Me, he is upon guidance."

Mawdoo' (Fabricated). Reported by Ibn Battah in al-Ibaanah [4/11/2], Khateeb, Nizam al-Malik in al-Amaali [13/2], Diyaa' in al-Muntaqaa 'an Masmoo'aatihi bimaroo [116/2] & Ibn 'Asaakir [6/303/1] by way of:

Nu'aim ibn Hammaad, who said: 'Abdur-Raheem ibn Zaid narrated to us from his father from Sa'eed ibn al-Musayyib from 'Umar ibn al-Khattaab from the Prophet (sallallaahu 'alaihi wa sallam).

This isnaad is *mawdoo'*.

Nu'aim ibn Hammaad is weak: Ibn Hajar said, "He makes many mistakes."

About 'Abdur-Raheem ibn Zaid al-'Ammee, al-Bukhaari said, "He was abandoned"; Abu Haatim said, "His ahaadeeth are abandoned: he is unacceptable in hadeeth - he used to undermine his father by narrating disasters from him"; Ibn Ma'een said, "He was an utter, filthy liar."

About his father, Zaid al-'Ammi ibn al-Hawaaree, Ibn Sa'd said, "He was weak in hadeeth."

Suyooti recorded this hadeeth in al-Jaami' as-Sagheer through the narration of Sijizzi in al-Ibaanah and Ibn 'Asaakir from 'Umar; Manaawi said in his commentary on al-Jaami' as-Sagheer :
Ibn al-Jawzi said in his al-'Ilal, "This is not authentic. Nu'aim has been disparaged; Ibn Ma'een has described 'Abdur-Raheem as an utter liar; it says in al-Meezaan: This hadeeth is false."

2.4) "Verily, my Companions are like the stars: so if you accept any of their sayings, you will be guided."

Mawdoo' (Fabricated). Ibn 'Abdul-Barr reports it in mu'allaq (suspended, i.e. an incomplete chain of narrators at the collector's end) form and Ibn Hazm reports it from him; the complete chain was provided by 'Abd ibn Humaid in *al-Muntakhab min al-Musnad* (86/1):

Ahmad ibn Yoonus informed me: Abu Shihaab al-Hannaat narrated to us, from Hamzah al-Jazree, from Naafee', from Ibn 'Umar from the Prophet (sallallaahu 'alaihi wa sallam).

Also, Ibn Battah narrated it in *al-Ibaanah* [4/11/2] by another chain from Abu Shihaab.

Ibn 'Abdul-Barr said, "This isnaad is not authentic; no one acceptable as proof has reported it from Naafee'."

This Hamzah is Ibn Abi Hamzah; Daaraqutni said about him, "*Matrook* (abandoned)"; Ibn 'Adi said, "His narrations are mostly fabricated"; Ibn Hibbaan said, "He would be alone in narrating things which are fabricated from reliable narrators, to such an extent that it is as if he did so deliberately - it is not permissible to narrate from him"; Dhahabi quoted some of his fabricated ahaadeeth in *al-Meezaan*, this being one of them.

Ibn Hazm said in *al-Ihkaam* (6/83), after declaring that this hadeeth (no. 2, with all its versions) is undoubtedly a lie since it also contradicts many aayaat of the Qur'aan, e.g. Najm (53:3-4), Nisaa' (4:82), Anfaal (8:46), the following:

"... therefore, it is absurd that the Messenger (sallallaahu 'alaihi wa sallam) would command us to follow every view expressed by the Companions, may Allaah be pleased with them all, for there were among them those who permitted something while others prohibited it: if the above were the case, trading in intoxicants would be permissible if one followed Samurah ibn Jundub; it would be permissible for someone fasting to eat snow if one followed Abu Talhah, but prohibited by following others beside him; to not take a bath due to incomplete intercourse would be obligatory if one followed 'Ali, 'Uthmaan, Talhah, Abu Ayyoob and Ubayy ibn Ka'b, but prohibited if one followed 'Aa'ishah and Ibn 'Umar; all these examples have been related to us with authentic chains of narration."

He then went on to explain at length some opinions expressed by Companions in which they were wrong about the Sunnah, both during the lifetime of the Prophet (sallallaahu 'alaihi wa sallam) and after his death. He then said (6/86),

"So how can it be allowable to blindly follow the opinions of people who make mistakes as well as get it right?!"

Before that, he had explained, under the heading Differing Condemned (5/64), the error of those who say, "Disagreement is a mercy", using as evidence the hadeeth, "**My Companions are like the stars: whichever of them you follow,**

you will be rightly-guided", by clarifying that the hadeeth is a lie for several reasons:

(i) it is not authentic with regard to its chain of narration;

(ii) further, the Prophet (sallallaahu 'alaihi wa sallam) could not have commanded us to follow something which he himself had declared erroneous at times; e.g. he pointed out Abu Bakr's mistake in interpreting a dream, 'Umar's error in another interpretation, and Abus-Sanaabil's going wrong in a verdict he gave; hence, it is not possible for him to order us to follow someone mistaken;

(iii) the Prophet (sallallaahu 'alaihi wa sallam) never spoke falsehood; his words were always truth: the comparison with the stars is clearly flawed, since for example, if someone intends to travel a certain route directed by the stars in the constellation of Capricorn, but instead follows the stars in Cancer, he will *not* be correctly-guided, but will stray far away from the correct path and err tremendously; therefore, it is obviously false to say that following any star will guide one correctly.

Ibn al-Mulaqqin gave a summarised version of Ibn Hazm's words in his *al-Khulaasah* [2/175], endorsed it and ended his discussion of the hadeeth saying: Ibn Hazm said,"This is an invented, fabricated, false narration, not correct at all."

APPENDIX 2

The authentic hadeeth:
"You are right in some of it and wrong in some of it."

from: Saheeh al-Bukhaari, Book of Dreams, English translation of the
meanings by Dr. Muhammad Muhsin Khan

Narrated Ibn 'Abbaas (Allaah be pleased with him):

A man came to Allaah's Messenger (sallallaahu 'alaihi wa sallam) and said,
"I saw in a dream, a cloud having shade. Butter and honey were dropping
from it and I saw the people gathering it in their hands, some gathering
much and some little. And behold, there was a rope extending from the
earth to the sky, and I saw that you held it and went up; then, another man
held it and went up and (after that) another (third) man held it and went
up, and then another (fourth) man held it, but it broke and then got
connected again."
Abu Bakr said, "O Allaah's Messenger! Let my father be sacrificed for you!
By Allaah, allow me to interpret this dream." The Prophet (sallallaahu
'alaihi wa sallam) said to him, *Interpret it.* Abu Bakr said, "The cloud with
shade symbolises Islaam, and the butter and the honey dropping from it
symbolises the Qur'aan, it's sweetness and some people learning much of
the Qur'aan while some a little. The rope which is extended from the sky to
the earth is the Truth which you (the Prophet (sallallaahu 'alaihi wa sallam)
are following. You follow it and Allaah will raise you high with it, and then
another person will follow it and will rise up with it and then another man
will follow it but it will break and then it will be connected for him and he
will rise up with it. O Allaah's Messenger! Let my father be sacrificed for
you! Am I right or wrong?"
The Prophet (sallallaahu 'alaihi wa sallam) replied, *You are right in some of
it and wrong in some of it.*
Abu Bakr said, "O Allaah's Prophet! By Allaah, you must tell me in what I
was wrong."
The Prophet (sallallaahu 'alaihi wa sallam) said, *Do not swear.*

(Related by Bukhaari and Muslim, and also by Abu Daawood, Tirmidhi,
Daarimi, Ibn Maajah, Ibn Abi Shaibah and Ahmad.)

100

APPENDIX 3

"The one who prayed badly" (radi Allaahu 'anhu)

In Hadeeth and Fiqh literature, this term refers to the Companion mentioned in the following hadeeth of Saheeh al-Bukhaari (*Book of Prayer, English translation by Dr. Muhammad Muhsin Khan*); many other narrations of this incident are found in the various collections of hadeeth, and provide an important source of instructions from the Prophet (sallallaahu 'alaihi wa sallam) regarding the correct way to pray:

Narrated Abu Hurairah (radi Allaahu 'anhu):

> The Messenger of Allaah (sallallaahu 'alaihi wa sallam) entered the mosque and a person followed him. The man prayed and then went to the Prophet (sallallaahu 'alaihi wa sallam) and greeted him; he returned the greeting and said (to him), *Go back and pray, for you have not prayed.*
> The man went back and prayed in the same way as before, and then returned and greeted the Prophet (sallallaahu 'alaihi wa sallam), who said, *Go back and pray, for you have not prayed,* three times.
> The man said, "By Him Who sent you with the Truth, I cannot do so any better than this, so please teach me."
> He said, *When you stand for the Prayer, say takbeer and then recite what is easy for you from the Qur'aan (from what you know by heart); then bow until you feel at ease in rukoo'; then raise your head and stand up straight, then prostrate until you feel at ease in sajdah; then sit with calmness until you feel at ease, and do likewise in all your prayers.*

[further narrations of this hadeeth found in the other works of Hadeeth such as Sunan Abi Daawood, etc. contain further details.]

APPENDIX 4

The weakness of the hadeeth about placing the hands below the navel.

from Irwaa' al-Ghaleel (353) & Ahkaam al-Janaa'iz (p. 118), by Shaykh al-Albaani

Abu Daawood (756), Daaraqutni (107), Baihaqi (2/310), Ahmad in his son 'Abdullaah's *Masaa'il* (62/2) and also in *Zawaa'id al-Musnad* (1/110), and Ibn Abi Shaiba (1/156/1) transmitted:

'an 'Abd ar-Rahmaan ibn Ishaaq *'an* Ziyaad ibn Zaid as-Siwaa'i *'an* Abu Juhaifah *'an* 'Ali (radi Allaahu 'anhu), who said, *"It is from the Sunnah during the prayer to place one palm on the other, below the navel."*

This is a da'eef (weak) sanad due to 'Abd ar-Rahmaan ibn Ishaaq (al-Waasiti al-Koofi), who is weak (see below). On top of that, it has *idtiraab* (shakiness) in it, for he has narrated it:

(1) once *'an* Ziyad *'an* Abu Juhaifa *'an* 'Ali (as above);
(2) once *'an* Nu'man ibn Sa'd *'an* 'Ali (transmitted by Daaraqutni and Baihaqi); and
(3) once *'an* Siyaas Abul Hakam *'an* Abu Waa'il, who said, "Abu Hurairah said: It is from the Sunnah ..." (transmitted by Abu Dawood [758] and Daaraqutni).

The Weakness of 'Abd ar-Rahmaan ibn Ishaaq al-Koofi in the eyes of the Imaams of Hadeeth

1) **Abu Daawood** said, "I heard **Ahmad ibn Hanbal** declaring 'Abd ar-Rahmaan ibn Ishaaq al-Koofi da'eef (weak)." *[This is why Imaam Ahmad did not accept this hadeeth of his, for his son 'Abdullaah said, "I saw that when praying, my father placed his hands, one on the other, above the navel."]*
2) **Nawawi** said in *Majmoo'* (3/313), and also in *Sharh Saheeh Muslim* and elsewhere, "They (the scholars of hadeeth) agree in declaring this hadeeth weak, because it is a narration of 'Abd ar-Rahmaan ibn Ishaaq al-Waasiti, who is a da'eef (weak) narrator, as agreed upon by the Imaams of *Jarh* and *Ta'deel* (Authentication and Disparagement of reporters)."
3) **Zayla'i** said in *Nasb ar-Raayah* (1/314), **"Baihaqi** said in *al-Ma'rifah*: 'Its isnaad is not firm, for it is a unique narration of 'Abd ar-Rahmaan ibn Ishaaq al-Waasiti, who is matrook (abandoned)'."
4) **Ibn Hajar** said in *Fath al-Baari* (2/186), "It is a weak hadeeth."

What further points to its weakness is that contrary to it has been narrated on the authority of 'Ali with a better isnaad: the hadeeth of Ibn Jareer al-Dabbi *'an* his father, who said, "I saw 'Ali (radi Allaahu 'anhu) holding his left arm with his right on the wrist, *above the navel*" - this isnaad is a candidate for the rank of *hasan*; Baihaqi (1/301) firmly designated it to be hasan, and Bukhaari (1/301) designated it with certainty while giving it in an abridged, ta'leeq form.

What is authentic from the Prophet (sallallaahu 'alaihi wa sallam) with respect to the position of the hands is that they should be on the chest; there are many ahaadeeth about this, among them is one on the authority of Taawoos, who said, "*The Messenger of Allaah (sallallaahu 'alaihi wa sallam) used to place his right arm on his left arm, and clasp them firmly on his chest during prayer*" - transmitted by Abu Daawood (759) with a saheeh isnaad. Although this is mursal, it is enough as proof for all scholars, with all their various opinions regarding the Mursal Hadeeth, since it is saheeh as a mursal isnaad and has also been related as mawsool in many narrations; hence, it is valid as proof for all. Some of the supporting narrations are as follows:

1) from Waa'il ibn Hujr: "That he saw the Prophet - sallallaahu 'alaihi wa sallam – put his right hand upon his left and place them upon his chest." Reported by Ibn Khuzaimah in his Saheeh (*Nasb ar-Raayah*, 1/314) and reported by Baihaqi in his Sunan (2/30) with two chains of narration which support each other.

2) from Qabeesah ibn Hulb, from his father who said:
"I saw the Prophet (sallallaahu 'alaihi wa sallam), leave [after completing the Prayer] from his right and his left, and I saw him place this upon his chest – Yahyaa (Ibn Sa'eed) described the right (hand) upon the left above the joint."
Reported by Ahmad (5/226) with a chain of narrators who are of the standard set by Muslim except for Qabeesah, but he is declared reliable by 'Ijli & Ibn Hibbaan; however, no one narrates from him except Simaak ibn Harb about whom Ibn al-Madeeni and Nasaa'i say: "Unknown" and Ibn Hajar says in *Taqreeb*: "He is 'Maqbool' [i.e. acceptable only if supported]." The hadeeth of one such as him are *hasan* as supporting narrations, and therefore Tirmidhi said after quoting the part of this hadeeth concerning taking the left hand with the right, "It is a *hasan* hadeeth."

So these are three ahaadeeth which show that the Sunnah is to place the hands on the chest, and one who comes across them will not doubt that together they are sufficient to prove this.

APPENDIX 5

The Weakness of the Hadeeth condemning Recitation behind the Imaam

from: Silsilah al-Ahaadeeth ad-Da'eefah wal-Mawdoo'ah (568-570) by Shaykh al-Albaani

1-"He who recites behind the imaam, his mouth is filled with fire."

Mawdoo' (Fabricated). Ibn Taahir quoted it in *Tadhkirah al-Mawdoo'aat* (p.93), and said, "The isnaad contains Ma'moon ibn Ahmad al-Harawi, an utter liar who used to narrate fabrications." More of his description is given in hadeeth 2 below. Ibn Hibbaan mentioned this hadeeth under his name in *ad-Du'afaa* (*The Weak Narrators*) and Dhahabi regarded it as one of his calamities!

Some Hanafis have been deceived by this hadeeth, arguing on its basis that any recitation behind the imaam is totally haraam! Abul Hasanaat al-Luknawi said in *at-Ta'leeq al-Mumajjid 'alaa Muwatta' Muhammad* (p. 99), "It was mentioned by the author of *Nihaayah* and by others as marfoo' with the wording, '...there is a burning coal in his mouth', and it is totally baseless."
He had said before that, "In no saheeh marfoo' hadeeth is there a forbiddance of reciting al-Faatihah behind the imaam; all that they quote as marfoo' regarding this is either baseless or not authentic", and had then mentioned this hadeeth with both wordings as an example.

The people of knowledge, both past and present, have differed regarding recitation behind the imaam, taking one of three views:

1- That recitation in loud and quiet prayers is obligatory.
2- That silence in loud and quiet prayers is obligatory.
3- That there be recitation in quiet, but not in loud, prayers.

This last view is the most balanced and closest to the truth, for in it, all the evidences can be accommodated such that none of them is rejected totally. It is the view of Maalik and Ahmad, and has also been prefered after analysis by some Hanafis, including Abul Hasanaat al-Luknawi in his aforementioned book.

Another example of Ma'moon al-Harawi's inventions is the following:

2- "He who raises his hands during the prayer, there is no prayer for him."

Mawdoo' (Fabricated). Ibn Taahir quoted it in *Tadhkirah al-Mawdoo'aat* (p. 87), and said, "The isnaad contains Ma'moon ibn Ahmad al-Harawi, an utter liar who used to fabricate ahadeeth."
Dhahabi said about him, "He brought calamities and disgraceful reports. He invented ahaadeeth, this being one of them, and related them apparently on the authority of reliable narrators."

It is clear to me from the ahaadeeth which Ma'moon al-Harawi has invented that he is a bigoted zealot of the Hanafi Madhhab, for all the ahaadeeth mentioned under his descriptions (in books of narrators) revolve around supporting Imaam Abu Haneefah and insulting Imaam Shaafi'i; amongst them is this one: a clear insult to the Shaafi'i view, which approves the raising of the hands on going down into rukoo' and rising from it (which is the truth without doubt), while obviously backing the Hanafi view which says that this is makrooh. This disgusting man was not even satisfied with the position of his Madhhab that raising the hands was makrooh: he even went to the extent of inventing this hadeeth, in order to propagate amongst the people that raising the hands actually invalidates the prayer!

Perhaps he also intended to support Makhool's narration from Abu Haneefah that he said, "He who raises his hands during prayer, his prayer is ruined", a narration which deceived Ameer Kaatib al-Itqaani, who compiled a treatise on the basis of it to argue the invalidation of the prayer by the raising of the hands! Similarly deceived was the one who trod his path and ruled that it was not permissible for Hanafis to pray behind Shaafi'is because the latter raise their hands! While all along, this narration from Abu Haneefah is utterly false, as 'Allaamah Abul Hasanaat al-Luknawi has verified in *al-Fawa'id al-Bahiyyah fi Taraajum al-Hanafeeyyah* (pp. 116, 216-7).

Shaikh 'Ali al-Qaari quoted this hadeeth in al-Mawdoo'at and then said (p. 81), "This hadeeth was fabricated by Muhammad b. 'Ukaashah al-Kirmaani, may Allaah disgrace him." Later (p. 129), he quoted Ibn al-Qayyim as saying, "It is fabricated."

This is contrary to what has been established (above) that the fabricator was al-Harawi; if it is proved, than perhaps one of them stole it from the other!

We can see from all this what lack of heed to the Sunnah, and abandonment of verification of narrations from the Prophet (sallallaahu 'alaihi wa sallam) and the Imaams, can do!

NOTE: About raising the hands on going into rukoo' and rising from it, many many ahadeeth have been narrated from the Prophet (sallallaahu 'alaihi wa sallam): they are actually mutawaatir in the eyes of the scholars; in fact, raising the hands with every takbeer is proven on his authority in many ahadeeth; whereas not raising the hands is not authentically-related from him except once via 'Abdullaah ibn Mas'ood (radi Allaahu 'anhu), but this is not suitable for putting into practice, for it is *naaf* (negatory). It is firmly established, in the eyes of the Hanafis and others, that the *muthbit* (affirmatory) takes precedence over the *naaf* (negatory); this is even when the affirmatory is on its own, let alone the case when it is a multitude of narrations, as in this issue! On the basis of this principle, and in the abscence of anything contrary, this renders it binding on them to adopt the raising of the hands, and not to stick zealously to the Madhhab after the establishment of proof. However, it is a pity that only a handful of the earlier or later ones have adopted it, so much so that not raising the hands has become a landmark for them!

Yet another of the inventions of this vile liar, this time a personal insult to Imaam Shaafi'i (Muhammad bin Idrees), is the following:

3- "There will be a man among my ummah known as Muhammad bin Idrees, who will be more harmful to my ummah than Iblees, and there will be a man among my ummah known as Abu Haneefah, who will be the lamp of my ummah."

Mawdoo' (Fabricated). Ibn al-Jawzi quoted it in *al-Mawdoo'aat*(1/457) via:

Ma'moon ibn Ahmad as-Salmi, who said: Ahmad ibn 'Abdullaah al-Juwaibaari narrated to us: 'Abdullaah ibn Mi'daan al-Azadi informed us from Anas, as marfoo';

and then said, "Fabricated; invented by Ma'moon or by Juwaibaari. Haakim mentioned in *Madhkal* that it was said to Ma'moon, 'Do you not look to Shaafi'i and his followers?' So he said, 'Ahmad ibn 'Abdullaah al-Juwaibaari narrated to us ...' etc., so it becomes evident from this that he is the fabricator of it."

The following addition appears in *Lisaan:* "Haakim then said, 'Anyone whom Allaah has granted the least amount of intelligence would testify that a hadeeth such as this is a fabrication attributed to the Messenger of Allaah (sallallaahu 'alaihi wa sallam)'."

The hadeeth does have other routes of narration, but these depend on liars and unknown reporters. Therefore, it is extremely bizarre that 'Allaamah 'Ayni should incline towards strengthening the hadeeth with those other routes, and that Shaykh Kawthari should support him! However, it is no surprise from the latter, for he was notorious for being submerged in zealousy for Imaam Abu Haneefah (rahimahullaah), even if it entailed insulting other Imaams; but it is very surprising from 'Ayni, for he was generally known not to go to such extremes. The opinion of these two has been refuted, with analysis of the other routes of narration referred to, in a unique way in 'Allaamah Yamaanee's valuable book, *at-Tankeel bi maa fi Ta'neeb al-Kawthari min al-Abaateel* (1/20, 446-9).

Analysis of the Ahaadeeth regarding the saying of 'aameen' by the Imaam and the Congregation

from: Silsilah al-Ahaadeeth ad-Da'eefah (951-2) by Shaykh al-Albaani

1- "When he said aameen, those behind him would say aameen, such that there was a lot of noise in the mosque."

There is no basis for the hadeeth with this wording as far as we know. Ibn Hajr said in *Talkhees al-Habeer* (p. 90), "I do not find it with this wording, but its meaning is related by Ibn Maajah in the hadeeth of Bishr ibn Raafi'":

2- "When he recited 'Not of those who received Your anger, nor of those who go astray', he said 'aameen', such that those close to him in the first row could hear [and the mosque trembled with it]."

Da'eef (Weak). Related by Ibn Maajah (1/281) & Abu Dawood without the addition (1/148), both via:

Bishr ibn Raafi' from Abu 'Abdullaah, cousin of Abu Hurairah, from Abu Hurairah from the Prophet (sallallaahu 'alaihi wa sallam).

Ibn Hajar said in *Talkhees* (p. 90), "Bishr ibn Raafi' is weak; the cousin of Abu Hurairah has been said to be unknown, but Ibn Hibbaan has declared him reliable."
Boosayri said in *Zawaa'id* (56/1), "This is a weak isnaad; Abu 'Abdullaah's condition is not known; Bishr was declared weak by Ahmad, and Ibn Hibbaan said, 'He narrated fabrications'."

Hadeeth 2 only gives a part of the meaning of no. 1, i.e. the saying of aameen by the imaam alone. As for the aameen of those behind, this could be the reason for the phrase "the mosque trembled with it (the sound)", but the hadeeth literally implies that the aameen of the Prophet (sallallaahu 'alaihi wa sallam) was the reason for this.

3- "When he finished reciting the Mother of the Qur'aan, he raised his voice and said 'aameen'."

Da'eef (Weak). Related by Daaraqutni, Haakim & Baihaqi.

All the above sources contain Ishaaq ibn Ibraaheem ibn al-'Alaa' az-Zubaidi, also known as Ibn Zibreeq, who is weak: Abu Haatim said, "An old man, no harm in him"; Ibn Ma'een described him in good terms; Nasaa'i said, "Not reliable"; Muhammad ibn 'Awf said, "I have no doubt that Ishaaq ibn Zibreeq used to lie." However, this wording is correct in meaning, for it has a supporting hadeeth of Waa'il ibn Hajar with a saheeh sanad.

(Since the text of this hadeeth does not imply the aameen of the congregation at all, it is incorrect to regard it as another version of hadeeth no. 2, as Shawkaani did.)

The only support for no. 1 is what Shaafi'i related in his Musnad (1/76) via Muslim ibn Khaalid from Ibn Juraij from 'Ataa', who said:

4- "I used to hear the imaams: Ibn az-Zubair and others after him would say 'aameen', and those behind would say 'aameen', until the mosque echoed."

This has two defects:

(i) The weakness of Muslim ibn Khaalid az-Zanji; Ibn Hajar said, "He was truthful, but made many errors."
(ii) The *an'anah* of Ibn Juraij, who was a *mudallis*; perhaps he actually took it from Khaalid ibn Abi Anoof, who narrated it from 'Ataa' as follows:

4.1- "I came across two hundred Companions of the Messenger of Allaah (sallallaahu 'alaihi wa sallam) in this mosque (i.e. Masjid al-Haraam, Makkah): when the imaam had said 'Nor of those who go astray', they raised their voices in aameen (*in one narration*: I heard the thundering sound of their aameen)."

Related by Baihaqi (2/59) & Ibn Hibbaan in *Thiqaat* (2/74); the alternative narration is from the former.

This Khaalid was described by Ibn Abi Haatim (1/2/355-6), but he did not include any authentication or disparagement. Ibn Hibbaan included him among the reliable narrators, but Ibn Hibbaan is well-known to be far from rigorous in such cases, so I am not satisfied that this narration is authentic. This is because if Ibn Juraij indeed took it from him, this constitutes only one debatable route; if not, we do not know from whom Ibn Juraij took it. It seems that Imaam Shaafi'i himself was not satisfied of the authenticity of this narration, for his position is contrary to it: he says in *al-Umm* (1/95), "So when the imaam completes reciting the Mother of the Book, he says 'aameen', raising his voice so that those behind may follow him: when he says it, they say it to themselves, but I do not like them saying it aloud"; had the above narration from the Companions been authentic in Shaafi'i's view, he would not have opposed their action.

Hence, the most correct opinion in this issue appears to be the madhhab of Shaafi'i: that the imaam, but not those following, should say 'aameen' loudly. Allaah knows best.

But then, I saw that Bukhaari mentioned the text (only) of the narration about Ibn az-Zubair in his Saheeh (i.e. in mu'allaq form), designating it with certainty. Ibn Hajar said in *Fath al-Baari* (2/208), "The connecting isnaad has been provided by 'Abd ar-Razzaaq from Ibn Juraij from 'Ataa'. He (i.e. Ibn Juraij) said, 'I said to him, "Did Ibn az-Zubair say aameen' at the end of the Mother of the Qur'aan ?" He said, "Yes, and those behind him also said aameen, until the mosque echoed." He then said, "Verily, aameen is a supplication".'" This is found in the Musannaf of 'Abd ar-Razzaaq (2640/2), and from this route, in Ibn Hazm's *al-Muhallaa* (3/364).

In this narration, Ibn Juraij has clarified that he took the narration from 'Ataa' face-to-face, so we are assured of the absence of *tadlees*, and the narration of Ibn az-Zubair is established firmly. Similarly is proven from Abu Hurairah; Abu Raafi' said:

5- "Abu Hurairah used to call to prayer for Marwaan ibn al-Hakam, stipulating that the latter would not get to 'Nor of those who go astray' unless he knew that Abu Hurairah had entered the row. So when Marwaan said 'Nor of those who go astray', Abu Hurairah would say 'aameen', prolonging it. He also said, 'When the aameen of those on the earth coincides with the aameen of those in the heaven, they are forgiven'."

Related by Baihaqi (2/59); its isnaad is saheeh.

Hence, since nothing is established from any of the Companions other than Abu Hurairah and Ibn az-Zubair contrary to their aameen aloud, this must be accepted. Presently, I know of no narration opposing this. Allaah knows best.

APPENDIX 7

The Two Rak'ahs After Witr

from: Silsilah al-Ahaadeeth as-Saheehah (1993) by Shaykh al-Albaani

1) The Messenger of Allaah (sallallaahu 'alaihi wa sallam) said, *Make the last of your prayer at night odd (witr).*
Related by Bukhaari & Muslim.

2) Abu Salamah asked 'A'ishah about the prayer of the Messenger of Allaah (sallallaahu 'alaihi wa sallam). She said, "He performed thirteen rak'ahs (in the night prayer): he observed eight rak'ahs *and would then observe Witr and then observe two rak'ahs sitting,* and when he wanted to bow, he stood up and then bowed down, and then observed two rak'ahs in between the *adhaan* and *iqaamah* of the Dawn Prayer."
Related by Muslim.

3) Thawbaan said, "We were on a journey with the Messenger of Allaah (sallallaahu 'alaihi wa sallam), when he said, *Truly, this journey is an exertion and a burden, so when each of you has prayed Witr, he should perform two rak'ahs; if he wakes up (then well and good), otherwise these two will be (the night prayer) for him.*

Related by Daarimi (1/374), Ibn Khuzaimah in his Saheeh (2/159/1103) & Ibn Hibbaan (683) from various routes going back to: Ibn Wahb, who said: Mu'aawiyah ibn Saalih narrated to me from Shuraih ibn 'Ubaid from 'Abd ar-Rahmaan ibn Jubair ibn Nufair from his father from Thawbaan, who said ...

Ibn Wahb has been backed up by 'Abdullaah ibn Saalih, who said: Mu'aawiyah ibn Saalih narrated to us ... etc., related by Daaraqutni (p. 177) & Tabaraani in *al-Mu'jam al-Kabeer* (1410). 'Abdullaah ibn Saalih is a shaykh of Bukhaari, so he can be used as evidence in supporting others' narrations.

This hadeeth is used as evidence by Imaam Ibn Khuzaimah, "that prayer after Witr is allowed to whoever wants to pray after it, and that the two rak'ahs which the Prophet (sallallaahu 'alaihi wa sallam) used to pray after Witr were not exclusively for him over his Ummah, for he has ordered us to pray two rak'ahs after Witr, an order of recommendation and preference, not one of obligation and compulsion."

Hence, it is clear to us from this hadeeth (because of his general order to his Ummah) that the two rak'ahs after Witr were not exclusively for him; it seems that the purpose of his command to make the last prayer at night odd was to prevent neglect of the one odd rak'ah, so this objective is not contradicted by the two rak'ahs after it, as established in his practice and his command. Allaah knows best.

APPENDIX 8

The Weakness of the Ahaadeeth Mentioning Wiping the Face with the Hands After *Du'aa'* (Supplication)

From Irwaa' al-Ghaleel (2/178-182) by Shaykh al-Albaani

1) "The Prophet (sallallaahu 'alaihi wa sallam), when he raised his hands in du'aa', he would not put them down until he had wiped his face with them."

Da'eef (Weak). Transmitted by Tirmidhi (2/244) & Ibn 'Asaakir (7/12/2) via: Hammaad ibn 'Isa al-Juhani from Hanzalah ibn Abi Sufyaan al-Jamhi from Saalim ibn 'Abdullaah from his father from 'Umar ibn al-Khattaab, who said: ...

Tirmidhi said after it, "This is a saheeh ghareeb hadeeth. We only know it as a hadeeth of Hammaad ibn 'Esa, for he is alone in reporting it; he has few ahaadeeth, but the people have reported from him."

However, this reporter is weak, as in *Taqreeb* of Ibn Hajr, who says about him in *Tahdheeb*:

> Ibn Ma'een said, "A good shaikh"[1]; Abu Haatim said, "Weak in Hadeeth"; Abu Daawood said, "Weak, he reports munkar ahaadeeth"; Haakim and Naqqaash said, "He reports fabricated ahaadeeth from Ibn Juraij and Ja'far as-Saadiq." He is declared to be weak by Daaraqutni. Ibn Hibbaan said, "He reports things which are the wrong way round on the authority of Ibn Juraij and 'Abdul 'Azeez ibn 'Umar ibn 'Abdul 'Azeez, such that it seems to those whose field this is that it is deliberate; it is not permissible to use him as proof." Ibn Maakoolaa said, "They declare his ahaadeeth to be weak."

Hence, the like of this reporter is very weak, so his ahaadeeth cannot be raised to the level of hasan, let alone saheeh!

---

[1] If Ibn Ma'een speaks favourably about a narrator, wheras the rest of the scholars declare him to be weak, then the statement of Ibn Ma'een is disregarded, the reason being that he was known for his strictness and severity in criticism: weak narrators would be very careful not to reveal their weakness before him; he would therefore pass judgment accordingly. This explains why he is alone in authenticating the narrator.

A similar hadeeth is:

"When the Prophet (sallallaahu 'alaihi wa sallam) did du'aa' and raised his hands, he would wipe his face with his hands."

Da'eef (Weak). Abu Daawood (1492) from Ibn Lahee'ah from Hafs ibn Hishaam ibn 'Utbah ibn Abi Waqqaas from Saa'ib ibn Yazeed from his father.

This is a weak sanad due to Hafs ibn Hishaam being unknown and the weakness of Ibn Lahee'ah (cf. *Taqreeb at-Tahdheeb*).

This hadeeth cannot be strengthened by the two routes of narration together due to the severity in weakness of the first one, which you have seen.

2) "When you call upon Allaah, then supplicate with the palms of your hands, and do not supplicate with their backs, and when you finish, wipe your face with them."

Da'eef (Weak). Related by Ibn Maajah (1181, 3866), Ibn Nasr in *Qiyaam al-Lail* (p. 137), Tabaraani in *Al-Mu'jam al-Kabeer* (3/98/1) & Haakim (1/536), from Saalih ibn Hassaan from Muhammad ibn Ka'b from Ibn 'Abbaas (radi Allaahu 'anhu) as marfoo'.

This is a weak sanad due to Ibn Hassaan, who is munkar in Hadeeth, as Bukhaari said; Nasaa'i said, "He is abandoned in Hadeeth"; Ibn Hibbaan said, "He used to have female singers and listen to music, and he used to narrate fabricated reports on the authority of trustworthy narrators"; Ibn Abi Haatim said in *Kitaab al-'Ilal* (2/351), "I asked my father (i.e. Abu Haatim al-Raazi) about this hadeeth, to which he said: 'Munkar'."

Ibn Hassaan has been backed up by 'Eesaa ibn Maimoon, who also reported it from Muhammad ibn Ka'b, as related by Ibn Nasr. However, this does not alter anything, since Ibn Maimoon is similarly weak: Ibn Hibbaan said, "He reports ahaadeeth, all of which are fabricated"; Nasaa'i said, "Not reliable."

This hadeeth of Ibn 'Abbaas is also related by Abu Daawood (1485), and from him Baihaqi (2/212), via: 'Abdul Malik ibn Muhammad ibn Aiman from 'Abdullaah ibn Ya'qoob ibn Ishaaq from someone who narrated to him from Muhammad ibn Ka'b, the wording being:

"Do not cover the walls. He who looks into the letter of his brother without his permission, verily he looks into the Fire. Ask Allaah with the palms of your hands, and do not ask him with their backs, and when you finish, wipe your faces with them."

This is a weak sanad: 'Abdul Malik is declared weak by Abu Daawood; it also contain the shaikh of 'Abdullaah ibn Ya'qoob who is unnamed, and therefore unknown - it is possible that he may be Ibn Hassaan or Ibn Maimoon, both of whom are mentioned above.

The hadeeth is also transmitted by Haakim (4/270) via: Muhammad ibn Mu'aawiyah, who said that Masaadif ibn Ziyaad al-Madeeni narrated to him that he heard it from Muhammad ibn Ka'b al-Qurazi. Dhahabi followed this up by pointing out that Ibn Mu'aawiyah was declared to be a liar by Daaraqutni, so the hadeeth is falsified.

Abu Daawood said about this hadeeth, "This hadeeth has been narrated via more than one route on the authority of Muhammad ibn Ka'b; all of them are feeble."

Raising the hands on doing Qunoot for a calamity is established from the Messenger of Allaah (sallallaahu 'alaihi wa sallam) in his supplication against the polytheists who killed seventy reciters - transmitted by Imaam Ahmad (3/137) & Tabaraani in *Al-Mu'jam as-Sagheer* (p. 111) as the hadeeth of Anas with a saheeh sanad. Similar is proved from 'Umar and others in the Qunoot of Witr Prayer. However, since wiping the face after Du'aa' al-Qunoot is not quoted at all from the Prophet (sallallaahu 'alaihi wa sallam), nor from any of his Companions, it is an innovation without doubt.

As for wiping the face after du'aa' outside of prayer, there are only these two ahaadeeth; it is not correct to say that they mutually strengthen each other to the rank of hasan, as Manaawi did, due to the severity of the weakness found in their routes of narration. This is why Imaam Nawawi said in *Majmoo'*, "It is not recommended", endorsing Ibn 'Abd as-Salaam, who said, "Only an ignorant person does it."

The view that wiping the face after du'aa' is not prescribed is strengthened by the fact that there are many authentic ahaadeeth about raising the hands in supplication, and in none of them is there a mention of wiping the face; this shows, Allaah Willing, that it is unacceptable and not prescribed.

GLOSSARY
(of terms as used in this book)

'an: In Hadeeth, "on the authority of".

'Asr: the Afternoon Prayer.

aayah (pl. aayaat): "sign", a verse of the Qur'aan.

Companion (Ar. Sahaabi): a Muslim who met the Prophet (sallallaahu 'alaihi wa sallam).

da'eef: "weak", inauthentic (narration).

Deen: the way of life prescribed by Allaah.

dhikr (pl. adhkaar): "remembrance", words by which Allaah is remembered and supplicated on doing various actions, including in prayer.

Fajr: the Dawn Prayer.

faqeeh (pl. fuqahaa'): a scholar of *fiqh*, jurist.

fatwaa (pl. fataawaa): religious verdict.

fiqh: the understanding and application of *Sharee'ah* (divine law) from its sources.

hadeeth (pl. ahaadeeth): a saying narrated from the Prophet (sallallaahu 'alaihi wa sallam) (whether authentic or not), regarding his words, actions, or attributes.

hadeeth qudsi: a narration by the Prophet (sallallaahu 'alaihi wa sallam) on behalf of Allaah.

Hajj: Pilgrimage to Makkah.

halaal: permitted under the *Sharee'ah*.

haraam: prohibited under the *Sharee'ah*.

hasan: "fine", used for a hadeeth which is authentic but does not reach the higher category of *saheeh*.

hasan li dhaatihi: a narration which is *hasan* in itself.

hasan li ghairihi: a narration which is *hasan* due to other supporting narrations.

iftiraash: to sit *muftarishan*.

ijmaa': "consensus"; a unified opinion of scholars regarding a certain issue.

ijtihaad: "exertion"; the process of arising at a reasoned decision by a scholar on an issue.

iq'aa': "squatting".

'Ishaa': the Night Prayer.

isnaad: the chain of reporters for a narrated saying, linking the collector of the saying with the person quoted.

isti'aadhah: "seeking of refuge" (with Allaah from Shaytaan).

istighfaar: to seek forgiveness (from Allaah).

madhhab: "position (opinion)" of a scholar.

Madhhab: "school of thought", the sum total of the legal rulings of the founder of that Madhhab, as well as those of his students and all scholars who adhered to his approach.

maqloob: "reversed", used for the text of a *hadeeth* in which an expression has been changed to its opposite, or for an *isnaad* in which names of reporters have been interchanged.

Maghrib: the Sunset prayer.

makrooh: "disliked"; *fiqh* terminology denoting an action which is discouraged, and one is rewarded for abstaining from it.

marfoo': "raised"; a narration attributed to the Prophet (sallallaahu 'alaihi wa sallam).

masaa'il (sing. **mas'alah**): "that which is asked about"; an issue in *fiqh*.

mawdoo': fabricated, spurious, invented (narration).

mawqoof: "stopped"; a narration from a *Companion*.

mawsool: "connected"; a continuous *isnaad*.

mu'allaq: "suspended"; a narration in which its collector omits part of the isnaad to previous authorities.

mudallis: one who practises *tadlees*.

muftarishan: (sitting) on the left foot, which is spread along the ground, with the right foot upright.

mufti: one who gives *fataawaa*.

muhaddith (pl. **muhadditheen**): scholar of the science of **Hadeeth**.

mujtahid: one who is qualified to pass judgments using *ijtihaad*.

munkar: "rejected"; a narration which is inauthentic in itself and also contradicts other authentic ones.

muqallid: one who practises *taqleed*.

mursal: "loose"; a narration in which a *Successor* narrates from the Prophet (sallallaahu 'alaihi wa sallam) directly, i.e. omitting the *Companion* from whom he heard it.

mutawaatir: a *hadeeth* which is narrated by a very large number of reporters, such that it cannot be supposed that they all agreed on a lie.

qiyaas: Analogical deduction of Islaamic laws. New laws are deduced from old laws based on a similarity between their causes.

qunoot: "devotion"; a special supplication while standing in Prayer.

radi Allaahu 'anhu/'anhaa/'anhum: "May Allaah be pleased with him/her/them".

rahimahullaah: "May Allaah bestow His Mercy on him."

rak'ah: one cycle of standing, bowing and prostrations during Prayer.

saheeh: "correct"; an authentic narration.

saheeh li dhaatihi: a narration which is *saheeh* in itself.

saheeh li ghairihi: a narration which is *saheeh* due to other supporting narrations.

Salaf: "previous"; the early Muslims, of the first three eras: the *Companions*, *Successors*, and their successors.

sallallaahu 'alaihi wa sallam: "May Allaah send blessings and peace on him", used for the Prophet (sallallaahu 'alaihi wa sallam).

sanad: same as *isnaad*.

shaadhdh: "unusual"; a narration which is authentic in itself but inconsistent with other authentic ones.

shaikh: teacher of a scholar or narrator of *hadeeth*.

Sharee'ah: The divine code of Law.

sharh: commentary on, or explanation of, a text other than the Qur'aan.

Successor (Ar. **Taabi'i**): a Muslim (other than a *Companion*) who met a *Companion*.

Sunnah: "Example, Practice"; the way of life of the Prophet (sallallaahu 'alaihi wa sallam), consisting of his words, actions and silent approvals. The Sunnah is contained in the various authentic *ahaadeeth*.

sunnah: an action of the Prophet (sallallaahu 'alaihi wa sallam).

surah: a chapter of the Qur'aan.

sutrah: "screen, covering"; an object ahead of the place of prostration, only beyond which may anyone pass.

tadlees: "concealment"; to mask the identity of one's immediate authority in narration, e.g. by using a less well-known name, or by saying "on the authority of ..." the next narrator along.

tafseer: explanation of the words and meanings of the Qur'aan.

tahajjud: voluntary, recommended prayer between the compulsory prayers of *'Ishaa'* and *Fajr*.

tahleel: to declare that there is no true deity except Allaah.

tahmeed: "declare the praise of", esp. to declare the Praise of Allaah.

ta'leeq: same as *mu'allaq*.

takbeer: "magnification"; to declare the Greatness of Allaah.

takhreej: to reference a hadeeth to its source and analyse its *isnaads*.

tarjamah: notes about a reporter of Hadeeth.

tasbeeh: to glorify Allaah, rejecting any imperfections attributed to Him.

tashahhud: from *shahaadah* (to witness); the sitting in Prayer, in which one bears witness that there is no true god except Allaah, and that Muhammad is His messenger.

tasleem: "to send peace on"; the Muslim salutation of peace.

taqleed: to follow someone's opinion; to follow a *Madhhab*.

Ummah: "nation"; the Muslims as a group.

'Umrah: the lesser pilgrimage to Makkah.

Witr: "Odd"; the last prayer at night, consisting of an odd number of *rak'ahs*.

Zuhr: the post-noon prayer.

AUTHOR'S BIBLIOGRAPHY

A) THE QUR'AAN

B) TAFSEER

2. Ibn Katheer (701-774 AH): *Tafseer al-Qur'an al-'Azeem*, Muhammad Mustafa publications, 1365.

C) THE SUNNAH

3. Maalik bin Anas (93-179): *Al-Muwatta'*, Daar Ihyaa' Kutub al-'Arabiyyah, 1343.
4. Ibn al-Mubaarak, 'Abdullaah (118-181): *Az-Zuhd*, ms.
5. Muhammad bin al-Hasan Shaibaani (131-189): *Al-Muwatta'*, al-Mustafaa'i, 1297.
6. Tayaalisi (124-204): *Al-Musnad*, Daa'irah al-Ma'aarif, Hyderabad Deccan, 1321.
7. 'Abd ar-Razzaaq bin Humaam (126-211): *Al-Amaali*, ms.
8. Humaidi, 'Abdullah bin az-Zubair (...-219): *Musnad*, ms.
9. Ibn Sa'd, Muhammad (168-230): *At-Tabaqaat al-Kubraa*, Europe.
10. Ibn Ma'een, Yahya (...-233): *Taareekh ar-Rijaal wal-'Ilal*, ms.
11. Ahmad bin Hanbal (164-241): *Musnad*, Al-Matba'ah al-Maymaniyyah, 1313; Matba'ah al-Ma'aarif, 1365.
12. Ibn Abi Shaibah, 'Abdullah bin Muhammad Abu Bakr (...-235): *Musannaf*, ms.
13. Daarimi (181-255): *Sunan*, Matba'ah al-I'tidaal, Damascus, 1349.
14. Bukhaari (194-256): *Al-Jaami' as-Saheeh*, Al-Matba'ah al-Bahiyya al-Misriyyah, 1348. Printed with its commentary, *Fath al-Baaree*
15. ------------: *Al-Adab al-Mufrad*, Matba'ah al-Khalili, India, 1306.
16. ------------: *Khalq Af'aal al-'Ibaad*, Matba'ah al-Ansaar, India.
17. ------------: *At-Taareekh as-Sagheer*, India.
18. ------------: *Juz' al-Qiraa'ah ("Article on Recitation")*, printed.
19. Abu Daawood (202-275): *Sunan*, Al-Matba'ah at-Taaziah, 1349.
20. Muslim (204-261): *Saheeh*, Muhammad Ali publications.
21. Ibn Maajah (209-273): *Sunan*, Al-Matba'ah at-Taaziah, 1349.
22. Tirmidhi (209-279): *Sunan*, ed. Ahmad Shaakir, Halab, 1356.
23. ------------: *Shamaa'il Muhammadiyyah*, with its commentary by 'Ali al-Qaari and 'Abd ar-Ra'oof al-Manaawi, Al-Matba'ah al-Adabiyyah, Egypt, 1317..
24. Al-Haarith bin Abi Usaamah (176-282): *Musnad - zawaa'iduh*, ms.
25. Abu Ishaaq al-Harbi, Ibraaheem bin Ishaaq (198-285):*Ghareeb al-Hadeeth (Difficult words in Hadeeth*, ms.
26. Bazzaar, Abu Bakr Ahmad bin 'Amr al-Basri (...-292): *Musnad - zawaa'iduh*, photocopy.
27. Muhammad bin Nasr (202-294): *Qiyaam al-Layl*, Matba'ah Rifaah 'Aamm, Lahore, 1320.

28. Ibn Khuzaimah (223-311): *Saheeh*, Al-Maktab al-Islaami.
29. Nasaa'i (225-303): *Sunan - Al-Mujtabaa*, Al-Matba'ah al-Maymaniyyah.
30. ------------: *as-Sunan al-Kubraa*, ms.
31. Al-Qaasim al-Sarqasti (255-302): *Ghareeb al-Hadeeth* or *ad-Dalaa'il*, ms.
32. Ibn al-Jaarood (...-307): *Al-Muntaqaa*, ms., Egypt.
33. Abu Ya'laa al-Mooseeli (...-307): *Musnad*, ms.
34. Rooyaani, Muhammad bin Haaroon (...-307): *Musnad*, ms.
35. Siraaj, Abul-'Abbaas Muhammad bin Ishaaq (216-313): *Musnad*, several vols. of it as ms. in the Zaahiriyyah Library, Damascus.
36. Abu 'Awaanah (...-316): *Saheeh*, Daa'irah al-Ma'aarif, Hyderabad Deccan, 1326.
37. Ibn Abi Daawood, 'Abdullaah bin Sulaimaan (230-316): *Al-Masaahif*, ms.
38. Tahaawi (239-321): *Sharh Ma'aani al-Aathaar (Explanation of the meanings of narrations)*, Al-Mustafaa'i, India, 1300.
39. ------------: *Mushkil al-Aathaar (Difficult words in narrations)*, Daar al-Ma'aarif, India, 1333.
40. 'Uqaili, Muhammad bin 'Amr (...-322): *ad-Du'afaa' (The Weak Narrators)*, ms.
41. Ibn Abi Haatim (240-327): *Al-Jarh wat-Ta'deel (Authentication and Disparagement of Reporters)*, India.
42. ------------: *'Ilal al-Hadeeth (Defects in Hadeeth)*, As-Salafiyyah, Egypt, 1343.
43. Abu Ja'far al-Bukhturi, Muhammad bin 'Amr ar-Razaaz (...-329): *Al-Amaali*, ms.
44. Abu Sa'eed bin al-A'raabi, Ahmad bin Ziyaad (246-340): *Mu'jam*, ms.
45. Ibn as-Sammaak, 'Uthmaan bin Ahmad (...-344): *Hadeeth*, ms.
46. Abul-'Abbaas al-Asamm, Muhammad bin Ya'qoob (247-346): *Hadeeth*, ms.
47. Ibn Hibbaan (...-354): *Saheeh*, Daar al-Ma'aarif, Egypt.
48. Tabaraani (260-360): *Al-Mu'jam al-Kabeer*, several vols. of it as ms., Zaahiriyyah Library, Damascus.
49. ------------: *Al-Mu'jam al-Awsat min al-jam' bainahu wa bain as-Sagheer*, ms.
50. ------------: *Al-Mu'jam as-Sagheer*, Matba'ah al-Ansaari, Delhi, 1311.
51. Abu Bakr al-Aajuri (...-360): *Al-Arba'een (Forty Hadeeth)*, ms.
52. ------------: *Aadaab Hamlah al-Qur'aan*, ms.
53. Ibn as-Sunni (...-364): *'Aml al-Yawm wal-Laylah*, Daa'irah al-Ma'aarif, India, 1315.
54. Abu ash-Shaikh Ibn Hayyaan (274-369): *Tabaqaat al-Isbahaaniyyeen*, ms.
55. ------------: *Maa rawaahu Abu az-Zubair 'an Ghair Jaabir (What Abu az-Zubair narrated from other than Jaabir)*, ms.
56. ------------: *Akhlaaq an-Nabi sall Allaahu 'alaihi wa sallam (Manners of the Prophet)*, Egypt.
57. Daaraqutni (306-385): *Sunan*, India.
58. Khattaabi (317-388): *Ma'aalim as-Sunan*, Ansaar as-Sunnah, Egypt.
59. Mukhlis (305-393): *Al-Fawaa'id*, ms., Zaahiriyyah Library, Damascus.
60. Ibn Mandah, Abu 'Abdullaah Muhammad bin Ishaaq (316-395): *At-Tawheed wa Ma'rifah Asmaa' Allaah Ta'aalaa*, ms.
61. Haakim (320-405): *Al-Mustadrak*, Daa'irah al-Ma'aarif, Hyderabad, 1340.
62. Tammaam ar-Raazi (330-414): *Al-Fawaa'id*, 2 complete copies as ms., Zaahiriyyah Library, Damascus.

63. Sahmi, Hamzah bin Yoosuf al-Jurjaani (...-427): *Taareekh Jurjaan (History of Jurjaan)*, printed.

64. Abu Nu'aim al-Isbahaani (336-430): *Akhbaar Isbahaan (Reports from Isbahaan)*, printed in Europe.

65. Ibn Bushraan (339-430): *Al-Amaali*, most of its sections, ms., Zaahiriyyah Library, Damascus.

66. Baihaqi (384-458): *as-Sunan al-Kubraa*, Daa'irah al-Ma'aarif, Hyderabad, 1352.

67. ------------: *Dalaa'il an-Nubuwwah*, ms., Ahmadiyyah Library, Halab.

68. Ibn 'Abd al-Barr (368-463): *Jaami' Bayaan al-'Ilm wa Fadlih*, Al-Matba'ah al-Muneeriyyah.

69. Ibn Mandah, Abul-Qaasim (381-470): *Ar-Radd 'alaa man Yunfi al-Harf min al-Qur'aan*, ms., Zaahiriyyah Library, Damascus.

70. Baaji (403-477): *Sharh al-Muwatta'*, printed.

71. 'Abd al-Haqq al-Ishbeeli (510-581): *Al-Ahkaam al-Kubraa*, ms.

72. ------------: *Tahajjud*, ms.

73. Ibn al-Jawzi (510-597): *At-Tahqeeq 'alaa Masaa'il at-Ta'leeq*, ms.

74. Abu Hafs al-Mu'aadib, 'Amr bin Muhammad(516-607): *Al-Muntaqaa min Amaali Abil-Qaasim as-Samarqandi*, ms.

75. 'Abd al-Ghani bin 'Abd al-Waahid al-Maqdisi (541-600): *Sunan*, ms.

76. Diyaa' al-Maqdisi (569-643): *Al-Ahaadeeth al-Mukhtaarah*, several vols. of it, ms., Zaahiriyyah Library, Damascus.

77. ------------: *Al-Muntaqaa min al-Ahaadeeth as-Sihaah wal-Hisaan (Selection of Authentic Ahaadeeth)*, ms.

78. ------------: *Juz' fi Fadl al-Hadeeth wa Ahlih (Article on the Excellence of Hadeeth and its People)*, ms.

79. Mundhiri (581-656): *At-Targheeb wat-Tarheeb (Encouragement and Deterrence)*, Al-Matba'ah al-Muneeriyyah, Egypt.

80. Zayla'i (...-762): *Nasb ar-Raayah (Hoisting of the Flaq)*, Daar al-Ma'moon, Egypt, 1357.

81. Ibn Katheer (701-774): *Jaami' al-Masaaneed*, ms.

82. Ibn al-Mulaqqin, Abu Hafs 'Amr bin Abil-Hasan (723-804): *Khulaasah al-Badr al-Muneer*, ms.

83. 'Iraaqi (725-806): *Tarh at-Tathreeb*, Jam'iyyah an-Nashr wat-Ta'leef al-Azhariyyah, 1353.

84. ------------: *Takhreej* of Ghazaali's *Ihyaa' 'Uloom ad-Deen*, Egypt, 1346.

85. Haithami (735-807): *Majma' az-Zawaa'id*: Husaam ad-Deen al-Qudsi, 1352.

86. ------------: *Mawaarid az-Zam'aan fi Zawaa'id Ibn Hibbaan*, Muhibb ad-Deen publ.

87. ------------: *Zawaa'id al-Mu'jam as-Sagheer wal-Awsat lit-Tabaraani*, ms.

88. Ibn Hajr al-'Asqalaani (773-852): *Takhreej Ahaadeeth al-Hidaayah*, India.

89. ------------: *Talkhees al-Habeer*, Al-Matba'ah al-Muneeriyyah.

90. ------------: *Fath al-Baari*, Al-Matba'ah al-Bahiyyah.

91. ------------: *Al-Ahaadeeth al-'Aaliyaat*, ms.

92. Suyooti (889-911): *Al-Jaami' al-Kabeer*, ms.

93. 'Ali al-Qaari (...-1014): *Al-Ahaadeeth al-Mawdoo'ah*, Istanbul.

94. Manaawi (952-1031): *Faid al-Qadeer Sharh al-Jaami' as-Sagheer*, Mustafa Muhammad publ.

95. Zurqaani (1055-1122): *Sharh al-Mawaahib al-Ladunniyyah*, Egypt.

96. Shawkaani (1171-1250): *Al-Fawaa'id al-Majmoo'ah fil-Ahaadeeth al-Mawdoo'ah*, India.
97. 'Abd al-Hayy Lucknowi (1264-1304): *At-Ta'leeq al-Mumajjid 'alaa Muwatta' Muhammad*, al-Mustafaa'i, 1297.
98. ------------: *Al-Aathaar al-Marfoo'ah fil-Akhbaar al-Mawdoo'ah*, India.
99. Muhammad bin Sa'eed al-Halbi (...-...): *Musalsalaat*, ms.
100. Albaani, Muhammad Naasir ad-Deen al-: *Takhreej Sifah Salaah an-Nabi*, ms., the original sourcework for this book, in which it is referred to as *al-Asl*.
101. ------------: *Irwaa' al-Ghaleel fi Takhreej Ahaadeeth Manaar as-Sabeel*, 8 vols., al-Maktab al-Islaami, published completely - All Praise be to Allaah.
102. ------------: *Saheeh Abi Daawood*, incomplete.
103. ------------: *Notes on 'Abd al-Haqq al-Ishbeeli's Ahkaam*, incomplete.
104. ------------: *Takhreej* of the ahaadeeth of *Sharh 'Aqeedah Tahaawiyyah*, al-Maktab al-Islaami.
105. ------------: *Silsilah al-Ahaadeeth ad-Da'eefah*, 4 vols., al-Maktab al-Islaami.

D) FIQH

106. Maalik bin Anas (93-179): *Al-Mudawwanah* (Maaliki fiqh), Matba'ah as-Sa'aadah, 1323.
107. Shaafi'i, Muhammad bin Idrees (150-204): *Al-Umm* (Shaafi'i), al-Matba'ah al-Ameeriyyah, 1321.
108. Marwazi, Ishaaq bin Mansoor (...-251): *Masaa'il al-Imaam Ahmad wa Ishaaq bin Raahawaih*, ms.
109. Ibn Haani, Ibraaheem NaisaAburi (...-265): *Masaa'il al-Imaam Ahmad*, ms.
110. Muzani (175-264): *Mukhtasar Fiqh ash-Shaafi'i*, printed on the margin of al-Umm.
111. Abu Daawood (202-275): *Masaa'il al-Imaam Ahmad* (Hanbali), al-Manaar, 1353.
112. 'Abdullaah bin al-Imaam Ahmad (203-290): *Masaa'il al-Imaam Ahmad*, ms.
113. Ibn Hazm (384-456): *Al-Muhallaa* (Zaahiri), al-Matba'ah al-Muneeriyyah.
114. 'Izz bin 'Abd as-Salaam (578-660): *al-Fataawaa*, ms.
115. Nawawi (631-686): *Al-Majmoo' Sharh al-Muhadhdhab* (Shaafi'i), al-Matba'ah al-Muneeriyyah.
116. ----------: *Rawdah at-Taalibeen* (Shaafi'i), al-Maktab al-Islaami.
117. Ibn Taimiyyah (661-728): *al-Fataawaa* (Independent), Farj ad-Deen al-Kurdi publ.
118. ------------: *min Kalaam lahu fit-Takbeer fil-'Eedain wa ghairuh* (*Discussion on Takbeer in the Two 'Eid Prayers*), ms.
119. Ibn al-Qayyim (691-751): *I'laam al-Muwaqqi'een* (Independent).
120. Subki (683-756): *al-Fataawaa* (Shaafi'ee).
121. Ibn al-Humaam (790-869): *Fath al-Qadeer* (Hanafee), Boolaaq ed.
122. Ibn 'Abd al-Haadi, Yoosuf (840-909): *Irshaad as-Saalik* (Hanbalee), ms.
123. ------------: *al-Furoo'* (Hanbalee).
124. Suyooti (809-911): *Al-Haawi lil-Fataawi* (Shaafi'ee), al-Qudsi.
125. Ibn Nujaim al-Misri (...-970): *Al-Bahr ar-Raa'iq* (Hanafee), Al-Matba'ah al-'Ilmiyyah.
126. Sha'raani (898-973): *Al-Meezaan* (according to the four madhhabs).

127. Haitami (909-973): *Ad-Darr al-Mandood fis-Salaah was-Salaam 'alaa Saahib al-Maqaam al-Mahmood*, ms.
128. ------------: *Asmaa al-Mataalib*, ms.
129. Wali-ullah Dehlawi (1110-1176): *Hujjat-ullaah al-Baalighah* (Independent), al-Muneerah.
130. Ibn 'Aabideen (1151-1203): *Footnotes on ad-Darr al-Mukhtaar* (Hanafee), Istanbul.
131. ------------: *Footnotes on al-Bahr ar-Raa'iq* (Hanafee).
132. ------------: *Rasm al-Mufi* (Hanafee).
133. 'Abd al-Haqq (1264-1304): *Imaam al-Kalaam feemaa yata'allaq bil-Qiraa'ah Khalf al-Imaam* (Independent), Al-Baladi, India.
134. ------------: *An-Naafi' al-Kabeer liman yutaali' al-Jaami' as-Sagheer*, Al-Yoosufi, India, 1349.

E) SEERAH (Biography of the Prophet sallallaahu 'alaihi wa sallam) and TARAAJUM (Biographies of the reporters of Hadeeth)

135. Ibn Abi Haatim, 'Abd ar-Rahmaan (240-327): *Taqaddamah al-Ma'rifah li Kitaab al-Jarh wat-Ta'deel*, India.
136. Ibn Hibbaan (...-354): *Ath-Thiqaat (Reliable Narrators)*, ms.
137. Ibn 'Adi (277-365): *Al-Kaamil*, ms.
138. Abu Nu'aim (336-430): *Hilyah al-Awliyaa'*, Matba'ah as-Sa'aadah, Egypt, 1349.
139. Khateeb Baghdaadi (392-463): *Taareekh Baghdaad (History of Baghdaad)*, Matba'ah as-Sa'aadah, Egypt.
140. Ibn 'Abd al-Barr (368-463): *Al-Intiqaa' fi Fadaa'il al-Fuqahaa'*.
141. Ibn 'Asaakir (499-571): *Taareekh Dimashq (History of Damascus)*, ms.
142. Ibn al-Jawzi (508-597): *Manaaqib al-Imaam Ahmad*, printed.
143. Ibn al-Qayyim (691-751): *Zaad al-Ma'aad*, Muhammad 'Ali publ., 1353.
144. 'Abd al-Qaadir al-Qurashi (696-775): *Al-Jawaahir al-Madiyyah*, India.
145. Ibn Rajab al-Hanbali (736-795): *Dhail at-Tabaqaat*, Egypt.
146. 'Abd al-Hayy Lucknowi (1264-1304): *Al-Fawaa'id al-Bahiyyah fi Taraajum al-Hanafiyyah*, Matba'ah as-Sa'aadah, Egypt, 1324.

F) THE ARABIC LANGUAGE

147. Ibn al-Atheer (544-606): *An-Nihaayah fi Ghareeb al-Hadeeth wal-Athar*, Al-Matba'ah al-'Uthmaaniyyah, Egypt, 1311.
148. Ibn Manzoor al-Afreeqi (630-711): *Lisaan al-'Arab*, Daar Saadir, Beirut, 1955 AC.
149. Fairoz Aabaadi (729-817): *Al-Qaamoos al-Muheet*, 3rd ed., 1353.

G) USOOL AL-FIQH (Principles of Fiqh)

150. Ibn Hazm (384-456): *Al-Ihkaam fi Usool al-Ahkaam*, Matba'ah as-Sa'aadah, Egypt, 1345.
151. Subki (683-856): *Ma'naa Qawl ash-Shaafi'i al-Matlabi, "idhaa sahh al-hadeeth fahuwa madhhabi" (The Meaning of Shaafi'i's saying, "When a*

hadeeth is found to be saheeh, that is my madhhab"), from Majmoo'ah ar-Rasaa'il, al-Muneeriyyah.

152. Ibn al-Qayyim (691-856): *Badaa'i' al-Fawaa'id,* Al-Matba'ah al-Muneeriyyah.
153. Wali-ullaah Dehlawi (1110-1176): *'Iqd al-Jeed fi Ahkaam al-Ijtihaad wat-Taqleed,* India.
154. Fulaani (1166-1218): *Eeqaaz al-Himam,* Al-Matba'ah al-Muneeriyyah.
155. Zurqaa', Shaikh Mustafaa (contemporary): *Al-Madkhal ilaa 'Ilm Usool al-Fiqh,* printed.

H) ADHKAAR

156. Ismaa'eel al-Qaadi al-Maqdisi (199-282): *Fadl as-Salaah 'alaa an-Nabi sallallaahu 'alaihi wa sallam,* with my checking, Al-Maktab al-Islaami.
157. Ibn al-Qayyim (691-751): *Jalaa' al-Ifhaam fi as-Salaah 'alaa Khair al-Anaam,* Al-Matba'ah al-Muneeriyyah.
158. Siddeeq Hasan Khaan (1248-1307): *Nuzul al-Abraar,* Al-Jawaa'ib.

J) MISCELLANEOUS

159. Ibn Battah, 'Abdullaah bin Muhammad (304-387): *Al-Ibaanah 'an Sharee'ah al-Firqah an-Naajiyah (Clarification of the Code of the Saved Sect),* ms.
160. Abu 'Amr ad-Daani, 'Uthmaan bin Sa'eed (371-444): *Al-Muktafaa fi Ma'rifah al-Waqf at-Taamm,* ms.
161. Khateeb Baghdaadi (392-463): *Al-Ihtijaaj bi ash-Shaafi'i feemaa asnada ilaih ...,* ms.
162. Harawi, 'Abdullaah bin Muhammad al-Ansaari (396-481): *Dhamm al-Kalaam wa Ahlah,* ms.
163. Ibn al-Qayyim (691-751): *Shifaa' al-'Aleel fi Masaa'il al-Qadaa' wal-Qadr wat-Ta'leel,* printed.
164. Fairoz Aabaadi (729-817): *Ar-Radd 'alaa al-Mu'tarid 'alaa Ibn 'Arabi,* ms.

122